WITHDRAWN

MERCHANTS
GUNS & MONEY
The Story of Lincoln County and Its Wars

Left: Revolver U.S. Colt Army Model, ca. 1860; caliber .44; six shot; barrel length 8 inches.

Right: Colt .41 Revolver, ca. 1875, also called the "Colt Lightning"; six shot; the preferred weapon of frontier characters such as William Bonney, a.k.a. Billy the Kid.

MERCHANTS
GUNS & MONEY

The Story of Lincoln County and Its Wars

JOHN P. WILSON

Museum of New Mexico Press

Manufactured in the United States

Support for this publication was made possible in part by a loan through the State of New Mexico's Office of Cultural Affairs Publications Revolving Fund.

Library of Congress Cataloging-in-Publication Data

Wilson, John P. (John Philip), 1935–
Merchants, Guns, and Money: The Story of Lincoln County and Its Wars.

  Bibliography: p.
  Includes Index.
  1. Lincoln County (N.M.)—History . 2. Outlaws—
New Mexico—Lincoln County—History. 3. Frontier and
pioneer life—New Mexico—Lincoln County. 4. Lincoln
County (N.M.)—Description and travel—Views.
I. Museum of New Mexico. II. Title.
F802.L7W55   1987   978.9′64   87-5790
ISBN 0-89013-171-6
ISBN 0-89013-172-4 (pbk.)

Typography by Business Graphics

Project Editor: Mary Wachs
Designed by Daniel Martinez

Museum of New Mexico Press
P.O. Box 2087
Santa Fe, New Mexico 87503

CONTENTS

LIST OF ILLUSTRATIONS

PREFACE

First and foremost I am obligated to Thomas J. Caperton, Director of the New Mexico State Monuments Division, who is an authority himself on the history of Lincoln. We talked about this project for at least two years before a contract was finally approved. He loaned books and records, provided encouragement and suggestions, and made available the Philip J. Rasch collection in his custody. Not least of all, his continuing patience when completion of this manuscript went far beyond the deadline date is most sincerely appreciated.

The advice and guidance received from Harwood P. Hinton while I was using the Maurice Fulton Papers at the University of Arizona and floundering for an explanation of the Lincoln County War were more helpful than any background reading. His perspective gained from long familiarity with many of the principals in Lincoln's history and his suggestion to "follow the money" aided immeasurably in my efforts to find rational explanations for the behavior of individuals during a violent decade.

Two colleagues who were working on their own books at the time this one was written contributed materially to the present volume. With Robert M. Utley of Santa Fe, who was writing a history of the Lincoln County War, there ensued quite a correspondence that sought to resolve a range of long-standing questions, such as the ownership of Tunstall's cattle and the nature and locations of his ranches. Utley furnished copies of certain documents from the National Archives, the Lincoln County Court House, and the Haley History Center, all much appreciated. In addition he made available a copy of the manuscript for his book *Four Fighters of Lincoln County*, since published by the University of New Mexico Press. Darlis A. Miller at New Mexico State University generously allowed me to use her notes, which included all available data from the National Archives on army contracts let in the Southwest and western Texas from ca. 1860 to 1880. These allowed me to track the extent of the L.G. Murphy & Co. and the Dolan and Riley contracts for army supplies. Dr. Miller also loaned me her copy of the Mehren (1969) M.A. thesis, which had comparable information for supplies provided to the Mescalero Apache Reservation. Finally, I used Dr. Miller's copies of the 1860, 1870, and 1880 U.S. Census agricultural schedules.

Very much appreciated was Philip J. Rasch's sharing of his knowledge and opinions gained from forty years of research, much of it focused upon Lincoln County and the individuals who had a part in the War. Many of the National Archives files were first used by Dr. Rasch. Donald R. Lavash, historian at the New Mexico State Records Center, helped particularly with legal questions, provided copies of relevant territorial laws and pursued the ephemeral traces of the Lincoln County Bank. Larry D. Ball at Arkansas State University, currently writing a book on the territorial sheriffs of Arizona and New Mexico, provided a number of leads, references, and copies of documents that would otherwise have been unavailable, and also resolved the mode and timing of succession to office by New Mexico sheriffs-elect.

The staffs of the institutions that I visited—the University of Arizona Special Collections Library, the University of New Mexico Special Collections Library, the Museum of New Mexico History Library, and the New Mexico State Records Center—were unfailingly helpful. Mr. Eric Pumroy of the Indiana Historical Society facilitated a loan of their Lew. Wallace Papers on microfilm. The Interlibrary Loan staff at the New Mexico State University Library cheerfully sought out elusive microfilms and journal articles; one such loan took almost two years to negotiate. Michael Miller at the New Mexico State Library in Santa Fe assisted greatly by lending all of the library's Lincoln County and Roswell newspaper microfilms for the territorial period. The National Archives staff in Washington responded to many requests for documents not found on microfilms by providing either copies or explanations. Robert W. Frazer and Andrew Wallace sent copies of other records from their research files together with helpful comments. Carol McKeag, CPA of Las Cruces, confirmed that my analyses of Murphy's ledger and the Murphy and McSween bank accounts were accurate.

To the extent that the interpretations in the following pages represent anything new, these are my own ideas unless otherwise acknowledged. In such a popular field as this one, a priority in ideas is sometimes difficult to establish. When colleagues actively share their sources or seek to resolve problems jointly, conclusions may well be simultaneously arrived at. When the various books being written at the present time are eventually viewed alongside one another, it's quite possible that there will be little real disagreement among the authors despite the substantial overlapping in their subjects and the partisanship among other writers in the past on Lincoln County War matters. With more information available than ever before, the field may be maturing to where old problems can be seen in a new light and even resolved. Still, individuals such as John Chisum and William Bonney apparently enjoyed being enigmas, and their roles and motives may be debated forever.

INTRODUCTION

This is a history of Lincoln, a town in southeastern New Mexico. It has always been a small town and for New Mexico not a particularly old one, but the violence of its early years ensured Lincoln a permanent place in the annals of the American West. It was the setting for a famous frontier conflict known as the Lincoln County War and for the exploits of a legendary western outlaw, Billy the Kid. This is a history of that community.

The story begins with its first settlement in 1855, coincident with the establishment of nearby Fort Stanton, and continues until 1913 when it finally gave up the county seat of Lincoln County to the newer town of Carrizozo. Lincoln's population probably never numbered more than a few hundred, predominantly Hispanic, citizens in a voting precinct that totaled upwards of 1,000 people. Today there are about fifty full-time residents.

The settlement or plaza bore two names originally—La Placita (the village) and Rio Bonito (pretty river). With the creation of Lincoln County in 1869, the town became the county seat, assuming the name Lincoln about 1873. Between 1878 and 1891 Lincoln County was a vast domain—all of southeastern New Mexico—and Lincoln's appearance is still very much a community of that period. Most buildings date to the nineteenth century and there are few recent intrusions. It is a town conscious of its past and increasingly concerned with its heritage. Lincoln State Monument maintains a number of historical buildings, while other structures have been renovated through private efforts.

Most of the books and articles written about Lincoln County stress the banditry of the Lincoln County War period beginning in 1878. Before and after that period, Lincoln had a fascinating history, which has largely gone unnoticed, a history largely built upon a series of conflicts. Several times these reached to the White House and the Supreme Court. The army usually regarded any civilian settlements in the neighborhood of a post as potential trouble spots, but for the commanders at Fort Stanton, eight miles to the west, Lincoln was sometimes a massive headache.

The problems in telling the story of Lincoln begin with the immense amount of information available. Sometimes it seems that every scrap of paper has survived, particularly from the period between 1873 and 1881 and especially from the time of the Lincoln County War, 1878–1879. In spite of this volume, the records must be used with care, since they are often incomplete and give unsubstantiated, conflicting, or even misleading versions of events.

One example is letters to newspapers, an important source. The correspondents who wrote them usually were seeking to achieve their own ends while painting their opponents in the blackest terms. The letter writers as well as the readers may have known the real issues or the actual course of events perfectly well, but without such first-hand knowledge the historian may have real difficulty in deciding whom to believe. Reminiscent accounts were subject to faulty memories, or to memories that improved with time. Finally, to sift through the romantic literature about the Lincoln County War and the activities of the Kid is a major task in itself. These difficulties and others underlie some of the differences between accounts by various writers.

The history given here has been written almost entirely from contemporary records. Documents that originated with the army at Fort Stanton were the largest and the most reliable source of information through 1879. After 1879 matters quieted somewhat and newspapers became more important. Sometimes a shortage of information hampered efforts to be even-handed; we may know only one side of a story. The chapters for the periods before the Horrell War and after the Lincoln County War were based mostly upon records not drawn upon by other writers.

The overwhelming dramatic appeal of the Lincoln County War has dominated the other aspects of Lincoln's past in the literature of the place. The story that emerges often floats between history and folklore. A writer pouring over the materials is tempted to produce yet another historical novel complete with plot twists and larger-than-life heroes and villains. Indeed, both the number of episodes and the cast of characters involved was immense, although some of the latter contributed little beyond getting themselves shot. With retellings, even their roles have changed.

To cut through some of the sensational aspects and present a more coherent and accurate story has been this writer's intention. Minor episodes and individuals who had brief or minor roles have been trimmed as necessary in attempting to allow attention to focus on the deserved principals. Endnotes and bibliographic references will lead the reader to the best sources for additional reading.

Early in the research this writer took the advice of historian Harwood Hinton, of the University of Arizona, to "follow the money" in seeking explanations of why people behaved in the ways they did in the rather bizarre world of Lincoln County. This thematic approach continues through 1878, and indeed the analysis of bank accounts, ledgers, and contracts has done much to clarify the actions and motivations of those who finally clashed in the Lincoln County War. After February 1878, economic analysis becomes less illuminating, since outlaws effectively ran the country for the rest of that year, settling their accounts with bullets. From 1879 Lincoln moved with alacrity toward stability in civil life, so much so that the major events of 1881—the last escape of Billy the Kid and his shooting by Sheriff Pat Garrett—were gross anachronisms from a world that was rapidly being forgotten. As points of high drama, these shootings soon became the province of novelists, playwrights, and historians.

PART I

". . . the water is clear as crystal and filled with cress."   Santa Fe *Weekly Gazette*, April 28, 1855.

Sharp's Pistol, ca. 1855; caliber .33 percussion; round rifled barrel; length of barrel 4½ inches.

∽ 1 ∽

THE FIRST SETTLEMENT
1855–1860

In 1846 the last outposts of settlement in eastern New Mexico were Manzano, at the eastern foot of the Manzano Mountains, and Anton Chico, in the upper Pecos Valley. The Mescalero Apache Indians claimed the country beyond, as far as the Pecos River. In particular they roamed the Capitan and Sacramento Mountains and the Sierra Blanca, as well as other ranges to the south through western Texas.

Two small streams, the Rio Bonito and the Rio Ruidoso, ran across the northern part of the Mescalero country. They united to form the Rio Hondo, whose waters continued east to the Pecos. The Rio Bonito had been named by 1851; the others received names soon after.[1] These streams had permanent flows and the Apaches who lived along them gained a livelihood primarily by hunting, gathering, and raiding, as well as by trading with the settlements.

Apache raids brought U.S. Army scouting parties and punitive campaigns into the Mescalero country. The first such force, sent out from Santa Fe in the summer of 1849, had two brushes with the Indians and found plenty of signs of their occupation. Two other expeditions followed in 1850, then came a peace treaty in 1852, more raiding, and two attempts to punish their depredations in 1854.[2] There was little actual fighting and sometimes the soldiers didn't even see Indians.

The army soon learned much about the geography of the country, and by October 1853 the military commander in New Mexico, Gen. John Garland, planned to establish a post in the Mescalero country. That spring a William D. Murphy had made known his intention to settle "at White Mountains."[3] While Murphy's plans apparently came to nothing, Indian Agent Michael Steck wrote that Mescalero chief José Cito

> has for three years past planted corn & squashes &c. He is one of the most influential men of his tribe and ought therefore to be encouraged at once in his enterprise: He wishes to settle upon the Rio Bonito east of the White Mountains and requested that he be furnished with hoes and axes.[4]

A band of Mescaleros ran off some 2,500 sheep near Anton Chico in December of 1854. The army took to the field to punish the raiders and got into a running fight, during which Capt. Henry W. Stanton rode into an ambush in what is now James Canyon and was shot out of his saddle. Two privates also lost their lives while a dozen Mescaleros, including Santa Ana, the most hostile of all, reportedly died in the same battle.

In response to the continued raids, General Garland established Fort Stanton in the heart of Mescalero country on the Rio Bonito. The official date was May 4, 1855. A month later the governor and ex-officio Superintendent of Indian Affairs in New Mexico made a peace treaty with the Mescalero Apaches.[5]

Bvt. Maj. James H. Carleton described the Rio Bonito country at this period, just before its settlement:

> The beauty and fertility of this country have not been exaggerated. . . . The hills,

which are some four or five hundred feet high, are nearly all of limestone, well rounded off, generally destitute of shrubbery, and well grassed to their summits. The
timber along the river is black walnut, box elder, hackberry, and small Mesquite
bushes; not very plentiful at that. . . . I have been nine miles below this point. The
valley is rich and fit for cultivation all the way. And hence upwards towards the
White mountains, where both the Bonito and Ruidoso have their sources, the Bonito
river bottom is very rich, at least for more than twenty miles which I have examined. . . . At one place, six miles above the junction of the rivers, in the bottom, is
where they [the Indians] planted corn, say two years ago; it is called the "Apache
Farm." It is irrigated entirely by the water from a formidable spring which comes
out of the bluffs, and runs along through the farm; the water is clear as crystal and
filled with cress.[6]

Settlers who arrived here in 1855 included the general's son, David S. Garland, and a
stalwart A.M. Clenny, who remained on his farm to the time of his death in 1898.[7] By the
end of August, the surveyor general of New Mexico could claim that Fort Stanton had been
established

in a Section of Country whose richness of soil and other inducements have caused
quite a number of families to locate there and form a Settlement. This settlement is
upon the public domain, and lies upon the rivers Bonito and Ruidoso near their junction, which forms the Rio Hondo.[8]

That same year another small group built houses and put in a crop of corn at the Patos
Springs, eighteen miles north of Fort Stanton.[9]

People flocked to the new country from all over. In February 1857 the commander at
Fort Stanton wrote that three men had asked for protection, claiming to be the representatives of forty others who proposed to settle on the river below that post. Two months later
he justified a large garrison in order to inspire fear in the Indians, so that they would resist
the temptation to raid "the numerous settlements of our people for twenty miles along this
river. . . ."[10]

Despite a few depredations, relations with the Mescaleros remained friendly until the
Civil War. Peace was always on trial, however, because the settlers sold liquor to the Indians, creating a potentially explosive situation. Before the first year was out, David Garland charged that Clenny intended to start a groggery and had set the wheels in motion.[11]
Charles Beach, the sutler's clerk, told Agent Steck that the citizens on the river were very
much annoyed by drunken Indians, echoing a complaint by the post commander.[12] This
culminated in a series of increasingly bitter letters by Capt. Thomas Claiborne accusing
practically everyone of being whiskey-traders, then running to the fort for protection if the
Indians threatened them: "Sir. There is no doubt that the influence which the whiskey selling Mexicans below this post exercise upon the Indians is in the greatest degree injurious
to the public interests."[13] And this, "There exists another and more potent cause of trouble, which . . . is the selling of whiskey to the Indians, by the Mexicans living on the river,
some eight miles below the post."[14]

Claiborne describes the extent of the problem:

This last place [La Placita] has had as many as sixty or even more Mexicans collected at it, while whiskey has been freely & openly sold & traded to the Indians, nor is
it confined alone to Mexicans. A Mr. Beckwith is reported as carrying on this traffic
on the borders of the reserve. A man named Hacket made his appearance 7 or 8
miles south west of this post with a cart load of Beer & Whiskey to ply a trade with
soldiers & Indians. . . . I sent out an officer to bring in absentees and to warn the
fellow off. He persisted five days longer & last Saturday before breakfast he had

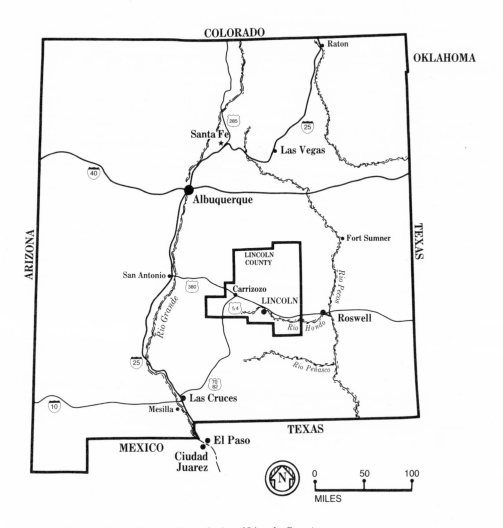

State of New Mexico, with present boundaries of Lincoln County.

the impudence to request me to let him have soldiers to guard his "ranche" while he could get a wagon & employ men to help him move away as he was afraid of the Indians. I told him preemptorily to clear out . . . he persisted; I told him to go to the devil and be off.[15]

Despite the captain's efforts, business evidently continued as usual, without precipitating an Indian war.

In this early period, a settlement was not necessarily larger than a ranch occupied by a single family. La Placita may have been the location noted by the surveyor general in 1855, but that may be attributed to the fact that it was the only settlement with a name.[16] Passing references in military reports and a petition from February 1859 showed that Anglo-Americans had small ranches scattered along the Rio Bonito valley for twenty miles or more and on the Ruidoso as well, while the Hispanic community was concentrated at La Placita, the precursor of modern Lincoln, some eight miles below Fort Stanton.[17]

Not everyone on the Rio Bonito was a depraved whiskey-seller; Col. B.L.E. Bonneville visited the settlements around Fort Stanton in late June of 1859 and found them in a thriving condition and increasing, predicting that there would be about 12,000 bushels of corn raised, in addition to wheat and oats.[18] He may have been slightly optimistic; 1859 and 1860 were very poor crop years in the territory and the 1860 Census agricultural schedule estimated 8,850 bushels of Indian corn from the Rio Bonito farms, with lesser amounts of wheat, beans, and potatoes.[19] The latter—706 bushels of Irish potatoes—were undoubtedly being grown with an eye to sales at Fort Stanton.

Establishment of this post was a powerful attraction for settlers to the area. The garrison could protect a farmer's improvements while providing a market for his products. Another market developed quickly when Agent Steck authorized the purchase of foodstuffs for the Mescaleros under his charge. Contract deliveries began at the Indian agency with the delivery of 200 fanegas (about 520 bushels) of corn in February of 1857 by Moore and Rees, corn contractors from Tecolote, New Mexico. By the end of that year at least four local men— Clenny, Charles Beach, Garland, and Timothy McGowan—were providing corn and beef for both the Indians and the troops at the post; contracts with McGowan and Beach alone called for the delivery of 2,500 fanegas of corn to the post quartermaster and commissary departments.[20] Contracts with the Indian agency from December 1857 through March 1858 added another 226½ fanegas of corn,[21] the total for both army and Indian agency requirements came to some 6,800 bushels. Part, if not most, of this corn would have been raised locally.

In 1858–1859 the post commissary and the Mescalero agency purchased another 1,591 fanegas (nearly 4,000 bushels) of corn between them—one-third of Colonel Bonneville's guesstimated total for the 1859 yield. The farmers and contractors sensed a healthy continuing demand and put some 1,092 acres into production—probably all under irrigation—in the Rio Bonito country as of 1860.[22] In a normal crop year, the harvest would have more than sufficed for all needs without the need to import grain.

Who were the people who first settled the Rio Bonito country? Documents out of Fort Stanton and the Mescalero agency, an 1859 petition by local settlers, and population and agricultural schedules from the 1860 Census all show that the population was unusual to the extent that both Anglo and Hispanic citizens were present, at a time when frontier communities in New Mexico typically had very few non-Hispanics. The Spanish-surnamed families were all native New Mexicans, but where they came from within the territory is not now known. The other family heads came from everywhere, but primarily from southern and border states. Two families from Canada suggest the extreme.[23]

Some, perhaps, had backgrounds similar to Hugh M. Beckwith. Forty-four years old in

1860, he reportedly had dry farmed a valley in the Sandia Mountains for three years; thence, by 1855, to a place called Beckwith's Ranch in the Rio Grande Valley about one mile north of old Fort Conrad. Sometime later in that decade he removed to the Rio Bonito, six miles below Fort Stanton.[24] After the Civil War the family lived for awhile at Missouri Plaza on the lower Rio Hondo, then in 1870 they established the first ranch in the Seven Rivers area, where Lakewood, New Mexico, now stands, in what would become the periphery of the Lincoln County War. Beckwith left the territory in 1878 and ended his days in Texas.[25]

Most of the fifty-four families (276 persons) in the 1860 Census had Hispanic surnames, but of the twenty-five family heads who gave their occupation as farmer, sixteen were non-Hispanic. When one looks at the values of both personal and real estate, both groups of farmers were substantial citizens, with personal estates worth between $2,500 and $10,000 and an average of forty-four acres under cultivation. Two of them, Hugh Beckwith and Moses Schnabacher, were clearly the leading entrepreneurs. In addition to his wife and four children, Beckwith's household included a miller, five laborers, a clerk, two herders, and six other persons with no listed occupation. Schnabacher may have lived on the Ruidoso; like Beckwith, he cultivated 100 acres, but unlike anyone else he was involved in livestock and freighting—with 1,800 sheep and 100 working oxen. His household included ten teamsters plus other laborers and servants—twenty-nine people in all.[26]

The overall population profile for the Rio Bonito indicates that about two dozen individuals, already relatively well-established types, came with their families and employees or *peones* to settle and develop the country and improve their own situations through contracts with the army and the Mescalero Apache agency. Some early residents (Beach, Garland, McGowan) were contractors, but evidently not farmers; Beach, at least, bought from local growers. By 1860, none of the three contractors had significant involvement in the local economy. The large quantities of feed delivered under contract at Fort Stanton may have reduced the opportunities for individuals to sell to the post in casual transactions, limiting the distribution of wealth.[27]

Occupations of the Rio Bonito settlers, other than farmer and laborer, included a musician, a seamstress, and a peddlar, all aged fifty or more, as well as a carpenter, a blacksmith, and an eighteen-year-old female with no specific livelihood. There was at least one saloon in the settlement, although the proprietor, Pablo Alderete, identified himself as a farmer.

The Rio Bonito country originally lay in Socorro County. So far as the commanders at Fort Stanton knew there was no civil authority, a situation that made it harder to deal with the troublesome whiskey trade. However, late in 1858 the commandant told departmental headquarters that the inhabitants on the Rio Bonito claimed to have "an authentic Alcalde & constable, and are endeavouring to exercise civil jurisdiction within, as well as without, this garrison & the Govt. reserve."[28] The officer at Stanton was perhaps doubly exasperated because the alcalde (actually Justice of the Peace) was Pablo Alderete, one of the accused whiskey sellers. Still, the claim was valid, since an act approved on January 15, 1858, created additional precincts in Socorro County, among them Rio Bonito, and Alderete had been commissioned Justice of the Peace as of September 20, 1858, following his election to office. A constable was elected at the same time.[29] David S. Garland received appointment to another civil office—postmaster—in May of 1857, that office being at Fort Stanton.[30]

Murder, and the benevolent treatment of accused murderers, was part of life at La Placita twenty years before the lawless years of the Lincoln County War. Four men in Captain Claiborne's company of the Regiment of Mounted Riflemen had gone to the Placita on a three-day leave and wound up with an unpaid bar bill at Alderete's saloon. They left and had gone about 1,000 yards when Alderete's son-in-law overtook them. Guns were drawn and a scuffle broke out; Pvt. Joseph Cummings' pistol went off and the son-in-law died with a bullet in his head. The soldiers broke and ran (evidently everyone was afoot) and one trooper made it back to the fort that night. There he told his tale.

Claiborne feared the worst, since the soldier thought that the Hispanics had Cummings and would kill him. The captain turned out twenty-five of his men and was back at the Placita by 11 p.m. that same night, where he proceeded to go through the houses. Alderete, Martin Sanchez, and José Torres all had blood on their clothes or their hands. The first two were "intimidated a little by me" as Claiborne gently phrased it, and Sanchez implicated others. The alcalde, Timothy McGowan, authorized incarceration of the four prisoners (including Theodosia Aragon) in the guard house at Fort Stanton.

The same morning, a corporal's guard who had remained to look for Cummings' body found it—hands tied, head split open in several places, throat cut and otherwise "horribly mangled"—in a little canyon in front of Alderete's house. The captain applied some more persuasion and got a confession out of Alderete, who now implicated six other men including several who had already fled.[31] As no court records are known to have survived from Socorro County for this period, the disposition of these cases cannot be known. Alderete and Aragon, we can surmise, got off, since the 1860 Census listed both as substantial citizens and family men in the Rio Bonito precinct. The general election that year saw Alderete reelected as Justice of the Peace.[32]

No accounts describing the appearance of La Placita before the Civil War are in evidence today, though something is known of its size. The 1860 Census, taken in October that year, listed forty-nine houses in the Rio Bonito precinct exclusive of Fort Stanton. While a map from the previous year placed Alderete's farm on the north side of the Rio Bonito, all maps from the 1860s showed the settlement at La Placita as south of the river, where Lincoln is today. One newspaper correspondent, less jaundiced than the army, reported that "the Rio Bonita, under the protecting arm of Fort Stanton, is fast becoming settled by a sturdy race of American pioneers. Many buildings are being erected, mills built, ranches opened, and everything betokening the settlement in real earnest, of a new country."[33]

Development of the country ground to a halt, or more likely went up in flames, with the opening of the Civil War. The Union garrison set fires at Fort Stanton and then beat a hasty retreat towards Albuquerque as Confederate Capt. James Walker's company arrived on the Rio Bonito.

~⌐ 2 ⌐~

CIVIL WAR ON THE
RIO BONITO

1861–1862

R elations with the Apache Indians began to deteriorate in early December of 1860 when
a band of miners, calling themselves the Pino Alto Rangers, attacked a body of Indians
on the Mimbres River in southwestern New Mexico and killed twenty-two of them, wounding and capturing many more. The Bascom affair at Apache Pass in Arizona in early February, in which a band of Chiricahua Apaches besieged a group of travelers at a stage station,
led to open warfare with the Southern and Chiricahua Apaches.[1] Meanwhile the Navajo
Indians raided south to the Jornada del Muerto and even near San Agustín Springs, twenty-
five miles east of Las Cruces, New Mexico.[2]

The Mescalero Apaches knew about these affairs and as 1861 dawned they commenced
to attack wagon trains and to rob livestock from citizens along the Rio Grande.[3] The monthly post return at Fort Stanton carried the following note for February 1861: "The Mescalero
Apaches have recently united, for hostile purposes, with the Mimbres Apaches and are
now prosecuting a war against the Whites."[4] On the Rio Bonito things remained quiet, and
the Indians stayed out of the way. Col. George B. Crittenden mounted a sweep through
their country during late March and early April of 1861.[5]

Not only did peace prevail in their home country, but fourteen Mescalero chiefs met with
the post commander on May 16, 1861, and amended their 1855 treaty, agreeing upon an
expansion of their hunting range and pledging themselves to prevent hostilities.[6] The Indians did continue to be restless, primarily because they were short of food. For the last four
years the Indian agent had encouraged the Mescaleros to plant and grow their own food,
but 1861 saw no aid forthcoming and permission denied for them to plant on the Rio Bonito.
Rations were handed out, but apparently not in sufficient amounts. The Mescaleros took to
hanging around the ranches along the Rio Bonito, leading the citizens to feel threatened in
their own security. A potential new trouble spot, at Jicarilla, about thirty miles north of
Fort Stanton, opened up in June with the discovery of gold placers that brought miners to
that area.[7]

The Superintendent of Indian Affairs for New Mexico wrote a report on the first of October, 1861, that well described the situation in the Bonito country over the previous two
months:

> At the time of the [Confederate] invasion the Mescaleras were receiving rations at
> Fort Stanton, and were conducting themselves well; but soon after the abandon-
> ment of the fort by the government troops they became involved in a quarrel with
> the Texans that brought on a fight, in which several Indians and some of the Texans
> were killed.
>
> Since then they have inaugurated a series of depredations upon the Mexican set-
> tlements, having killed one man and stolen a considerable amount of property. After
> Fort Stanton was abandoned by the government forces it was, for a short time, held

9

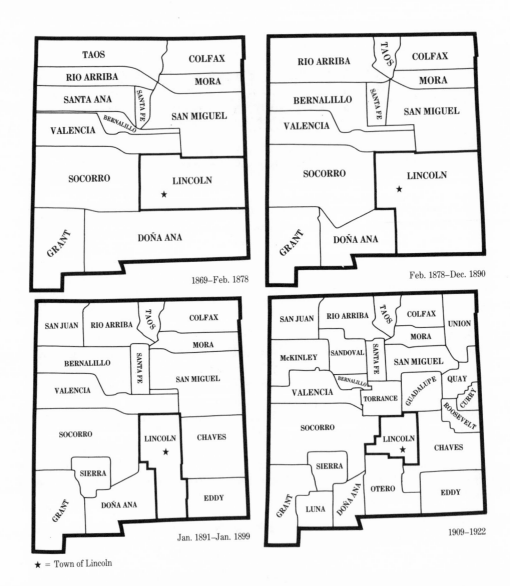

★ = Town of Lincoln

Changes in Lincoln County boundaries, 1869–present (maps from Coan, 1922).

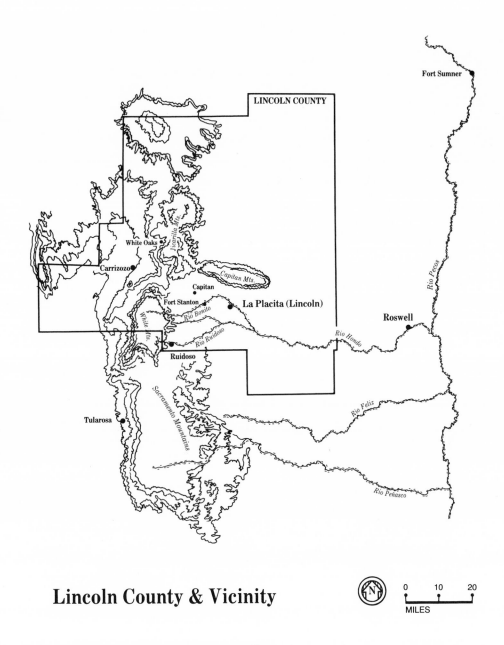

Lincoln County & Vicinity

MILES

Lincoln County and vicinity, showing 1909 county lines.

by the Texans; and when they left the Indians, smarting under the injuries they had received from the invaders, very soon assumed a hostile attitude towards the citizens on the Rio Bonito, who had settled under the protection of the fort. These settlers have made many valuable improvements on the Bonito, and their crops promised an abundant yield the present season; not less, it is said, than five thousand fanegas [twelve thousand bushels] of corn, besides a heavy crop of potatoes and other vegetables. These products would have been quite sufficient to have supplied all the demand for such articles at Fort Stanton. All this has been deserted and lost by the settlers in consequence of the hostility of the Indians.[8]

By the first of July, 1861, the army garrisons in southern New Mexico had been warned to expect demonstrations and an invasion from Texas. Fort Fillmore, on the Rio Grande a few miles below Las Cruces, received the bulk of the forces being gathered to confront the Texans while two companies of infantry and two from the Regiment of Mounted Riflemen were sent to Fort Stanton, where Lt. Col. Benjamin S. Roberts, R.M.R., commanded.

Roberts' own testimony best described the situation at Fort Stanton. His regiment had a high proportion of Southern-born officers, several of whom, including Colonel Crittenden and Captain Claiborne, had harangued the troops and sought to convince Roberts himself to leave with them and go to Texas. This subversive threat was a serious one, but evidently no one yielded to their pleas; a year later Roberts overdramatized the situation in his testimony before a congressional committee.[9] Despite his claims to the contrary, most army officers remained loyal to the Union and a paymaster had been sent to Fort Stanton in May of 1861.[10]

Ordered to put his post in the best condition for defense, Roberts reported as follows: "I have so far progressed with the defenses of this Post, as to feel secure against any attempts upon it by the Texans; unless they attack with artillery." He had one troop out towards the Pecos, the other in the direction of Fort Fillmore, and meanwhile sought to conciliate the Mescaleros. He wrote, "I have pleasure in reporting my convictions of the loyalty of my entire command. All the officers have renewed their oath of allegiance, and there is universal cheerfulness and contentment at the Post." Unfortunately there were a few problems in the neighborhood:

> There are a few secessionists and bad men in the settlements below, and I shall be glad of your directions either to cause their arrest, or remove them from this Indian Territory. They are trespassers here and may do mischief. I have already destroyed several whiskey establishments, and sent off the Indian dealers and traders in that staple of the country.[11]

All plans were cast aside after July 25, 1861, when Lt. Col. John R. Baylor's 260 Texas Confederates marched into Mesilla, New Mexico, and skirmished with the Union garrison from Fort Fillmore. Two days later Baylor's men pursued the retreating federal troops to San Agustín Springs and captured them there. Several of the U.S. soldiers slipped away and one or two made it to Fort Stanton with news of the surrender. By his own report, Roberts abandoned that post after destroying the supplies he could not carry away, setting the four companies on the road for Albuquerque and Santa Fe.[12]

Baylor had a different account:

> On the 10th of August an express reached me from Fort Stanton stating that the news of the capture of Major Lynde's command had created a stampede among the United States troops, who hastily abandoned the fort after having destroyed a considerable portion of their supplies and Government property of all kinds, and all would have been destroyed but for a storm of rain, which extinguished the fire intended by the enemy to destroy the fort. The few citizens living near the fort took pos-

House and torreon, or defensive tower, at Manzano in late 1880s. This is similar to the torreon erected in La Placita around 1863. Courtesy Aultman Studio, Trinidad, Colorado.

session of it, and saved a valuable lot of quartermaster's and commissary stores. The Mexicans and Indians in large numbers demanded the right to pillage the fort, which was granted. The citizens, being too weak to resist, not knowing that they would get aid from me or not, were forced to abandon the fort to the Mexicans and Indians.[13]

All of this supposedly happened on August 2. Six days later, according to a more vivid recounting in the *Mesilla Times*, an express arrived at Mesilla,

> bringing the intelligence of the hasty abandonment of Fort Stanton by the United States troops. This occurred shortly after the surrender of San Augustin; two fugitives from Lynde's command fled to this post and gave information of that affair. The garrison was panic stricken, and, supposing the whole Confederate forces would be down upon them, immediately evacuated the fort.
>
> They set fire to the fort in several places before they left. Forty Arizonians, under the command of Capt. Hare, immediately took possession in the name of the Confederacy, put out the fires, and kept guard over the property. The express asked for immediate assistance, as between Mexicans and Indians they had their hands full in protecting the stores. The property and stores are estimated to be of $300,000 value.[14]

Baylor sent Capt. James Walker's company ("D," Second Regiment Texas Mounted Rifles) to occupy the post: "Most of the commissary and quartermaster supplies were saved and a battery. . . . The families there were at the mercy of Indians and Mexicans, and I thought it proper to garrison the post, at least until I could learn the wishes of the Government."[15]

Roberts' destruction had been much less thorough than he reported. According to the *Mesilla Times*, "Capt. Walker's command captured at Fort Stanton and in that vicinity, fifty-one wagon loads of quartermaster and commissary; thirteen wagon loads were captured at Mansano, within a day and a half's march of Albuquerque."[16] The newspaper was wrong about Manzano, which was nearly at Albuquerque's doorstep but never seriously threatened. Capt. Saturnino Barrientos' scouts were watching the routes from Fort Stanton. Barrientos wrote from the Sierra Gallinas late in August to tell Colonel Canby, the federal commander in Santa Fe, that according to his best information the Texans intended to take Manzano "pronto." Hugh Beckwith, Pablo Alderete, and several others from the Rio Bonito had sworn allegiance to the invaders:[17] Canby had already learned that the Texans were at Fort Stanton and that . . . "a man named Beckwith and others in the neighborhood of Rio Bonito have joined these troops . . . allegedly increasing their numbers to about 150."[18]

On the wretched 12th of August, as a literary but anonymous correspondent from the Rio Bonito put it, the Texans had marched in at 3 p.m. The writer's description of what happened then was far different from the Confederate versions:

> El dia 13 me nombró el pueblo paraque á su nombre pidiera garantías sobre sus vidas, intereses y familias, las cuales concedió depico, porque en la misma noche todos sus satelites andaban forzando puertas, violando mujeres y niñas, y lo menos que nos han hecho es saquearnos hasta lo que no teniamos, con el pretesto de ser todo propiedad del antiguo gobierno.[19]

In essence, the writer is saying, "On the 13th (of August) the people asked me to be their spokesman and request guarantees for their lives, interests and families, which he (the Confederate commander) granted. He went back on this because the same night his creatures were roving about forcing doors, raping women and children, and the least that they did to us was to rob us of everything, under the pretext that this was all right under the old (Union) government."

Whatever their treatment of civilians, the Confederate tenure at Fort Stanton was a rough one. Four men were sent to the Gallinas Mountains to watch for any advancing Federal troops. Indians surprised them instead, killed and scalped three of the men while the fourth one escaped by spurring his horse down an almost perpendicular slope and galloping away amidst a shower of arrows.[20] As the *Mesilla Times* told it,

> We have received from Capt. Walker, particulars of the late massacre of three of his company [by] the Kiowa Indians. A spy party of 4 men were sent out on the 2d of Sept. On the 3d, while at dinner near the fork of the Albuquerque and Fort Union roads, eighty-five miles from Fort Stanton, they were suddenly surrounded by thirty or forty Indians, supposed to be Kiowas. After four hours hard fighting, three of the Americans were killed, and the fourth, Sargeant T.A. Saunders, succeeded in making his escape having a very fast horse. The names of those killed are, Jas. Emmemcher, Jas. Mossee, and T.G. Pemberton; all of Lavaca County, Texas. Emmenecher was the last one that fell, having received many wounds. As soon as he fell, he was surrounded by Indians, who commenced torturing him with arrows, etc., to which he returned scorn and contempt, and showed them when dying, an undaunted spirit. His last words heard by his comrade, were taunts to his persecutors. When his body was found, his tongue and eyes had been cut out, most probably while still alive. Those who visited the scene for the purpose of burying the dead, report that at least ten or twelve Indians must have been killed. Behind every pine tree in the vicinity, was blood.[21]

Another party went back to bury the dead and returned to the fort on September 8. That day was a long one, since

> the same evening word was brought into the fort that the Indians had attacked the Placito, a Mexican settlement 10 miles below the fort. I was ordered to take fifteen men there and protect the citizens; did so; had an engagement with them [the Indians], and killed five. Returned to the fort amidst a pouring rain at 2 a.m.[22]

This brief report was apparently the only account of how the Confederates helped to defend La Placita. Later in the morning of September 9 the Texans abandoned Fort Stanton and started back towards the Rio Grande.

The citizens on the Rio Bonito, surrounded now by hostile Indians, were in an untenable position. Most of them did the only thing they could do and abandoned the country themselves; scouts from Captain Barrientos' company met them some miles out from Manzano and were told that they had left "on account of risk from Indians."[23] Colonel Canby still expected that the Confederates might advance by way of the Pecos River and he continued to keep scouts out in that country. Early in January 1862 one patrol just in from the Rio Bonito found no signs of Texans but reported "there are still remaining there a number of families." Charles Beach had abandoned his ranch only as of December 25, 1861, blaming Indian depredations.[24]

Long before then another murderous incident took place. When most of the Rio Bonito settlers left about mid-September, their crops were still growing in the fields with a promise of an abundant harvest. Some two weeks later Capt. Isaiah Moore reported from his camp near Manzano that "it is almost certain that there are no Texans at Stanton. Twenty-five men left here the other day to gather their crops in that country."[25] This party was almost certainly the one whose fate a distant newspaper reported later:

> Indian Massacre.—The overland mail which arrived at Kansas City on the 17th brought intelligence of a terrible massacre by the Indians at Fort Stanton. It is stated that on the approach of the Texans to that post in the summer, all the citizens in the vicinity fled to the settlements, leaving their homes, crops, and everything else

behind. After the Texans abandoned the place, the Apache Indians took possession, and had command of all the country around. The full party, numbering twenty men, determined to revisit the neighborhood, and obtain what they could of the remaining crops, when the whole number fell into the hands of the savages, and were brutally murdered.[26]

The victims must have been from many of the families formerly in the Rio Bonito. Few of the earlier settlers returned after the Civil War.

Several civilians with known rebel sympathies received special treatment. Pablo Alderete, a principal in the murder of a soldier two years before, reportedly swore to defend southern principles to the last drop of his blood, then went to Mesilla "and was very active as one of their partisans." He was soon taken prisoner and forwarded to Albuquerque.[27]

Hugh Beckwith involved himself with a scheme, supposedly masterminded by a former territorial secretary who went south. This involved sending or planting letters designed to raise doubts about the loyalty of New Mexican leaders and to subvert the raising of volunteer regiments. In one such letter to J. Francisco Chaves, who was the governor's stepson and already a major in the Second Regiment, New Mexico Volunteers, Beckwith wrote from Fort Stanton "feeling assured of your loyalty and patriotism in behalf of the Confederate States of America" and expecting to see him at this post very shortly. The writer well knew that this would probably be read by others before it reached Chaves, who was hardly a southern sympathizer. The potential damage to the Union war effort by circulating such letters was substantial. Canby was aware of this campaign and evidently intercepted other correspondence of the same type.[28]

For the moment Beckwith lay beyond reach, but before 1862 was out a military commission instituted proceedings against him, while a civilian grand jury indicted him for selling whiskey to the Apaches and inciting them to rise against the government. On top of this, his property was attached in a civil suit. Canby's successor, Brig. Gen. James H. Carleton, ordered Beckwith's ranches on the Rio Bonito and upper Hondo seized and held for government purposes. These were not returned, but Beckwith seems to have escaped other punishment.[29]

A third person, Charles Beach, was in even less favor. Carleton wrote: "I consider Mr. Beach an improper person to reside in the Mescalero country, so he will be forbidden under any circumstances from settling there."[30] Beach was eventually vindicated of the charges against him; in later years a person by that name held army contracts at Camp Date Creek, Arizona. As of 1866 the old Beach and Beckwith farms were rented out with one-third of the produce going to Fort Stanton, one-third to the owners, and one-third to the renters.[31]

From January through the fall of 1862 the Mescalero Apaches continued to roam and raid the Rio Bonito country. Once the Confederate Army of New Mexico had been defeated and expelled from the territory, the Indian problem could be faced again. Chief Manuelito came forward in early September to ask for peace, telling Col. Christopher Carson that he was authorized to speak for the entire Mescalero nation, planned to make a treaty, and wanted the U.S. troops and the New Mexicans to return and settle on the Rio Bonito.[32] Carson thought the offer was made in good faith but General Carleton chose war instead.

A third threat in the spring of 1862, severe flooding by the Rio Grande, left many people in the Mesilla Valley destitute. A number of families moved to the site of Tularosa, where the Santa Fe *Gazette* reported that fifty or sixty settlers from La Mesilla had established themselves "and have commenced agricultural labors."[33] According to later newspaper accounts,

the first settlement . . . was made in Tularosa in 1862. The settlers were fugitives from the Mexican settlement of Picacho which had been destroyed by a sudden rise in the waters of the Rio Grande. They were few in numbers and lived in constant dread of an attack by roving bands of the murderous Apaches, who held full sway over the surrounding country. The oldest was Santos Saiuz [*sic*; Saenz] of Tularosa, who died a few days ago at the advanced age of 92 years.[34]

Señor Saenz' obituary claimed that "he was the first settler in this section of New Mexico, coming to Tularosa in June, 1862, 37 years ago. Peach trees planted by him in 1863 are still alive and bearing in Tularosa."[35] Before the year was out, settlers began returning to the Rio Bonito as well.

~ 3 ~

RESETTLEMENT

1862–1869

The last Confederates disappeared back into Texas in July of 1862, just as the 1,400 federal reinforcements, called "the Column from California," arrived in New Mexico. Their commander, General Carleton, was no stranger to the Southwest. In September of that year he assumed command of the Military Department of New Mexico. Because of active or threatening Indian hostilities on all sides he kept the troops on a war footing with the southern part of the territory under martial law.

As one of Carleton's first acts, he sent Col. Christopher Carson with five companies of New Mexico Volunteers to regarrison Fort Stanton. They were ordered to make war on the Mescalero Apaches, killing the men and taking the women and children as prisoners.[1] Carson launched a campaign that turned out to be brief, but effective and humane. By early December it had ended and Carson could claim that

> the happy effect this change will have upon this part of the country, by far the best grazing, and no doubt the most productive in the Territory, is already beginning to be felt. Settlers are arriving every day from all parts of the Territory, and of that class that will develop the resources of the country. . . . Below the military reserve on the Rio Bonito and Riodoso, settlements are springing up rapidly and a large quantity of wheat is already in the ground. . . . Before spring I anticipate an influx of emigrants into this section of the country that will have no parallel in the history of the Territory.[2]

At the time Carson sent this bit of euphoria, the 240 Apaches in his custody were being readied for transfer to their new home at Fort Sumner on the Pecos River. By February 1863, some 350 Apache Indians were being held there; in early September the number had risen to 436.[3] Indian raids continued nonetheless, complicated now by Navajos depredating within the old range of the Mescaleros.[4]

The settlers who drifted back to the Rio Bonito had reason to be optimistic. With the Mescaleros mostly out of the way and the threat of Indian raids in general much reduced, this was a good country for raising crops and grazing livestock. The reestablishment of Fort Stanton also guaranteed a steady market for the local farmers. That market might have increased tremendously if General Carleton's original plan to collect the Mescaleros together, make a definite treaty with them, and then let them return to a reservation in their own country had been carried through. Instead, by March of 1863 he had decided to keep the Indians on a reservation at Fort Sumner permanently.[5] In the Jicarilla District, miners were returning to work the gold placers.[6]

Colonel Carson sent another promotional letter about the Rio Bonito country less than a month after his first one:

> I am happy to state that there no longer exists any reason why the prolific valleys of the Bonito, Pecos and their tributaries should remain uncultivated, and the resources of this section of the Country, so rich in mineral wealth and fertility remain undeveloped. . . . Since the arrival of my Command at this post several "Ranches" and

grazing camps have been established thro' the Country, and not one instance has come to my knowledge of even a sheep having been stolen by Indians.[7]

This state of peace was a sometimes thing and resettlement may have been rather slow. Indians raided the farmers on the Ruidoso in May 1863 and killed one man; two months later they attacked some herders at the Placita and killed another.[8] It was likely in this period that the settlement of La Placita built its *torreon*, a three-story stone tower built for defense against Indian raids.

In September a scouting party reported Joseph Storms cultivating corn at his ranch near the junction of the Bonito and Ruidoso and no signs of Indians in that country for months.[9] Another letter out of Fort Stanton claimed that the citizens had a bad time of it that first season:

> The majority of the inhabitants in this vicinity are almost in a starving condition not for want of money to buy the necessities of life but for want of some where to procure them. There is no store in this vicinity where flour can be purchased hence the suffering amongst the inhabitants. . . . The wheat crops will be matured in a few weeks from this time which will in a great means alleviate the suffering in this vicinity.[10]

The post commander did issue small quantities of flour to the distressed citizens.

Stories that claim La Placita and the Bonito country were settled by people from Manzano may actually refer to the post-Civil War period.[11] We do not know where within New Mexico the settlers, many of whom were laborers, came from beginning in 1855. When the families abandoned the Rio Bonito late in 1861, many of them did withdraw to the Manzano area. Two years later Manzano was in poor shape, as the Surveyor General of New Mexico learned from a caller one evening:

> [Frank] Higgins from Mesilla called this evening to see me in relation to land matters in his district. A Mexican from near Manzana called with him and wished to know what he had to do to secure rights in the Rio Bonito valley, where he and some eighty heads of families proposed to move to next spring. He says for three years the water has so failed at Manzano that they have raised hardly anything, *and the whole* people are obliged to move. I gave him all the information required and he went his way rejoicing.[12]

Whatever the number that left Manzano that spring, the community still had an estimated population of 300 as of 1866.[13]

Relations with Indians in the Bonito country continued hostile, especially after they escaped from Fort Sumner on the night of November 3, 1865. There were raids and murders even in the town of Placita; during one two-week period the Indians attacked at different points "on the Rio Bonito Placita" and killed one woman, three boys, and six men.[14] More people died in raids along the Ruidoso.[15] Despite the hostilities, settlers not only stuck it out but improved their holdings to the point where it was estimated that in 1865 "The corn crops in this section are better than they have been for years and it is estimated that 2500 or 3000 fanegas of corn can be bought here and some 1500 at the Tuloroso."[16]

One peculiarity of the Rio Bonito is that very little description of the settlements there or of the countryside exists from any period. One exception was the long letter by a Brev. Maj. Lawrence G. Murphy, then a volunteer officer commanding at Fort Stanton, dated June 10, 1866.[17] Murphy was winding up some five years of service with the New Mexico Volunteers on top of ten years of enlisted duty in the regular army. He would remain a leading figure, first at Fort Stanton and then at Lincoln, New Mexico, until his death in late 1878.

REPORT OF MAJ. LAWRENCE G. MURPHY—June 10, 1866
SHOWING THE POPULATION, AGRICULTURAL RESOURCES, FARMING IMPLEMENTS, FLOUR MILLS, ETC. OF TULAROSA, AND RIOS RUIDOSO, HONDO, AND BONITO

Place	Population		Corn		Wheat		Beans		Flour Mills	Wagons	Ploughs	Stock			Remarks
	American	Mexican	No. of acres planted	No. of fanegas supposed to yield	No. of acres planted	No. of fanegas supposed to yield	No. of acres planted	No. of fanegas supposed to yield				Horses and Mules	Cattle comprising Oxen & Cows	Sheep and Goats	
Tularosa	4	496	1,000	10,000	30	300	100	1,000	2 small, water-power	22	None but the old class of wooden Mexican ploughs	51	274	2,000	There are about 2,000 acres of land that could be placed under cultivation, but owing to bad management, and no system for a supply of water, this is not done. Each settler has alloted to him a piece of ground 960 yards long and 400 yards wide, in the vicinity of the town.
Rios Ruidoso and Hondo	40	80	1,002	13,000	90	900	60	600		10	American ploughs used only by Americans	30	70		
Rio Bonito	5	300	500	3,000	75	750	50	500	2	10		60	200	300	
Total	49	876	2,502	26,000	195	1,950	210	2,100	4	42		141	544	2,300	

Murphy may have visited Fort Stanton as early as 1862, though his command of that post began in April 1866, lasting a few months. His information about events before 1865 was mostly in error, while for the spring of 1866 it was precise and probably quite accurate. The figures in his table (see page 21) showed that accurate records existed of the acreages cultivated and the crops grown in the Rio Bonito area, including the Tularosa country. The 1,352 acres of farmland along the Bonito and Ruidoso were nearly twenty-four percent greater than the amount cultivated in 1860.

The settlements in 1866 evidently continued the pre-Civil War pattern of scattered farms along the main valleys with humble dwellings and settlers who depended upon the military both for protection and as a market for their grain. The native Hispanic and eastern migrant (Anglo) populations were both well represented, the former living along the Rio Bonito while the latter settled in the Ruidoso and Hondo valleys.

Land tenure was by right of possession. Although titles to improvements had been passed by quitclaim deeds as far back as 1858, there was no legal mechanism for obtaining a patent on a tract of land until a survey had been made. For most of the Bonito and Hondo valleys, the exterior boundary surveys and subdivisions of townships were done in 1867. In Octo-

Lily Casey Klasner's remembrances of her youth in Lincoln were lost for many years and eventually published in the memoir My Girlhood Among Outlaws. *Courtesy University of Arizona Press.*

ber surveyor Robert Willison found the Plaza San Patricio on the lower Rio Ruidoso to be "a settlement of about 40 families, who are cultivating the land along the Rio Ruidoso for a distance of about 3 miles on each side of the town."[18] San Patricio also had a church, or more likely a small chapel. Willison wrote at the same time that "the Placita del Rio Bonito is a town containing about 60 houses."[19] Six months earlier another surveyor, Hiram Fellows, had claimed that "the town of Placita in the SW corner of the Township [T9S R16E] contains some Forty houses and 21 Stores."[20] These "stores" must have been small affairs, probably operated in one room of a family home.

The best description of early-day Lincoln is provided by Lily Casey Klasner, whose writings in the 1920s about places and events of her girlhood in Lincoln County were eventually collected in her book *My Girlhood Among Outlaws*. Her memory, where there is other information to check it against, was quite accurate. She arrived in what was still Socorro County as a five-year-old child in 1868, and retained vivid memories of the trip:

> In 1868, Lincoln was not known as Lincoln, but was called simply La Placita. . . . I distinctly remember my first visit to La Placita. One day in 1868 Father announced that he was going there the next day for a meeting of the citizens of that section on some matter of business, and he offered to take Mother and the children along. . . . Alec Duval had a sort of hotel in connection with the La Placita branch of L.G. Murphy & Co.'s store, and we took accommodations there for the night. We children did not object to the continuation of our visit, for it gave us time to ramble around and see something of the town.
>
> Scattered along the two sides of a crooked stretch of road were twelve or fifteen houses which might be credited with a certain degree of pretension. They were adobe, flat-roofed, angular in shape, and one story in height. In the rear of the houses fronting on the street were a number of *jacals*, that is, houses of a simpler type made by standing up cedar or juniper posts and daubing them together into walls by applying mud. Both sorts of houses were plastered on the outside with mud and whitewashed inside with a gyp [gypsum] solution, called by the Mexicans *jaspe*.
>
> The population of the town was predominantly Mexican, most of them getting their livelihood by farming tracts of land up and down the valley of the Bonito which flows by the edge of the town and furnishes abundant water for irrigation. The business section of La Placita consisted of a few stores. José Montaña had a store and saloon, and Jacinto Sánchez a store in which Antonio Avan Sedillo worked. Captain Saturnino Baca, who later became one of the conspicuous citizens, had not then moved to the town, but was living some miles to the west in the vicinity of the old Antonio Torres place. Mariano Trujillo was the most prominent citizen of the village; . . .
>
> Alec Duval ran a saloon which was also a branch of the L.G. Murphy & Co.'s store. Pete Bishop, a large, bald-headed old man, ran a regular saloon in the town; that is, his place was exclusively for the dispensing of alcoholic liquors.[21]

The Placita was on the right (south) bank of the Rio Bonito, with ranches above and below the town.[22] So far as is known, the village has always stood at the same location.

Several aspects of the Rio Bonito community in the late 1860s are worth emphasizing. One is that it was a very small community, perhaps with three hundred people in all, on the ranches and in the town. Nor was everyone there entirely as a matter of his or her own choice; some and perhaps most of the residents were either sharecroppers or laborers of some kind. Major Murphy alluded to this in an 1866 letter:

> Mexican citizens who settled here in 1862, are still peddling at their fifteen or twenty acres, most of them on shares, and all of them in the same condition as regards wealth as they were in then. He would be a great benefactor to his people who would make them understand that it would be better for them to cultivate their own ground

than to go in shares and cultivate the ground of another man. I told them that two or three men own the whole of the farming land at Placitas, and I know of instances where men have from one hundred to two hundred acres under cultivation to which they did not contribute an hour's work but half the produce will be theirs, and the real tillers of the soil have not a particle of claim to it, and may be set adrift as soon as the crop is gathered.[23]

Finally, there was the impact of Fort Stanton on the local economy. Murphy continued:

Remove the troops (within the next couple of years) and the market for the produce of the farmers is destroyed, and the incentive of gain which is now attracting settlers, and which induces them to take so much risk will be taken away.

In his Annual Report for 1869–1870 the secretary of war portrayed the situation even more starkly. While from a military point of view Fort Stanton was wholly unnecessary, its economic importance could not be underrated:

Certainly it would be safe to say that not more than twelve or fifteen hundred persons have settled in all that region near Fort Stanton for the fifteen years of its existence, and these settlers found their sole market at the fort. Far from being self sustaining, the settlers could sell nothing except to the post, and if it goes they must go also, and that entirely irrespective of Indians.[24]

At this period the Mescaleros were still hostile. The first movements toward a reservation dated from the spring of 1871.[25] The secretary was correct in saying that without Fort Stanton there was no market for local products and therefore no basis for the settlements to sustain themselves, whether the Indians were raiding or not.

On January 16, 1869, the governor of New Mexico signed an act to create and organize the County of Lincoln. Saturnino Baca was president of the special legislative committee to which the bill had been referred. The committee reported in favor of passage and the Legislature adopted the committee report by a roll call vote of twenty-two in favor, none against. Lincoln County at that time consisted of the former eastern part of Socorro County. Only in February 1878 was the new county enlarged to include almost the entire southeastern quarter of New Mexico (see page 10).[26]

Army records continued to refer to the principal settlement in Lincoln County as the Placita until about 1873. The Lincoln post office dates from September 19, 1873, and the name change from La Placita to Lincoln may have been in compliance with a post office order.[27]

Until 1869 the Rio Bonito country had been a precinct of Socorro County. Now in March 1869 the acting governor ordered an election for the offices of probate judge and sheriff in Lincoln County. This was held on April 19, with Lawrence G. Murphy elected probate judge and Mauricio Sanchez as sheriff, both receiving their commissions on May 12. At the first general election that fall, Murphy won reelection as probate judge while William Brady received the necessary votes to become sheriff.[28] From then until their deaths in 1878, these two men were among the most widely known citizens of the county.

Service in the army at Fort Stanton had brought Lt. Col. Emil Fritz of the California Volunteers together with Captain Brady and Major Murphy of the New Mexico Volunteers, each of whom commanded Fort Stanton at various times between 1864 and 1866 and settled there after mustering out. Capt. Saturnino Baca served at Stanton and later returned to live on the Rio Bonito, while former Pvt. George W. Peppin took up a ranch on the Rio Ruidoso in 1867.[29] These five worked closely with one another and had prominent roles in the Lincoln County conflicts of the 1870s. The partnership of Fritz and Murphy, as L.G. Murphy and Co., became a dominant economic power for a time.

PART II

"The town of Lincoln, the County Seat, shows considerable enterprise and prosperity . . ." **Mesilla Valley Independent, October 13, 1877.**

". . . L.G. Murphy & Co. were absolute monarchs of Lincoln County and ruled their subjects with an oppressive iron heel." **Deposition of A.A. McSween, June 6, 1878.**

Remington Revolving Rifle, ca. 1866–1872, caliber .38; six shot, single action; barrel length 28 inches.

∼ 4 ∽

THE RISE AND DECLINE
OF THE HOUSE OF MURPHY

1867–1873

The Lincoln County War of 1878–1879 was not a cattle or a range war, nor even a feud. Essentially it grew out of a struggle for economic power in a land where hard cash was scarce and federal contracts for the supply of provisions, especially beef, for the military posts and Indian reservations were the grand prizes. The competition for these contracts became bitter and frequently ruthless.[1]

On one side in this competition was the firm of L.G. Murphy & Co., known as the House of Murphy or simply "The House." Opponents of Murphy & Co. painted the House in the blackest of terms:

> I am informed that Lawrence G. Murphy and Emil Fritz doing business under the style of L.G. Murphy & Co. had the monopoly for the sale of merchandise in this County, and used their power to oppress and grind out all they could from the farmers and force those who were opposed to them to leave the County. For instance the farmers would buy merchandise of them at exorbitant prices, and were compelled to turn in their produce in payment thereof at prices that suited L.G. Murphy & Co., and if a farmer refused so to do, they were subjected to litigation and the whole judicial machinery was used unwittedly [sic] to accomplish that object. The result of these proceedings were that L.G. Murphy & Co. were absolute monarchs of Lincoln County and ruled their subjects (the farmers & others) with an oppressive iron heel. This state of affairs has existed for some time, at least ten years.[2]

An officer at Fort Stanton alleged that Murphy & Co. had swindled the government outrageously in the matter of Indian supplies; that the prices of their goods sold to enlisted men at Fort Stanton were extortionate; that their tradership was a den of infamy and its toleration a disgrace to the public service.[3]

Lily Klasner said much the same in the perspective of fifty years:

> The firm of L.G. Murphy & Co. . . . not only supplied the whole of Lincoln County with the necessities of life, but it held the population in what was approximate peonage. . . . Only those who have experienced it can realize the extent to which Murphy & Co. dominated the country and controlled its people, economy, and politics. . . . All Lincoln County was cowed and intimidated by them.[4]

Since the House rarely sought to refute such charges, they were generally believed. More recent writers have repeated these claims, if less colorfully.

For the ten years of L.G. Murphy & Co.'s existence—1867–1877—it was the best-known institution in Lincoln County and the center of more than one controversy. The people who claimed that the company swindled, extorted, monopolized, and so forth were not, it must be recognized, disinterested parties themselves. To determine the role of the House of Murphy during the most violent decade in Lincoln County's history, the firm's operations must

Post trader's store at Fort Stanton, ca. 1886. The building was built by Emil Fritz and L.G. Murphy in the 1860s. Courtesy Rio Grande Historical Collections, New Mexico State University.

be assessed carefully. Only then can Murphy & Co. and those who opposed them be viewed in the true light of understanding.

Fortunately there is plenty of evidence, including L.G. Murphy & Co.'s own ledger covering eighteen months in 1871–1872 when the company was probably at its peak. A daybook for most of 1873; their bank records beginning in 1871; listings (complete or nearly so) of their contracts with both the army and the Indian Superintendency in New Mexico; and even partial income tax accounts supply much documentation.[5] From these records, much can be inferred about the operations of the House.

Murphy, as has been suggested, had a military background in staff positions. In the Fifth U.S. Infantry he had worked his way up to being quartermaster sergeant of the regiment. In the New Mexico Volunteers he served as a regimental quartermaster, recruiting officer, regimental adjutant, and in 1865 as acting agent to the Apache Indians at Fort Sumner.[6] Supplies and logistics were his speciality. According to Lily Klasner, Murphy was a natty dresser, quick-tempered and generous on occasion. He also had a habit of heavy drinking. A dreamer and a planner, he let others put his schemes into action.[7]

Emil Fritz, the other partner in the House, was a few years older and evidently less outgoing than Murphy, but his energy and businesslike attitude complemented Murphy's qualities in the seven years of their partnership. (Fritz had tuberculosis and left Lincoln in the spring of 1873 to revisit his old home in Germany, where he died on June 24, 1874.)[8] The two had served together at Fort Sumner and also at Fort Stanton prior to their discharges in September 1866. While at Fort Sumner they undoubtedly met J.A. LaRue, the post trader and later the Indian trader there. LaRue at the time was a very successful businessman, having paid taxes on an income of $7,000. in 1865.[9] Fritz and Murphy may well have attempted to model their operation upon his. LaRue probably did give them their start, as the largest single liability carried over to the L.G. Murphy & Co. ledger on May 1, 1871, was a debt of $21,505.38 to J.A. LaRue. The partnership still owed LaRue more than $16,000. when the books were balanced again on August 31, 1874, indicating that either Murphy and Fritz never worked this off or LaRue continued to finance them.[10]

L.G. Murphy & Co. probably began business in April 1867, paying $22. in taxes on sales of $22,000. in merchandise from that date through 1868. This was a relatively unimpressive start, as Henry Lesinsky & Co. of Las Cruces often did that much business in a month during this same period. Murphy may have bought out the interests of L.B. Maxwell, who had been a licensed wholesaler and retailer of both liquor and merchandise at Fort Stanton since the first of May, 1863.[11]

Upon starting their business, the new firm promptly made application to remain at Fort Stanton as the post trader. They received a recommendation, but the order granting such permission was delayed until April 28, 1868.[12] Fritz in the meantime proposed to rent lands not required for government purposes at Fort Stanton, presumably as a site for the post trader's store, but Murphy resolved the situation temporarily by filing a preemption claim.[13] Their building must have been started soon after permission came through, at a location described as "up-stream some distance and just around the point of a little cañon that led down to the river."[14]

The two partners seemed to be verging on prosperity, despite their modest start. Murphy paid taxes on a personal income of $1,850. for 1868 and on $1,500. in 1869,[15] indicating that the two men were taking a large portion out of their business as personal profits. Even before the post tradership came through, they had discovered army contracting and received one-year contracts from September 1, 1867, to furnish both fresh beef and beef on the hoof for the Fort Stanton garrison.[16] These were "supply as needed" contracts with very good unit prices. (Since we do not know the amounts delivered, the ultimate dollar values are unknown.) Things improved in 1868 when they were awarded a $9,390. contract to furnish lumber for rebuilding Fort Stanton, followed by one in 1869 to supply 250,000 pounds of corn for $7,775.[17] By this time they were probably acting as subcontractors for other suppliers as well. The only hint of controversy during this early period came in early 1869 when two freighters swore that they had delivered twenty-six sacks of flour to Lawrence G. Murphy instead of to the commissary officer at Fort Stanton. Apparently this didn't even lead to an investigation.[18]

Murphy was removed as post trader by the secretary of war in the fall of 1870. The reasons were not stated.[19] That same year Congress changed the law governing post traders.[20] Murphy & Co. applied for reinstatement and were recommended by the officers at Fort Stanton, but the Department of the Missouri omitted this firm from their list of requested reappointments. Murphy's politics may have been the reason; in Washington the adjutant general replied to an inquiry by saying that Fritz and Murphy had always been "virulent opponents" of the Republican Party and that Murphy "as Probate Judge [of] Lincoln Co. [had] stolen out Republican votes to make it appear the county was Democratic." The New Mexico congressional delegate had another candidate in mind—a good Republican.[21]

Perhaps Murphy foresaw the outcome when he offered in August to sell his building to the army for use as a hospital—for $12,000. The structure was commodious, with eighteen rooms and 6,882 square feet of space under the roof. The post surgeon thought that it would do well as a hospital, but the district quartermaster declined the offer.[22]

This left L.G. Murphy & Co. with their building and still as the de facto post traders. From 1870 the army made a series of short-term post trader appointments; some of the people never showed up while others suffered removal. Bliss & Lombard did function in that capacity for about a year, but they were removed after Murphy bought them out in April 1872.[23] The House of Murphy stayed on at Fort Stanton, kept the competition at bay, and as of March 30, 1871, held an Indian Department license to trade with the Mescalero Apaches.[24] They had a branch store at La Placita as well.

Murphy and Co. entered the 1870s serving still a third clientele, the settlers of the Rio Bonito country. The twenty-one stores at the Placita in the 1867 Census must have been pretty ephemeral, since the 1870 Census listed the eighty-five male heads of households below Fort Stanton and above the Robert Casey (Lily Klasner's father) Ranch on the Rio Hondo only as farmers, laborers, and a single musician.[25] As late as 1872, Lt. Col. August Kautz wrote with reference to Murphy & Co. and Bliss & Lombard that "these two establishments being the only trading posts, all the settlers are at present compelled to come here for their supplies and the troops are materially benefitted by this fact and the competition of the two traders at the Post."[26] Actually, Elisha Dow was a merchant in Lincoln at the time and small stores existed at the Casey Ranch and at Blazer's Mill on the Ruidoso, as well as in Tularosa and San Patricio. Later in the decade Isaac Ellis, Juan Patron, and José Montaño all had stores at Lincoln in competition with the House.

Murphy & Co. offered services as well as goods. For the traveler they operated a restaurant (Samuel Wortley's Mess), a lager beer saloon supplied by their own brewery, a billiard room, and probably accommodations. For the settlers and officers at the fort they allowed purchases on credit, apparently without limits or terms of settlement—a bad system and almost unheard of in an economy where money was scarce. Enlisted men evidently had to pay in cash since none had accounts in the Murphy ledger. Because of this, the army's complaint that soldiers were charged outrageous prices cannot be checked. Finally, the House of Murphy was effectively a branch bank where a person could deposit money, if he had any, arrange to have it transferred, or even borrow on occasion. At one time Murphy was also postmaster at Fort Stanton.

Murphy and Fritz were much more than storekeepers: they were mercantile capitalists.[27] In an economy where capital was generated by writing promissory notes and money scarcely circulated, the merchant credit system was the cornerstone of every settler's livelihood, as well as the source of the condemnation Murphy & Co. inspired in their years of doing business in Lincoln County.

Murphy and Co.'s own ledger and daybook are excellent sources for examining both the business practices and life in general in the Rio Bonito country during the early 1870s. Murphy's clerks entered the value of every item purchased and of every service rendered.[28] Lily Klasner cited their prices accurately in her memoirs—thread, 25¢; baking soda, 50¢; tobacco, 50¢—except that coffee and sugar cost up to 62½¢ per pound.[29] For the gourmet the shelves held spiced oysters and champagne, while whiskey (apparently from Kentucky) at $1.25 a bottle and locally brewed beer at $1.00 to $1.25 per gallon must have seemed like bargains. For dry goods and other merchandise items, we know only the sale prices and not the markups, but the partners sold food staples such as beef, bacon, sugar, and coffee on credit at approximately 100 percent more than they allowed. This was a reasonable margin, then as now. If it applied to their other goods, then allegations that the House charged exorbitant prices would seem to have little basis. Their prices to cash customers we of course do not know.

Murphy & Co. ran a number of subsidiary businesses. One of these, Samuel Wortley's Mess, was a restaurant (and possibly a boarding house) with a varied, even extravagant, bill of fare. Another enterprise, the Rio Bonito Brewery, must have been a boutique or vanity operation, to judge by the large number of charges on its account and the low volume of sales—301 gallons in January of 1872 but otherwise much less. The merchandise consigned to their branch store at the Placita indicated a low volume of business there.

Family men such as William Brady and Saturnino Baca made frequent purchases of cloth, sewing supplies, foodstuffs, and children's clothing from the House. Christmas was celebrated with a big dinner and modest gift giving. At the Lincoln (Wortley) Hotel on Christmas, 1884, guests were well feasted with roast duck, chicken, pork, sweet potatoes, and all the "usual ornaments, both plain and scalloped, liquid and solid."[30] William Brady took home four bottles of champagne ($16.) on December 24, 1872, but no gifts. Another customer purchased some ribbon, two dolls, a skirt, a perfume box, and one pomade jar (probably facial cream) that same Christmas. Several other men bought children's clothing.

With virtually all of their customers buying on credit and taking out occasional small loans, one might expect that Murphy & Co. required settlements on the accounts. When the ledger opened May 1, 1871, individuals already owed the House some $26,000.00, Saturnino Baca's $4,842.21 debt being by far the largest owed by anyone. Yet he and everyone else went merrily along letting their tabs run. James J. Dolan probably kept the books at that time. He included a monthly balance for the entire merchandising business. For May–December of 1871 the sales exceeded receipts by over $25,000., while in 1872 this difference came to more than $38,000.[31]

In August 1872 the Santa Fe *Daily New Mexican* reported

Maj. Murphy was attending yesterday to the wants of Fort Stanton—that delightful retreat on the banks of the Rio Bonito—and Spiegelberg Bros. were attending to the wants of Murphy. The consequence was a wholesale raid upon the wholesale department and a literal jamming and choking of the sidewalk with goods, compelling pedestrians to "take the street for it." The whole affair gave the liveliest satisfaction: Maj. Murphy was delighted to get goods so cheap; Spiegelberg Bros. were tickled to make so grand a sale; Fort Stanton has reason to rejoice at obtaining such a supply of the best, finest and latest styles of goods, useful and ornamental.[32]

The Mescalero Apaches negotiated a peace settlement with the army at Fort Stanton in June of 1871. This photograph was taken ca. 1880s. Photo Archives, Museum of New Mexico.

This photograph, taken in 1883, shows Mescalero Chief San Juan. Photo Archives, Museum of New Mexico.

Had the Spiegelbergs seen Murphy's ledger or the negative balance in his bank account, they might have been groaning instead. From the firm's own books it appears that L.G. Murphy & Co. was somewhat less than a monopoly that ground down the farmers and held people in peonage. If the partners foreclosed for debts, the ledger didn't reflect it.[33]

Nearly everyone did make payments on their accounts, the farmers mostly in produce such as corn and hay, wheat and barley, and occasionally cattle, usually delivered during the fall and early winter months. Saturnino Baca was the only one who grew potatoes (which he sold to the Mess) and made charcoal (for the brewery). These payments in produce, when compared with Murphy's known contractual obligations and the 1870 Census records, tell us a considerable amount about the Rio Bonito country.

The agricultural schedule for the 1870 Census listed only twenty-one sheep and some 260 "other" cattle for Lincoln County Precinct No. 1, less than the number of working oxen. On the other hand the valleys of the Rio Bonito, Ruidoso, Hondo, and Tularosa were literally a corn belt. Everyone grew corn and most farmers probably considered it their cash crop, which any merchant would receive and credit against the farmer's debts. In the four years since Major Murphy's survey of the Rio Bonito, estimated corn production had approximately tripled—to almost 1,300,000 pounds—while for all of Lincoln County the total was more than 7,300,000 pounds.[34] Where did all of this corn go?

A small proportion was probably eaten and somewhat more used locally for livestock feed, but without purchases by the army there would have been no market for most of it. New Mexico was overproducing corn and the price was tumbling. Murphy & Co. had two good contracts for corn during the 1871 crop year, the time covered by their ledger. From November 1871 through February 1872 they purchased almost 940,000 pounds of corn from a total of fifty-three suppliers, crediting the accounts with 3¼–3½¢ per pound for the first month or so and dropping the price to 2½¢ per pound for most deliveries after mid-December. During the calendar year, from October 28, 1871, through October of 1872, they furnished almost 928,000 pounds to buyers—more than 95 percent of it to the U.S. Army. For this they received 3½¢ per pound from the quartermaster at Fort Stanton and 4½¢ for delivery at the Tularosa post, but they had to pay 1½–2¢ per pound as freight charges to the latter point.[35] So while their corn purchases and sales were almost in balance, they handled these at no more than cost. Was this any way to run a business?

From their standpoint, yes. If they had bid any higher they would probably have lost the contracts. Corn, in fact, dropped in price through the remainder of that decade. It gave Murphy's creditors a means of paying against their accounts, whereas without corn most farmers would have had little or nothing to barter. Finally and perhaps most importantly, Murphy & Co. received vouchers in payment that were as good as cash. These they could use to settle their own accounts with mercantile houses in northern New Mexico and Colorado. The Rio Bonito country produced nothing else that they could ship out and expect to sell even at cost.

If the corn grown in 1871 was even approximately as much as the amount estimated in the 1870 Census schedule, then the 940,000 pounds bought by the House was almost three-quarters of the corn produced on the farms along the Rio Bonito. However, only ten of their fifty-three suppliers were farmers from that valley. The others lived elsewhere along one of the major stream valleys. Not only were less than one-fifth of the Bonito farmers directly involved in the deliveries, no more than half of all the fifty-three suppliers delivered what would appear to have been an entire crop—more than 8,000 pounds of corn per farmer. The others brought in from one to three wagonloads apiece, applied these to their accounts and presumably disposed of the balance elsewhere. While the latter group may have included sharecroppers, these figures suggest that Murphy & Co. had little real grip on either the people or the economy. Lily Klasner's explanations as to how the firm exploit-ed local people probably reflect serious misunderstandings; from the ledger we see that in 1871 her own father delivered 43,111 pounds of corn to Murphy and received between 2.7¢ and 3¼¢ per pound for it.[36]

Such analyses should prompt the reader to ask why this company wasn't going bank-rupt, given their losses on individual accounts and the non-profit situation with army corn contracts. Eventually it did, but for the time being there were other factors at work. Both partners undoubtedly realized what was happening, but they also knew that maintaining the appearance of success in business was very important, and they did this very well. If a person or a company wants to be thought of as the only show around, then it has to act the part. Nothing in the correspondence from the 1870s suggests that Murphy & Co. ever thought of themselves as less than the biggest and the best. Even their worst detractors would probably have conceded on the first.

Another factor was that the partners had still other things going for them. In 1870 Mur-phy held at least seven army contracts, for supplies ranging from corn to charcoal, to a total value of $40,752.[37] In 1871 the firm topped this by almost $4,400., while in both years they subcontracted to the firms who held fresh beef contracts at Fort Stanton.[38] The con-tracts in all cases went to the person who offered the lowest price.[39]

With June of 1871 the good times really arrived, or so they thought. After nearly ten years of hostilities, the Mescalero Apaches negotiated a peace settlement and began to come in and live by the fort. The army issued rations to them until about July 1, when the Indian agent arrived and took up quarters in the only available space—the premises of L.G. Mur-phy & Co.[40] The House did hold an appointment as a licensed trader with the Mescaleros and quickly began to manipulate what for them was an ideal situation. It was another two years—May 29, 1873—before President Grant finally issued an executive order to estab-lish the Mescalero Apache Indian Reservation.[41]

Both the Superintendent of Indian Affairs in New Mexico, Nathaniel Pope, and the Mescalero agent, one Andrew Jackson Curtis, gave Murphy and Fritz considerable credit for having induced the Indians to come in and make peace.[42] Indeed, Murphy had been their military superintendent at Fort Sumner six years before, but any contacts in the inter-im must have been slight. As it was, Curtis had some 325 hungry Apaches at hand by early September and ample authority to feed them.[43]

Initially, Pope contracted with Murphy to furnish the agent with beef, corn, and other supplies at the same rates paid by the military. The general policy was to issue one pound of beef and one pound of corn meal per person per day, in proximity to the Murphy store. However, there was no regular issue day and the rations were given to representatives elected by various groups who appeared and requested the rations for that group. After the initial census it was therefore impossible to determine the exact number of Indians settled around the fort.[44]

Murphy had responsibility for furnishing the rations and for issuing them. Not surpris-ingly, the numbers of Mescaleros fed on paper began to increase wildly. Curtis' 325 Apaches rose to 569 by October 1871. As of April 1872, by Murphy's inflated account, there were 1,312 Indians at the Agency, and in August, 1,895, all peaceful and contented. Curtis had once estimated a probable total of 760, but at the end of his tenure in March 1873 he report-ed 2,679 Mescalero Apaches, "a rapidity of increase" remarked his successor, Samuel B. Bushnell, "which leaves rabbits, rats and mice in the shade."[45]

L.G. Murphy & Co. was the sole contractor for supplies to the Apaches in 1871 and through October of 1872. As the numbers of Indians and rations multiplied, so did the size of vouchers:[46]

June 1871	———————————	$158.25.
July 1871	———————————	$845.97.
August 1871	———————————	$1,512.97.
September 1871	———————————	$3,048.98.
October 1871	———————————	$2,343.60.
November 1871	———————————	$2,268.00.
December 1871	———————————	$2,268.00.
January 1872	———————————	$3,871.00.
February 1872	———————————	$4,323.55.
March 1872	———————————	$5,076.30.
April 1872	———————————	$4,923.80.
May–July 1872	———————————	$12,418.42.
August–September 1872	———————————	$11,543.30.

Acting under instructions from Washington, Superintendent Pope advertised in September 1872 for proposals to supply beef and corn. Emil Fritz received the corn contract at a very reasonable price of $2.60 per 100 pounds. Van Smith won the beef contract at $4.49 per 100 pounds, considerably less than the 7¢ per pound being paid to Murphy. Nevertheless, the House provided a considerable proportion of the beef ration in November at the old price—costing the Indian Bureau an additional $2,359.35.[47]

It was the off-contract purchases, those made in lieu of existing contracts, from the principals of L.G. Murphy & Co. that should have raised eyebrows, but for a long time this did not happen. At the end of November, coinciding with the Murphy firm's loss of their sole-source status, Agent Curtis received permission to issue sugar, coffee, and flour to the Indians. Until July of 1873 this was done by authority of the New Mexico Superintendent of Indian Affairs, i.e., with no contract.[48] In February 1873 alone, Murphy supplied 6,291 pounds of coffee, 9,437 of sugar, and 31,458 of flour at a cost of $5,504.89, enough to ration a hypothetical 2,247 Indians. This largess continued through July, with the number of beneficiaries never less than 1,990. During Curtis' term in office, June 1871 to February 1873, the purchases from Murphy & Co. amounted to a grand total of some $125,000.[49]

When the new Superintendent of Indian Affairs, L. Edwin Dudley, took office on December 14, 1872, the Mescalero Agency purchases rolled right along. All of the coffee-sugar-flour vouchers were marked purchased by authority of the Superintendent of Indian Affairs. In due course Dudley approved these and they were paid by the government. Dudley likewise approved the open-market purchase of 155,000 pounds of corn from Murphy, Fritz, and Dolan in the early summer of 1873, although a new contract with Murphy and Fritz had been signed on June 26, 1873.[50] Since Dudley visited the agency from time to time, his complaints about the agents simply signing vouchers made out by Murphy and allegations that Murphy had taken charge of affairs have a hollow ring to them, especially after he castigated Samuel B. Bushness, Curtis' successor, for making private inquiries about the amount of issues the House delivered.[51]

Several weeks after that episode, early in June 1873, Bushnell took the unusual step of writing directly to the Commissioner of Indian Affairs and urging him to invalidate half of Dolan's and Fritz's vouchers, they being the ones whose names appeared on most of the vouchers for off-contract purchases.[52] This perhaps cost Bushnell his job, but it may have marked the beginning of the end for what some were calling the "Indian Ring." Official Washington was now alerted to problems at the Mescalero Agency. Meanwhile, for Murphy & Co., the money continued to roll in, at least theoretically.

Did all of this new-found wealth, much of it for rations never issued, finally make Murphy & Co. an economic power? Not for a minute. Their banking records at both the First

Personnel of L.G. Murphy & Co., ca. 1868–1873. Left to right: J.J. Dolan, bookkeeper; Col. Emil Fritz; W.W. Martin, clerk; Maj. L.G. Murphy. Photo Archives, Museum of New Mexico.

and the Second National Banks of Santa Fe showed a company whose financing, for months at a time, came partly by large checking account overdrafts. These overdrafts began in April or May of 1872. At its worst this deficit ran $39,733.05 on October 1, 1873, while on the 29th of the same month the account had a $11,738.11 surplus—the highest ever—thanks in part to a $20,000 note (loan) credited to it. The money that the Indian Bureau paid out from 1871 through 1873 for rations, real and fabricated, Murphy used to pay on an incredible array of bills probably accumulated for years past.[53]

There were other reasons why feeding Indians on paper or having a monopoly didn't make Murphy and Fritz wealthy men. For one thing, they didn't receive much of the money. Vouchers and promissory notes were transferable, much like drafts, and often used to settle accounts. By 1873 individual vouchers to Murphy & Co. were being endorsed over to a wholesale house or to a bank, an indication that the firm had cash flow problems. Finally on August 28, 1874, Murphy executed an assignment to the First National Bank of Santa Fe of all vouchers issued to L.G. Murphy & Co. for supplies of any kind furnished to the Indian Department in New Mexico.[54]

The following day, their First National Bank account was credited with $15,000. After this, it became virtually inactive for the next two years.[55] What happened in this interim is that as vouchers were paid, the money went to the bank to pay off Murphy's loans or through the bank to his creditors. The House was still cash-poor. Any government delays in making payments for its vouchers simply added to this debt burden.

There were other problems, from Murphy's standpoint. Prices for corn and beef were declining rapidly. Corn, at least, could be obtained on barter, but all of the coffee, sugar, and flour for filling contracts had to be purchased by Murphy, on credit, and eventually paid for. Even if most of these goods were sold, rather than distributed as Indian rations, the receipts from these sales would have been largely in barter goods such as corn, rather than in money.

Again, the off-contract purchases of Indian supplies required approval from the Superintendent of Indian Affairs, who later had to approve the vouchers *and* add his endorsement as to why the purchases were necessary. To browbeat an Indian agent into signing a voucher might be one thing, but coercion of a superintendent into doing the same is scarcely creditable. His approval, assuming a certain willingness, could be gained much more efficiently through bribery. This of course meant splitting the money and reducing the share to the House.

The army generally supported the continuance of L.G. Murphy & Co. at Fort Stanton, with or without their designation as post trader.[56] The Mescalero agents—Curtis, and then Bushnell—were distraught and found themselves under fire when they complained both about being compelled to accept Murphy's hospitality, since the Indian Bureau had no buildings, and his obstinate insistence upon managing the affairs of the agency. Dudley, to his credit, insisted that a reservation be set aside for the Mescaleros and that buildings be provided for the agency.[57] One of those who stood to gain by such an arrangement was Lawrence G. Murphy.

As of May 29, 1873, the Indians had a reservation, and on June 13 Emil Fritz and Lawrence G. Murphy executed a quitclaim deed to Dudley in consideration of $8,000. for the eighteen-room structure known as the sutler's buildings on the Fort Stanton Military Reservation. A voucher for the money was issued July 1, 1873.[58] The partners moved their merchandise operations to the Placita in July, but continued to occupy the building.[59] They were not about to loosen their grip on supplying rations for the Mescaleros if they could possibly avoid it, especially as their bank account was almost $25,000. in the red on July 1 and sinking deeper.

Post headquarters at Fort Stanton, ca. 1870s. Third from left, Fritz; far right, Murphy. Photo Archives, Museum of New Mexico.

The army by this time smelled a rat, perhaps a very dead one. It had watched the abuses at the Indian agency and evidently made its own decision that Murphy & Co. had worn out their welcome. What was needed was an incident. It happened on May 18 when James Dolan, Murphy's clerk, drew his revolver and allegedly fired a shot at Captain Randlett when Randlett sought to stop Dolan from abusing a "Mr. Reilly." This incident had its own background, as "Reilly" was probably John H. Riley, agent for Van Smith, the beef contractor to the Mescalero Agency. During the preceding six months, Murphy & Co. had furnished the beef on Smith's behalf, but in late April or May, Smith commenced filling the contract himself. Murphy had a technique to regain control of this situation, which was to cause a forfeiture of delivery by issuing a writ (Murphy was then Probate Judge) and attaching the seventy-six head of cattle that Riley delivered on May 8. The antagonism was between Dolan and Riley, but Randlett nearly got in the way. The near result of the shooting was that Randlett had the guard take Dolan into custody and had Murphy arrested as well when he tried to interfere. Both men were released the next day.[60]

The long-term consequences were more interesting. In view of Van Smith's default in delivery (!), the Indian agent had to purchase beef in the open market. He did so on May 31, buying 55,741 pounds of beef from Emil Fritz for $2,787.05.[61] The cows, ironically, were Van Smith's originally. Dudley certified the voucher, adding that he believed the contractor had been prevented from making his delivery because of interference by L.G. Murphy & Co. After this, Dudley was called upon to add endorsements to satisfy the objections to payment raised by the government auditors.[62] Finally, in a long letter of October 3, 1874, the ex-superintendent made the damning admission that "I called upon the Military Authorities to restore the cattle to the Agent, and the Sheriff at once delivered them up."[63] For the past year and a half, Fritz had really had no claim to payment, and Dudley knew it.

Eventually someone, probably Emil Fritz, did receive the money for these cows, as the voucher was marked "paid."[64]

The conclusion that is easily drawn from this trail of mishandled finances for Mescalero Apache supplies, which includes at least one voucher that bears an obviously dishonest certification, is that L. Edwin Dudley, Superintendent of Indian Affairs for New Mexico, was on the take. The corruption reached high, and an outspoken officer, Maj. Wm. Redwood Price, said as much in defending one of the Indian agents:

> I understand that Dr. Bushnell, Agent of the Mescaleros, has been removed from his position. If such is the case, he has fallen victim to the machinations of the Murphy ring whose ramifications must reach to the office of the superintendent at Santa Fe.[65]

The army had its own methods for dealing with these situations. Two months after the May 18 incident, Randlett was arrested and charged with assault stemming from that affair. Hopping mad, he fired off two incensed letters, to the secretary of war and to the adjutant general of the army, that left no one in doubt as to his feelings towards Murphy & Co. or the local civil authorities:

> The Officers of the Civil law here are nearly all parasites of Murphy's. The Magistrate and Probate Judge before whom Dolan's case was examined it is said and so believed by everybody I know, holds a relation to Murphy the most unnatural and disgustingly brutal. The people of the County are nearly all considered Peons of Murphy's.[66]

The endorsements and letters by Randlett's immediate commanding officer, Captain Chambers McKibbin, were classic acts of fence-straddling, which he was later called upon to explain. Otherwise the army chain of command right up to the secretary of war supported Randlett. Somewhat after the fact, the secretary ordered the commander at Fort Stanton to remove Murphy, Fritz, and every man in any way in their employ from the post and to *keep them off the reservation.*[67]

Murphy belatedly offered a slickly worded reply to Randlett's denunciations, but in support of his own position he offered testimonial letters from army officers and others that were mostly several years old and had limited relevance. The secretary's order stood, and by November affairs at the Indian agency were coming under control. The number of Apaches fell to about 250.[68]

One circumstance that helped Murphy and Fritz to hold on so long was the army's belief that the firm had an appointment from the Department of the Interior as Indian traders, while the Indian Bureau thought that the partners were Post traders at Fort Stanton. The two traders undoubtedly fostered these misunderstandings, when actually there was no designated Post trader or Indian trader at Fort Stanton.[69] The two departments finally got together late in August and discovered this.

After that, things moved quickly. According to Major Price, "A communication was given them directing them to vacate in twenty four hours, at which time if they had not removed, measures would be taken to effect their removal. They moved in the time specified to the town of Placita on Bonita Creek, nine miles East of the Post."[70]

Superintendent Dudley was at Fort Stanton at the time. Not to be outdone, he likewise claimed credit for ousting Murphy & Co. Dudley also gave the date of the event—September 2, 1873.[71] After June 1874 the House of Murphy held no more contracts to supply the Mescalero Agency, although they did act as subcontractors and made occasional sales when the Indian agent bought goods on the open market. Their creditors eventually seem to have received payment for the vouchers, perhaps after considerable delays.[72]

The Murphy-Dolan store in Lincoln, ca. 1887; later the Lincoln County Courthouse. This photo, taken approximately thirteen years after construction was completed, shows Sheriff James Brent (center) and his deputies. Courtesy Special Collections, University of Arizona Library.

In La Placita, now beginning to be called Lincoln, Murphy temporarily quartered in a three-room adobe. (A.A. McSween, a lawyer whose role in the Lincoln County War becomes pivotal, purchased this some four years later and enlarged it into a twelve-room house.)[73] Meanwhile, construction got underway on the building that would house Murphy & Co., soon to be known as the Big Store or the House. Murphy moved to Lincoln without Fritz, who had left in early June to visit his old home in Germany. After his death the following year, James J. Dolan became a partner in the concern, as of August 31, 1874.[74]

Then, as now, the Murphy-Dolan store (still known as L.G. Murphy & Co.) was the most impressive building in town. Two stories in height, with approximately 2,800 square feet on each floor, it boasted red brick fireplaces and a shingle roof. Originally it housed the mercantile operations, offices, residence, and sundry operations for L.G. Murphy & Co. Murphy evidently intended to replicate the kind of establishment the firm had had at Fort Stanton, since the ground floor included a large store, billiard parlor, bar, store room, and offices, while the upper story had a lodge room and living quarters. The House mess, now operated by F.H. Ricken, had a separate building.[75]

Construction of the Big Store probably began in the fall of 1873. Its progress was chronicled, rather sketchily, in the daybook. The first purchase on October 7 was for three pounds of glue. One month later Paul Dowlin's sawmill on the Rio Ruidoso furnished some $2,742. worth of lumber. This was the only major purchase of materials, the last item being "1 large lock, No. 415" for $2.50 on January 22, 1874. Labor costs, not always clearly segregated in the daybook, contributed most of the building expense. At the most these probably amounted to just over $4,000. Since no purchases of adobes or shingles were listed, these costs were presumably part of the labor. Most of the workmen received $4. a day with the carpenter topping the list at $5. The new building probably cost a little more than $7,000. and as of August 31, 1874, it was valued at $8,000.[76] Newspaper accounts and other reports out of Lincoln at this time did not mention the new Murphy building, probably because all the news focused on the Horrell War, which some papers began calling the Lincoln County War.

Until the fall of 1873, the history of L.G. Murphy & Co. was much more closely tied to Fort Stanton than to the town of Lincoln. However, an explanation of the devious operations and financial weakness of the firm in its early years is necessary for one to understand what happened a few years later during the actual Lincoln County War. The roots of that conflict rested in the attempts of L.G. Murphy & Co. and its successor after March 1877, J.J. Dolan & Co., to carry on in the old ways under changed economic circumstances. The results were disastrous, in part because of the lawless elements drawn into the county.

Fritz and Murphy have come down through history as a couple of heartless villains who exploited and dominated Lincoln County, grinding people down while growing rich from contracting. Yet in their own time they were probably rather typical; generous as well as greedy, calculating but not evil, open if not entirely honest in their business dealings, eager to seize advantages or opportunities and willing to reduce or eliminate competition by any reasonably legitimate means. The main support for La Placita's school in 1871, including Juan Patron's salary as schoolmaster, seems to have been Murphy's donation of his salary as probate judge.[77]

Their most flagrant breach—inflating the numbers of Mescalero Apaches to balloon the billings for rations—they probably rationalized as justified so long as they could get away with it. In their mercantile business and in subsidiary enterprises such as the brewery and the mess, their fiscal records indicate that they were poor businessmen, almost always in the red and not particularly concerned about it or inclined to change their ways. They must have received dunning letters without number—and probably threw them into the fireplace.

If there was a consistent theme in their behavior, it was a quest for money. They dealt with local people by barter arrangements, not even pressing them for settlements on their accounts. While they held mortgages on property and crops, their foreclosures (beginning in 1874) probably gained them little more than the lands themselves.[78] Everything that generated cash or its equivalent (vouchers, drafts) they did try to monopolize. If Fritz or Murphy had been asked why, they might have said—"We need it, they don't."

The House needed all of the cash equivalents it could get to settle bank loans and debts with the wholesale dealers in northern New Mexico and Colorado. At that period Lincoln County produced nothing that could be shipped out and sold profitably. Mexican silver dollars were the common currency in the Southwest and at Lincoln even these may have been uncommon. The only sources of cash were contracts with the army and the Indian Bureau, and for awhile Murphy & Co. did monopolize these, bartering with local farmers for the necessary corn, hay, barley, and firewood. Contracts received through competitive bidding were not necessarily profitable, while some of their subcontracting must have been done at cost, simply in order to gain cash and to keep the business from others.

By the end of the 1870s, New Mexico and Lincoln County had witnessed major changes; mining was under way and a railroad had arrived. With it came outside financing of the range cattle industry—all new sources of money that soon made the conflicts in Lincoln obsolete.

Coincident with the appearance of the innovative Colonel Colt's Peacemaker in 1873, a .45 revolver that used metallic cartridges, Lincoln experienced a great increase in violence.[79] The combination of hard liquor and improved firearms created instability in the region. Many of the resulting incidents were random acts of violence, unrelated to anything that happened before or after. Some, of course, coincided with more significant events in Lincoln's history.

～ 5 ～

THE HORRELL WAR

1873–1874

The year 1873 initiated what Lily Klasner aptly called "the Reign of the Six Shooter."[1] Late in the spring there was a fight on Tularosa Creek over water rights. When troops were called, an angry Hispanic crowd from Tularosa fired on them. Captains Randlett and McKibbin arrived with reinforcements from Fort Stanton and the crowd dispersed. McKibbin proceeded on to Tularosa, which he threatened to enter by force if necessary, hanging the priest if fired upon.[2] His aggressive ways may have influenced the army's drafting of a general order that prohibited the use of troops to enforce the laws of a state or territory, except by order of the president.[3] More trouble over rights to the Tularosa water flared now and again into the twentieth century.

About the time of the so-called Tularosa Ditch War, five Horrell brothers rounded up their cattle and set out for New Mexico with their families and a dozen or so kinsmen and hangers-on, leaving four dead state policemen, a jail break, and a relieved citizenry behind in Lampasas County, Texas. The Horrells bought a homestead on the lower Ruidoso at what would become known as the Dick Brewer place during the Lincoln County War.[4]

On December 1, 1873, Ben Horrell and an ex-sheriff of Lincoln County named L.J. Gylam went to Lincoln with three other men, perhaps on business, but more likely just for a spree. They started drinking and firing off their guns, thoroughly upsetting the peace of the community. The constable, Juan Martinez, demanded their weapons. These they surrendered, but about an hour later the re-armed Texans congregated at a house of ill repute and began firing in every direction, threatening the authorities and the whole community, particularly the probate judge. The constable came back with four or five members of the Police Guard. While an interpreter was making explanations, a Texan named Dave Warner suddenly shot Martinez and killed him instantly. Warner was killed in the return fire. Gylam and Ben Horrell evidently broke from the house and ran as far as the Rio Bonito, but could get no further. Both were shot down.[5] According to reports reaching Fort Stanton, the fight

> resulted in the death of three of the Texans, and one Mexican—all accounts agree in the statement that the Texans were murdered in cold blood, one at least whilst on his knees—badly wounded, had surrendered and begged for mercy was inhumanly murdered by having been pierced by nine balls—his body then taken and thrown across the creek near the town—of course this exasperated the friends of the Texans. . . .[6]

The post commander's bias against Hispanic settlers was all too evident in his other remarks, and typical of officers at that time. However, this paled beside the murderous antagonism shown by the Horrell clan. Three days later Seferino Trujillo and another prominent local man were found murdered at the Horrell ranch.[7]

Lincoln County was about to be gripped by a race war. Gov. Marsh Giddings, the district judge, Lawrence G. Murphy, and the army at Fort Stanton all realized this and sent off appeals for instructions or help, each explaining in his own way about the several groups of people living in Lincoln County.[8] One was the Spanish-speaking New Mexicans, universally called Mexicans, which was concentrated at the town of Lincoln. The valleys below, principally on the tributaries of the Pecos, "are being settled by Americans, principally from Texas, many of them hard working peaceably disposed Citizens, who have taken up ranches, and desire to be peaceable law-abiding Citizens."[9]

Then there was the source of the recent trouble: "Another element is the Texas cow boys—who bring in large herds of Texas Cattle—some to go north others remain on the large tracts of fine grazing lands in this region."[10] Within a few years this group would be known as the "Pecos men." There were also the families of men such as contractor George Peppin, William Brady, Hugh Beckwith, J.B. "Green" Wilson, and "Ham" Mills, all of whom had married New Mexican women and settled in the area during the 1860s. They were generally considered to be part of the Mexican community, and equally the targets of the Horrells' hatred.

The murders of Seferino Trujillo and the other man prompted Sheriff Mills to organize a posse. With or without warrants he set off to arrest the Horrells, aided by about twenty-five well-armed citizens. The Horrells refused to surrender to such an armed mob. The sheriff's party withdrew, apparently without shooting. Tensions continued to build and over the next several weeks the two sides became armed camps.[11]

On December 20 a wedding was about to be celebrated in Lincoln. That night while a *baile* (dance) was in progress in the building known as Chapman's Saloon, also used for the courthouse, the Horrells and their compatriots suddenly appeared and poured a volley into the celebrants through the windows and doors. Juan B. Patron, the father of Juan Patron, and three others died on the spot. Three others, including two women, were dangerously wounded. The Texans rode off and denied any involvement.

Civil authorities went into shock, except to petition for military protection. The governor, after hearing that the probate judge had resigned and the sheriff had put himself elsewhere, contented himself with a vain wish that "the Military authorities would undoubtedly go to the aid of the civil if there was any active civil authority in the county." The letters and petitions went all the way to Washington, but the response was a firm refusal of authority for troops to interfere in the affairs of civilians.[12]

Governor Giddings did proclaim a $500. reward for the capture of three Horrell brothers and two other men. The district judge issued arrest warrants for them, but he also advised the sheriff that an attempt to serve these with a Mexican posse would result in a serious loss of life. In this standoff, Major Price agreed to hold the warrants once he reached Fort Stanton either until the court met or he received further instructions, in the meantime notifying both parties that they had to keep the peace.[13]

January saw armed groups on both sides roving through the country and firing on one another. Several reports used the term "guerilla warfare." When Price arrived at Fort Stanton, his first letter reported the receipt of a letter from Robert Casey, who asked that a detachment be sent to Casey's ranch until the difficulties between the Americans and the Mexicans had passed. Lily Klasner's reminiscences noted that six soldiers were sent.[14]

On January 20 Sheriff Mills finally set out from Lincoln with sixty men to arrest the Horrells. A series of letters by Price told what happened next:

> The Mexican Posse returned to the Placita on Friday night [January 23]. They had surrounded the house of the Texans and had shot down or driven off all their horses. During the night of the 20th the Texans left their hiding place and gathered up their families moved quietly down the Hondo. James Dolen (clerk of Murpheys) and Chas. Miller (his agent for the delivery of corn at this Post) were the austensible purchasers of their cattle, the notes for the payment of which had been deposited in Murphey's

safe, before they knew that it was one and the same concern. Turner was warned that he would be murdered, if he did not at once leave the Country as soon as the cattle was turned over. He was shot by a man in ambush from behind a stone wall.

Ben Turner, a brother-in-law to the Horrells, was killed at Picacho. The major continued:

The man who killed him came to the Placita, boasted of the act and it was proposed to raise a purse of $100 for him. He is well known having murdered a Mexican a short time since. No attempt was made to arrest him.

Their provisions were all carried away, and the house the Texans occupied was burned shortly after they left. Parties who have seen them since the death of Turner say that their entire number twenty-two, took a solemn oath, that they would work together and while five of them lived they would be revenged.

Under these circumstances it is impossible to do anything by "Moral suasion." . . . Lt. Wilkinson who has just returned from the Plaza says that the town is deserted, that Murphy was very drunk, but told him that Jimmy Dolen was heading the Posse and they had gone down after the Texans. . . . I believe that martial law is the only method of stopping the disturbances.[15]

After signing off on this cliffhanger, Price reopened it the next morning to add a P.S.:

I have just learned that Steve Stanley was shot but not dangerously in the Placita last night. He is half Brother of the Sheriff Mills. The Sheriff Mills I believe was also in the Placita. It is not known by whom Stanley was shot. He was drunk and was in the dark.

While army headquarters in Santa Fe waited for the next chapter in Price's saga, the *New Mexican* ran a series of short articles and notes based mostly upon rumors and misinformation. Price then resumed his report on January 28:

There seems to have been a pretty general spree in the town of Placita, on the night of the 25th inst. [this month]. . . . Steve Stanley (half Brother of the Sheriff) was shot but not dangerously; he was drunk and very abusive, brandishing his pistol and hitting several men on the head and in the face with it. The next day a man named Gill was reported wounded at a house three miles this side of Placita. He says Stanley shot him, and he ran that far in the direction of the Post. He had been heard to say that he would rather pay the fine than serve on the Sheriff's Posse. The same night they got a young man named Little, beat him terribly and had a rope around his neck to hang him. He got away and reached Casey's Ranche. Joe Flum forage agent at the Jicarillas was also badly cut in the head.

Murphy has been drunk for a week. He is now in bed sick from the effects of it, but continues drinking. His store is the rendevous of all the Sheriff's parties, and all supplies are furnished from there. After Mills the Sheriff had been to the Post on Saturday last he returned to the Plaza. Another Posse was organized and headed by James Dolen moved down the Valley. The house on the Ranche owned by the Haralds was burned and all their [?] including six hundred bushels of wheat was hauled to the Plaza.

Today Mills the Sheriff and Juan Patrone the County Clerk started for Santa Fe, which I believe leaves the County without a Civil Officer. During the previous absence of Patrone to Santa Fe a meeting was held and all the County Offices except Sheriff declared vacant. Murphey conducted the meeting. He was appointed Probate Judge, Brady (I believe) Alcalde, and Jimmy Dolen County Clerk. After consideration it was concluded to be illegal, and did not go into effect.

Here Price was getting into something else. Murphy's name kept surfacing in one connection or another during the Horrell War as he sought to manipulate things to his own advantage, at least during his more sober moments:

> Murphey however saw the Harolds and assured them that if they would come to the Placita and submit to a trial before a commission, composed of himself, Brady and a Mexican named Montoya, that he would give him his word of honor they would be acquitted.

The major's conclusion not only pulled the rug from under any assistance that Sheriff Mills might have been able to get from the Military District, but he left the boys in the district headquarters on the edge of their chairs again:

> I today rode down to Casey's Ranche 25 miles east of here as an escort to Gen. G.A. Smith, U.S. Internal Revenue Collector. At that point I learned that three Mexicans had been killed by Texans about 40 miles farther East on the Honda, also that a large number of Texans were congregating and were going to make an attack on the town of Placita. Murphey and his clerks are almost the only white men left there. I consider Mills perfectly incompetent as sheriff and the possibility of getting law or Justice before any Tribunal except the District Judge is and has been simply impossible. Unless there is some order for the Military authorities to interfere there will be much bloodshed and lawlessness before the next mail can reach you.
>
> The Texans have the support of the cattle men on the Pecos River. They are perfectly lawless and visiting their revenge on the Mexicans as a race. The town of Placita is composed of some of the worst Mexican element in the Territory. Most of the men have no austensible means of livelihood, getting their living from the expenditures of the Post and the Indian Department.[16]

On this positive note Price again put down his pen. Would Lincoln still be there in another week?

Meanwhile the secretary of war had consulted with President Grant over a very large package of letters that originated at Fort Stanton and Lincoln during December and January, forwarded by Governor Giddings and the secretary of the interior. Most of these have been cited.[17] The secretary answered that troops could be used by a U.S. Marshal, on his application, to aid in enforcing orders from U.S. courts, but that they would not interfere in civilian affairs, specifically not in Lincoln County.[18]

Price wrote his last letter on February 5:

> On the 30th ult. [last month] the Texans moved up the Honda. A short distance from Casey's Ranche they killed Joe Haskins. He is a brother-in-law of the Sheriff, Ham Mills, also of Steve Stanley—he was concerned in the killing of Gylam, Warner and young Harrold, which took place in Nov., and was the commencement of the present troubles.
>
> The Texans numbered between 50 and 70 and moved up to within a mile of the town of Placita. From parties who saw them when they went back, I learn they had a disagreement among themselves, that a few among them wished to attack and burn the place killing and plundering indiscriminately—that the Harrold brothers did not want to do it, and fearing they could not control the party they turned back. They say they only want the authors of their troubles and name twelve men, some of whom are as follows; Murphey, Mills, Juan Patrone, Juan Gonzales, Dolan, Stanley, Haskins, Joe Warnock, Montanya and one or two other Mexicans. They say it is only a question of time, that they will kill them sooner or later. It is presumed their attempts will be made in small parties and when least expected.[19]

The *Mesilla News* learned from a private letter that Joe Haskins was taken out of his bed about 8 p.m. one night and murdered by the Texans, after which they started down the Hondo, plundering horses and mules along the way.[20] So far as Lincoln itself was concerned, the Horrell War had ended. Two weeks later the commander at Fort Stanton reported that everything seemed to have quieted down and the Texans had left the country.[21]

Their departure was anything but quiet. The *New Mexican* carried a front-page story that four of the desperadoes stole four mules and two horses at Roswell, then met up with Robert Beckwith of Seven Rivers and took his horse, saddle, and pistol, later divesting him of eight head of horses and mules as well. A posse set off in pursuit and when it returned to Seven Rivers on February 20 or 21 it had recovered eight of the horses and mules. With respect to two of the outlaws, "they say that Zach Crompton and Still will steal and murder no more; that some one shot them near Waco Tanks, and that their bodies may be found on the road leading from the Pecos river to El Paso."[22] The other two *compadres* were last seen with some citizens of old Mexico in hot pursuit.

The Horrell War left an evil heritage in addition to the ill feelings between ethnic groups in Lincoln County. Both the county probate judge and the justice of the peace at Lincoln had fled Lincoln County during the fighting. To replace them and restore peace, the Murphy bunch set up the meeting that Price mentioned in his January 28 letter. This actually took place on January 13 and saw a committee consisting of Murphy himself, José Montaño, and William Brady each appointed to act in any cases that involved the powers of the vacant offices, with J.J. Dolan as their secretary.[23] This troika was of course illegal, but it might have seemed like a good idea at the time since no one knew but what Lincoln might be burned around their ears before nightfall. Later, on March 2, a special election for probate judge and precinct offices saw L.G. Murphy returned as probate judge and Pablo Pino y Pino elected justice of the peace.[24]

A more curious outcome was that Capt. James Randlett found himself indicted by the Lincoln County grand jury as an accessory to the four murders on December 20, 1873. The Horrell brothers and others were indicted for the same murders, but Randlett's contribution seems to have been limited to one of his inflammatory letters to district headquarters. He was probably at Fort Stanton at the time of the shootings. Randlett saw Murphy's hand behind the grand jury's action as a way of evening the score for Randlett having initiated Murphy's removal from Fort Stanton. Randlett, with his usual explicitness, observed that the grand jury had "not an atom of Evidence to sustain an indictment. Murphy's Parasites did the job with the object to subject me to anoyance and expense, and if possible to get me out of his way here."[25] At his trial in Socorro County, the jury returned a verdict of not guilty without leaving their seats.[26]

Murphy undoubtedly benefitted from the Horrell War, beyond earning the opportunities to harass Randlett and to gain his own reelection as probate judge. In a later affidavit, Juan Patron said that

> Murphy & Co. aided and abetted the "Harroll" party and the result was that the Harroll party left the country leaving however all their property in the hands of Murphy, such as cattle lands &c. There are people who say that this was one of the ends Murphy was working for.[27]

Why the Horrells included Murphy on their death list isn't at all clear. He was one of the few who could have bought out their interests. Price's January 25 letter implied some conflict, by the Horrell's decision to sell their cattle to Dolan and Miller "before they knew. . . ." The Murphy & Co. daybook on January 19, 1874, logged the purchase of 1,098 head of cattle from Horrell Bros. & Co. by C. Miller & Co. There were only three steers in that herd, the other animals being cows, calves, yearlings, and two-year-olds. The prices received were on the low side, but not unreasonably so for a forced sale. The total price, which covered four yoke of oxen and thirteen horses as well, came to $9,802.50.[28] Miller's promissory notes to Samuel Horrell were executed at Lincoln on January 26, 1874. Scarcely a week later, Miller sold his interest in the stock to Dolan. Miller's two largest notes, each for $3,762., cleared payment via the L.G. Murphy & Co. account at the Second National Bank of Santa Fe on December 24, 1874.[29]

The Horrell War also planted the seeds for trouble beyond anything that Lincoln County had seen up to that time. The country was already plagued with horse thefts, usually laid to the Comanches and the Mescalero Apaches, although white men in turn raided the Indians. Horrell followers who remained in the Pecos country supposedly were the persons who introduced cattle rustling.[30]

Finally, the army established a precedent for dealing with civil disturbances. When Sheriff Mills and his posse rode off on December 5 to confront the Horrells, the Fort Stanton commander ordered Captain McKibbin to take thirty men and camp near the Horrell ranch. This show of force, it was hoped, would prevent an actual outbreak, but under no circumstances was the captain to allow himself or the troops to be drawn into the quarrel. That situation, as we've seen, resolved itself, probably without shooting. On December 24 another army captain received orders to take all available men and bivouac within about one-half mile of La Placita, "to prevent by their presence, if possible, a riot between the American and Mexican citizens of the country."[31] This followed on the murders there the night of December 20 and again it was hoped that the troops' presence would preserve the peace, without the army becoming involved. Once more nothing happened.

In the aftermath of the Horrell War the army saw two precedents where it had stepped in and preserved the peace, quieting civil disorders simply by its presence. Whether showing the flag this way actually had much to do with preventing a war remains to be seen, but the army probably gave full credit to its actions. When Lt. Col. N.A.M. Dudley tried to apply the same policy in Lincoln four and a half years later, the results were disastrous— arson, murder, and chaos for Lincoln and recriminations that reached all the way to Washington. The difference was that the army could bluff its way through 1874; by July of 1878, however, its bluff had been called.

~ 6 ~

A TRADITION
OF VIOLENCE

1874–1877

Horse stealing was certainly not unique to Lincoln County, but Lincoln may have had more or better horse thieves than most places. In one of his reports on Indian affairs, Major Price observed that

> at the Fort Stanton Reservation affidavits were handed me of over four hundred horses that had been stolen by those Indians from Cattle men, during the previous nine months, many of which were recognized as in the hands of the Indians.[1]

Later that same year, an anonymous correspondent at Lincoln indicated that the situation was no better:

> There has been many more horses stolen lately, in fact so many that we don't know the number, nor all the persons from whom they were stolen, as this nefarious business goes on by wholesale. The Apache Indians have been stealing lately, and now white men are stealing; and sometimes the two classes of thieves above mentioned steal from each other. The Apaches say if the whites are going to steal all the stock back as fast as they steal it, it does them no good, and they are talking of signing the temperance pledge, and joining the church.
>
> But, seriously, if this stealing is not stopped in some manner, the people will soon take the law in their own hands, and hang every man they can catch with a stolen horse: the trial will be fair and the punishment rapid.[2]

The Apaches were frequently charged with such thefts, but as the writer implied they were far from helpless.

Both the stealing and the accusations went on, John S. Chisum being a particular target of both.[3] Chisum had located along the Pecos River in 1872 and through the decade he was probably the most widely known cattleman of the Southwest, with herds numbering about 80,000 by 1875. When U.S. Indian Inspector E.C. Watkins investigated charges of wrongdoing at the Mescalero Agency,

> testimony was taken on the subject of the stealing of horses from the Indians by men in the employ of John S. Chism, as I found at Agent Godfroy's office an account for over forty-seven thousand dollars against the Government in favor of this same John S. Chism, for damage by reason of the thefts by the Indians, and referred to him (Agent Godfroy) for investigation and report. I think the evidence shows conclusively that in the matter of horse stealing, Mr. Chism is far ahead of the Indians, and that a balance should be struck in their favor. . . . The testimony shows conclusively that John S. Chism,— whose agent and advisor [Alexander A.] McSween was,—was systematically robbing the Indians of their horses, through the instrumentality of men whom he hired for that purpose.[4]

49

Murders and Political Chicanery

Another practice that continued alongside larceny in horses was the settling of personal disputes by gunfire. According to the *Daily New Mexican*, a deputy sheriff named Lyon Phillipowski came into the L.G. Murphy & Co. store late in the evening of October 21, 1874, very much intoxicated, and proceeded to insult William Burns, the clerk. Burns sought to deflect the insults but Phillipowski drew his pistol and threatened Burns' life, then went outside and challenged Burns.

Burns got a pistol and stepped out; Phillipowski began shooting and the two blazed away at each other until the deputy fell mortally wounded. He died the next day. The coroner held an inquest and returned a verdict of justifiable homicide.[5]

One month later José Domingo Valencia and Daniel Fisher were both drunk in the dining room at Samuel Wortley's Hotel in Lincoln. Two shots were heard, after which Fisher was found shot through the chest and in his last agonies. Valencia was held until the coroner's jury met the next morning, then sent to Fort Stanton to await the grand jury. The newspaper correspondent commented "it was a cold blooded affair."[6]

The year 1875 began on a positive note with the *Mesilla News* congratulating L.G. Murphy on pushing through to completion one of the finest buildings in the territory, namely his new store and residence.[7] After this it was all downhill.

In January the territorial auditor reported that "that banner democratic county of New Mexico, Lincoln, has paid no tax into the territorial treasury for the past two years."[8] Murphy, as probate judge, was the chief executive officer for Lincoln County. Letters, excuses, slurs, and overwrought literary allusions began to fly between Murphy (a Democrat) and the Santa Fe *New Mexican* (staunchly Republican). In a letter which the *New Mexican* generously allowed "that he was no doubt hanging on the ragged edge of irresponsibility, when he wrote it," Murphy excused the non-payments by saying that ex-sheriff L.J. Gylam had robbed the county of over $20,000. A sheriff at that time was also the tax collector, but the paper reminded everyone that Murphy was the responsible officer and the sheriff's bondsman as well. Gylam had been one of the first casualties in the Horrell War. The "big dog of the political tan-yard down in Lincoln" tried to wiggle out of this one, while the paper kept up the exposé.[9]

When the April term of the district court convened at Lincoln, the grand jury could not find any of the bonds required of county officers and brought indictments against the current sheriff, county clerk, treasurer, and the justice of the peace at Lincoln. As the sad result of all this, reported the press,

> We regret to say that owing to the failure of the officers to collect and take care of the county taxes, it has been impossible to take any steps towards the erection of a jail, court house or school house, but trust that the action of your grand jury in indicting the officers above named will have a salutary effect in the collection of taxes, and soon enable us to erect the necessary buildings.[10]

Apparently only Sheriff Mills came to trial, and he was sentenced to pay costs. Murphy tendered his resignation as probate judge to Governor Giddings, but the governor failed to act upon it.[11] At the general election in September, Florencio Gonzales replaced Murphy as the probate judge and continued to hold this office through the next several elections.[12] In a follow-up article later that year, the *New Mexican* reported that the delinquent tax payers in Lincoln County had all come forward and paid their taxes to about $6,000.[13]

Another murder on the first of August led to the first and most celebrated legal hanging in Lincoln County. Robert Casey, an outspoken opponent of L.G. Murphy & Co., had gone to Lincoln to attend a political convention that seemed likely to break the grip of the Murphy machine. (The convention ended with a defeat for Murphy and Dolan.) Casey ate lunch at Wortley's Hotel with William Wilson, who until a few days before had been in his employ, and later made ready to return to his ranch on the Rio Hondo.

Lily Klasner gave a fascinating, highly colored account of the whole affair, essentially the same as was reported in the newspapers.[14] Casey at some point had either been confronted or ambushed by Wilson, perhaps as a result of Casey's attack on the Murphy organization at the convention. Casey was wounded with a shot in the body. The two ran around opposite sides of a house and met again, whereupon Wilson blasted Casey with a shot in the face. Casey held onto life until about 2 p.m. the next day. The crowd that gathered evidently sympathized with Wilson, who surrendered to the sheriff. After a preliminary hearing the accused was sent to the Fort Stanton guard house.[15]

The Hanging of William Wilson

The territorial newspapers had a field day with the murder and later with the trial, where Wilson was sentenced to be hanged. And hang he did on the 10th of December, from a gallows built the same morning. During the period that Wilson was incarcerated and awaiting execution, there were suspicions that "friends" would either help him to escape or try to get him off completely. None of these efforts came to anything, and on the appointed day officers and men from Fort Stanton were present in force to see that justice was carried out. The prisoner appeared, garbed in his funeral clothes, and Sheriff Saturnino Baca read the death warrant, subsequently declaring that the execution would be stayed for one half hour. The crowd protested so loudly that the sheriff proceeded with his duty.[16]

Lily Klasner's version of the actual hanging could have been the way it happened. Though only twelve years old at the time, her keen observations made for vivid recollections. That Wilson's victim was her own father may have intensified the youngster's perceptions.

> When everything was ready for the trap to be sprung, Wilson took the opportunity given him to say something, to turn to Major Murphy and say bitterly, "Major, you know you are the cause of this. You promised to save me, but . . . ." Before he could say more, Major Murphy kicked the trigger that sprung the trap door, and Wilson's body shot down through it until the rope was taut.[17]

As Lily recalled years later, Wilson swung for a full 9½ minutes before he was cut down and placed in a coffin. After awhile someone noticed that he was still breathing. The Murphyites allegedly tried to interfere and prevent Wilson from being hung a second time. The army took charge then and allowed the crowd to tie another rope around Wilson's neck, draw the body from its coffin, and suspend it from the gallows for another twenty minutes, until any possibility of repeating the first mistake was past.[18]

The very next day another act of violence rang out as Tomás Archuleta, a servant of Lincoln lawyer Alexander McSween, visited the home of one Copetona, a woman of doubtful reputation recently from Las Cruces. Two men from Doña Ana County were there as well. A fight ensued and while one of the Doña Ana men held Archuleta by the hair and ears the other drove a knife into his back, killing him almost instantly. The woman and one man were incarcerated, while the knife-wielder headed out of town on a stolen mule. The murdered man's two brothers and friends set off in pursuit, as did the officers of the law.[19]

In commenting on the year's violence at Lincoln, the *Mesilla News* observed that "tragedies such as [these] . . . have ceased to excite the passions of the people of Lincoln county. They are accustomed to the smell of blood."[20]

Top left: A serene portrait of Saturnino Baca and daughter Carlotta, ca. 1869. In 1875, as sheriff, Baca presided over Lincoln's first hanging.

Top right: Charlie Bowdre and wife — one of many outlaws drawn to Lincoln County by its lucrative cattle industry.

Left: A youthful portrait of John Chisum (right) with brother Walter and mother Sallie. Chisum became the Southwest's most widely-known cattleman. Top and left, Photo Archives, Museum of New Mexico.

Land Titles on the Rio Bonito

Lincoln experienced at least two newsworthy events in 1875 that did *not* involve either outright larceny or the sound of six-guns. Back in 1867–1868, lands along the Rio Bonito and Rio Hondo had been surveyed, which made them eligible for entries under the home-steading, preemption, and other land-entry laws. At the time there was little interest in purchasing the properties, nor did the public auction of areas along the Rio Hondo—the only public land sale ever held in New Mexico—stir much excitement.[21] The settlers, or squatters, preferred to hold lands simply by occupation. The improvements were all that they actually owned and the title to these could be transferred by a quitclaim deed. For the more insecure, a preemption or homestead claim gave one possession of up to a quarter section while "proving-up," or making good, on it.[22]

This informality came to a halt in 1875 when Marcos Estabrook and Elisha Dow, the latter, as we've seen, a store-owner at San Patricio on the lower Ruidoso, sought to preempt nearly the entire town of Lincoln, "taking in every body's houses, cultivated lands, &c."[23] These lands had been offered but not sold at the public auction in 1870 and were therefore subject to purchase at private entry any time—something that any lawyer would have known. A Mesilla attorney, John D. Bail, evidently made the appropriate entries and received patents for lands at Lincoln the following November. Bail sold his holdings to L.G. Murphy the same day. Murphy, in turn, disposed of the properties between January and April of 1877 either to J.J. Dolan and John Riley, who sold them to McSween, or directly to Alexander McSween.[24]

On the face of it, it looked like Murphy might have been acting the part of a public-spirited citizen in buying out Bail's interests and keeping ownership of the townsite in local hands. For Murphy, generosity was not out of character. In his daybook there was a backdated entry that credited L.J. Gylam's account with $887.14 three days prior to his death at the beginning of the Horrell War. The House also paid for Gylam's coffin and for coffins at $12. each for the four people gunned down on the night of December 20, 1873.[25] These credits cost Murphy little in real money but they could have meant quite a lot to the families involved.

It follows, then, that claims made against Murphy, such as "he would get the Mexicans in debt to him, take their notes and mortgages, and the next year he would foreclose and rent their places out," ought to be reviewed carefully.[26] Klasner, among others, accused Murphy of this questionable practice.[27] The first Lincoln County record book shows a fore-closure and sale only against Joseph Storms, in April 1875, although Saturnino Baca, Florencio Gonzales, and the Phillipowskis did quitclaim or mortgage property to Lawrence Murphy.[28] For him to have taken property or driven someone who could not pay rent or other debts off their land would have made no economic sense in a country with little cash and where agricultural produce was the principal means of settling debts; this would simply have deprived people of their means of paying. Renting the land to another party would only have compounded the problem, and L.G. Murphy & Co. would likely have found itself owed even more with no better hope of collecting. There is little or no evidence that the House of Murphy behaved as an evil landlord, even allowing that the partners were poor businessmen.

The McSweens Arrive in Lincoln

The year 1875 was also newsworthy for the arrival of Alexander A. and Sue McSween on March 3, two characters whose names would soon be inextricably tied to the Lincoln County War. The two had married at Atchison, Kansas, on August 23, 1873, then had gone to live

Alexander A. McSween

Sue E. McSween

at Eureka. In the fall of 1874 they left Kansas to look for better opportunities. At Punta de Agua, New Mexico, they heard of Lincoln and came on, penniless and hauled in a farmer's wagon, intending to make Lincoln their El Dorado.[29] At the time, McSween, thirty-one years old, was starting out as a lawyer; his wife was two years his junior.

Apparently he had little trouble in establishing a practice. John Chisum employed McSween from the first time Chisum saw him, while a Lincoln County War reminiscence claimed that the Murphy interests engaged McSween upon his arrival in Lincoln.[30] Both are probably true enough. Later that year, a letter from Chisum's first ranch at the Bosque Grande mentioned that McSween was the only lawyer who would come for such little accounts and if he didn't collect anything he got no pay.[31] Nevertheless, he must have done well enough by Chisum, since he opened an account at the First National Bank in Santa Fe in March 1876, with a $2,000. draft from R.D. Hunter. Hunter was the principal in a beef commission firm at St. Louis that had bought out most of Chisum's interests in the fall of 1875.[32]

During the first two years, McSween attracted no special attention as he built his law practice; letters and other records from the period suggest that he was certainly competent. During 1877, however, McSween's role changed dramatically as he took an active part in the plunge towards the incredible violence known as the Lincoln County War. As historian Robert Utley has written, McSween was a central character then:

> He may even have been *the* central character. This War was uniquely the making of McSween and the other people who fought it. . . . McSween contributed decisively to its origin and progress.[33]

L.G. Murphy & Co.: The House Without Money

The Lincoln of 1875 was changing, although not necessarily for the better. One very important change was in the economic circumstances of the premier business house, namely L.G. Murphy & Co. The House had lost its monopoly in rationing the Mescaleros at the same time that their numbers dropped to more realistic levels. Competitive bidding on Indian supplies began late in 1872, which caused prices to drop drastically—from the $7.00 per 100 pounds for beef, that Murphy had won as supplier, to $4.49 per 100 pounds under Van C. Smith's beef contract. Smith had problems in making deliveries, but even the beef bought on the open market was purchased at $5.50 per 100 pounds.[34] These prices were "net on the hoof," meaning live weight, in contrast with the army policy of deducting fifty percent from the live weight for wastage, when paying for beef cattle. Corn, which Murphy provided as corn meal at 5¢ per pound, never cost more than 3¢ a pound under competitive bidding— shelled and in 100-pound sacks.

Murphy & Co. continued to bid on and win a few corn contracts at prices scarcely higher than their own costs, but the House evidently never held a contract again for beef, flour, or other supplies for the Mescaleros. From their standpoint the prices were a disaster. John Chisum was awarded one contract for delivering 1,000,000 pounds of beef on the hoof at $1.98 per 100 pounds, beginning in September 1874. Even at that low price the Indian agency could use only about one-third of the amount.

For the next year, beginning in July 1875, William Rosenthal of Santa Fe submitted an even lower bid of $1.63 per 100 pounds of beef. The Indian Bureau began requiring an average weight of at least 850 pounds per steer in 1876, which meant that Rosenthal received less than $14. for an average cow. Until this time Murphy had probably subcontracted to deliver some supplies, but with the first Rosenthal award L.G. Murphy and John H. Riley became his agents for supplying beef to the agency.[35]

The next annual beef contracts also went to Rosenthal, for $3.86 per 100 pounds in 1876, and $3.78 in 1877.[36] Filling these orders required substantial numbers of cattle; 607 head weighing 545,992 pounds were delivered between December 1876 and June 1877.[37] The price would have been between $32. and $33. per animal, still leaving only $12. to $13. per steer for all expenses and a profit for Rosenthal and Murphy, had they been able to purchase beef at a reasonable cost.

At this period Murphy & Co. had no significant livestock holdings of its own; instead, the firm bought cattle from other people to meet its obligations.[38] With such low prices, the House could not furnish beef cattle under someone else's contract and still expect to make a profit. After 1872, L.G. Murphy & Co. probably made money only on occasional open market sales. Otherwise the profit margin was very thin, or nonexistent. For that matter, no one could make a profit delivering beef steers at prices of less than 4¢ per pound, with the probable exception of John Chisum, the man who raised most of the cattle. Chisum, at this period, valued a beef steer at $20.00 and consistently delivered on his own contracts in Arizona and to R.D. Hunter for $2.50 per 100 pounds.[39]

Lily Klasner provided at least a partial answer to the question of where the House obtained beef early on in its contracting:

> At first it bought the cattle from herds passing through. By the time a herd reached Lincoln some cattle would be so exhausted that they were worth little and the company bought them at a very low price and placed them on its ranch near Carrizozo. Since there were no fences they could not put the animals near the Fort because the half-starved Indians might have stolen them. . . . [40]

This could have been the basis for building a herd, but would have entailed a delay and additional expenses. For their short-term needs, a cattle-feeding operation was no solution. Another possibility was that the House filled its fresh beef contracts with meat from cows or young cattle, animals worth from one-half to two-thirds the value of steers. This might explain why Murphy bought almost 1,100 head of such stock from the Horrells. Army proposals sometimes allowed the delivery of either dry cows or steers.

After some delivery delays in 1877, this situation came to a head in the spring of 1878 when all of the beef suppliers began to delay, default, or go out of business—due only in part to the violence at that time.[41] The real problem was that none of them were making money. Someone always underbid the House for the Indian contracts and then used Murphy as a subcontractor, a role which he came to accept for two very good reasons: it kept the business from competitors and it provided some cash for settling his own debts.

An alternative to provisioning the Indians was to contract with the army for its corn, hay, and beef needs. For the army beef contracts, a very important bit of missing information is the actual quantities delivered, since the contractors agreed to provide fresh beef and/or beef cattle on demand. Without knowledge of the amounts delivered, the value of these contracts is not known.

Prior to 1876, the Murphy firm had subcontracted with some of the actual contract holders to deliver beef at Fort Stanton. Murphy's bank records from 1873–1874, when the prime contractor (C.H. McVeagh) received 8¢ per pound for fresh beef and cattle, showed only a few hundred dollars a month in vouchers from McVeagh.[42] Army contracts directly with Murphy & Co. or with the individual partners left the business no better off. J.J. Dolan and then John H. Riley held the beef contracts at Fort Stanton from July 1876 through June 1879, during which they furnished beef cattle at 5¢ to 6¢ per pound.[43] Even with the improved prices over the Indian contracts and the elimination of one level of profit, the economics were not good inasmuch as many fewer cattle were needed for the small army garrisons.[44] The reasons for continuing in this situation were to keep other people out and to generate some cash. Sooner or later a company doing business this way would bankrupt itself, which was exactly what happened.

A Lesson in Frontier Economics

Frontier business conditions and economics could become very rough, apart from any desperadoes involved. They became even more so as firms struggled to maintain themselves in the depression that followed the Panic of 1873. Worsening economic conditions made army and Indian contracts all the more desirable, especially in this corner of the New Mexico Territory where they offered nearly the only cash sources. The Murphy business was effectively uncapitalized and chronically short of cash. The desirability of such contracts, combined with business practices of the period and the economics of contracting, were at the roots of the Lincoln County War. Historian Maurice Fulton's observation was accurate: "Scratch beneath the surface and you will find one thing as the prime mover in most of the Lincoln County troubles—money."[45]

One incident illustrated this point and the interrelatedness of business methods with contracting, cattle, and Lincoln County people. The incident was the arrest of McSween and Chisum at Las Vegas, New Mexico, on December 27, 1877. McSween was accused of embezzling the proceeds of a $10,000. insurance policy on the life of Emil Fritz, the deceased partner in L.G. Murphy & Co. McSween posted bond and was free in a few days. Chisum, however, lingered in jail until early March of 1878.[46]

While there, Chisum was served with papers in several lawsuits, one of which was a judgment against him for some $2,370. granted by a district court in Bernalillo County, south of Santa Fe, in favor of William Rosenthal in Santa Fe. Rosenthal had bought up some old notes from the defunct partnership of Wilbur, Chisum, and Clark, a meat-packing firm in Arkansas. The notes evidently had a face value of about $18,000., but since a Texas court had previously cleared John Chisum of any liability, the notes must have traded at a substantial discount.[47] This was in a period when even the federal greenbacks paid to soldiers were commonly discounted at rates of fifteen, twenty, and up to fifty percent on the frontier.[48]

During his stay in jail, Chisum wrote a fascinating autobiographical essay, but he refused to budge on paying the judgments and eventually was freed on bail. The real issue in the Rosenthal complaint was never voiced. This revolved around the plaintiff also being the person who held the beef contract for the Mescalero Apache Agency—his third year with that contract, in fact. Chisum did not mention this connection. By the fall of 1877 the Rosenthal firm had gotten into deep trouble, due in part to the very low prices in their beef contract. Then they hit upon an ingenious solution.

Chisum being the man with the beef cattle, they bought up his old notes at a cheap price and then sought to squeeze him to satisfy the judgment they obtained from a New Mexico court, perhaps even to the face value of the notes. If Chisum could have been coerced into delivering cattle to meet Rosenthal's contract, to at least the value of the judgment against him, Rosenthal might have come away looking very well indeed, depending upon what he had paid for the notes. Chisum would have taken a beating. The scheme was sufficiently transparent that Chisum didn't see a need to explain it to anyone else, and by hanging tough he forestalled any collection in his lifetime.[49] By April 1878 it was Rosenthal, and not Chisum, who was in trouble, unable to continue making deliveries.[50]

This whole episode was probably not untypical in the business world of that time, though such dealings have been misunderstood by later observers, for whom such practices are out of their realm of understanding. While this contest was resolved without gunfire, practices not too dissimilar were what led to the Lincoln County War. With the war it was hidden motives, misrepresentations, incomplete understandings, and silence about the real issues at the time, combined with a reluctance to probe very deeply in looking for causes, that helped to obscure the reasons for the violence of the period. The surest route to a better understanding is simply to follow the money.

After 1874 L.G. Murphy & Co. and its successor, J.J. Dolan & Co., saw their bank statements reflecting much less income, while their bills continued. As of February 1876 the Murphy firm was greatly indebted to Spiegelberg & Bros.[51] The partners borrowed money, but even so their bank accounts showed anything between a negative balance of more than $10,000. and a positive one of a few hundred dollars from month to month. After Murphy began to fade from the business scene and the firm became J.J. Dolan & Co. in April 1877 the financial situation didn't change.[52] Dolan and partner Riley received a few minor army contracts for bran, beans, and wood plus a ruinous one for 300,000 pounds of corn at $1.69 per 100 pounds, but their long-term interests were as beef contractors for the army post and as subcontractors for the Indian agency.[53] Their business policies followed the mold cut by L.G. Murphy; his practices were their practices, and his solutions were likewise adopted.

How to Make It As a Beef Contractor

Of all the supplies needed by the army and the Indian Bureau, beef cattle clearly gave contractors the most problems. Unlike other commodities, cattle could rarely be obtained by barter. It was possible to buy stock from legitimate sources, but because of the low contract prices with the Indian agency and the relatively few animals required by the army, a contractor who did this was practically guaranteed no profit for his work. When a beef supplier's business was already in a slump or failing, what was to be done?

Sharp practices such as William Rosenthal's attempt to manipulate Chisum were one possible solution. John Riley was credited with another one:

> Riley would condone such practices as stampeding fat cattle that were being delivered following sale, and then replacing them with skinny animals before they were returned following the stampede.[54]

This might work once. There was still another answer to the problem of how to supply cattle at a low price and make money at it. This was to cut costs by stealing cattle yourself or by buying them from rustlers. The evidence that both L.G. Murphy & Co. and J.J. Dolan did this is overwhelming, though they were far from being the only ones.[55]

Rustlers delivered stolen cattle at $5. per head, while stockmen could not afford to sell the same class of cattle for less than $15. a head.[56] With rustled cattle a person might make money even at the $1.63 per 100 pounds rate that Rosenthal received under his beef contract with the Mescalero Agency in 1875–1876, a price, incidentally, that undercut John Chisum's $1.98 per 100 pounds for the year previous.[57]

When a contractor's agents were willing to pay $5. a steer with no questions asked, a coterie of suppliers soon formed.[58] Many of them were later included among "the Pecos men." Billie Wilson, one of the minor Lincoln County *banditos*, observed that

> the Beckwith family made their boasts that they came to Seven Rivers a little over four years ago with one Milch Cow borrowed from John Chisum; they had when I was there Year ago one thousand six hundred head of cattle.[59]

This rate of increase exceeded even the numbers of Indians at the Apache Agency under

Murphy's stewardship, but these cows were real. Chisum's "warriors," as his cowboys were called, protected their boss' interests; nevertheless, cattle stealing from his herds became acute by the late fall and early winter of 1876. There was a current saying that "No one can live at Seven Rivers who does not steal from Chisum's range."[60] From Seven Rivers it was a relatively short drive to either Fort Stanton or the Mescalero Agency.

The Pecos War

All of this led to a number of bloody incidents along the Pecos. Chisum decided to clean up the situation by leading an attack on the Beckwith ranch, the stronghold of the cattle thieves. On the way there, Chisum's warriors collected some horses and mules later claimed as Beckwith's. The result was the Pecos War of April 1877, which ended after Chisum's men began to rebel at the siege of the Beckwith ranch, saying that they had been hired to herd cattle and not to fight or be killed. No one was hurt, but Deputy Sheriff Andrew Boyle later served a number of those involved in the assault with warrants for riot, larceny, and other offenses. The way that Boyle saw the situation, Chisum and another rancher were trying to extend their range south of Seven Rivers to include all of the Pecos River valley. Boyle wrote a long letter on this affair published in the first issue of the *Mesilla Valley Independent*.[61] He also recovered the horses, which led one warrior, Charles Brady, to make it clear that feelings ran as high as ever:

> May 27, 1877
> South Spring River
>
> Mr. Andrew Boyle; Dear Sir, you red headed s— of - b—— if you do not bring them horses back you stole you shall hear the gentle report of my needle gun; that is the kind of a hair pin I am, this thing of being on a sheriff's posse for a band of horse thieves may do in some places but it has got too thin with me, yours, on the first dark stormy night.[62]

Later that year a fan of Boyle's at Lincoln dubbed him

> the famous Pasha Boyle, the distinguished historian of the "Pecos War," having by that history gained by clear right to be called the champion falsifier of 1877.[63]

This exchange illustrates as well as anything the problems in deciding what to believe when every incident had several sides to it and nearly everyone who survived that period later sought to portray their own actions as honorable and high-minded, while their opponents' behavior was lower than low.

"The Boys" and a Boy Named Billy

The local talent who fought the Pecos War were about to be reinforced by some of the most notorious hard cases in the Southwest. During August and September of 1877 a band of organized outlaws known variously as "The Boys," "The Banditti," or "The Jessie Evans Gang" plundered their way through Lincoln County, stealing the horses and mules at the Mescalero Agency and at Dick Brewer's ranch on the Ruidoso.

At the same time a confirmed bandit named Frank Freeman and a would-be desperado, Charles Bowdre, rode into Lincoln and loaded up on liquor at José Montaño's store. They then proceeded to tear up the store, nearly shot off an army sergeant's head, paraded the streets shooting and yelling, broke into the McSween house and riddled the furniture, including Sue McSween's new sewing machine, and declared they would burn the house down if

William H. Bonney, alias Billy the Kid. The only authenticated photograph ever made of the Kid, presumably taken at Fort Stanton ca. 1879. Photo Archives, Museum of New Mexico.

John Chisum (who was stopping there at the time) or his corpse wasn't turned over to them. The sheriff managed to arrest both of these desperate characters, but Freeman escaped. During all of this the local citizens had become "greatly enraged and highly excited," as one newspaper account put it, but they stayed out of the way. About a week later Sheriff William Brady and a posse of fifteen cavalrymen hunted Freeman down and killed him.[64] Newspaper correspondents claimed that this plague of bandits had come to the Southwest from Doña Ana and Grant counties.

The Boys and Jessie Evans turned towards the Rio Grande with their stolen horses and evidently continued west into Grant County. Just five days after Sheriff Brady ended Freeman's rampage, another promising young gunman shot down his first man, a blacksmith named F.P. Cahill, at Camp Grant in Arizona.[65] When Evans and the Banditti commenced to pillage their way eastward again, the boy from Camp Grant rode with them at least as far as the Rio Grande. The *Mesilla Valley Independent* called the seventeen year old Henry Antrim.[66] In time he would also be called "Kid," "Kid" Antrim, William Bonney, and Billy the Kid. When he first turned up at Seven Rivers sometime in the fall of 1877 he was, as Lily Klasner's brother Robert Casey recalled sixty years later, what you might call "a bum . . . nothing but a kid and a bum."[67] Apparently he did not have a bad name at the time, though his criminal days, by most accounts, had begun at least two years prior.[68] Probably no one knew that a few weeks earlier he had helped to steal some miners' horses in the Burro Mountains south of Silver City, New Mexico, and attempted to hold up a stagecoach seven miles east of Cook's Canyon.[69] A year after he first appeared on the Pecos, Casey's judgment of Billy was modified considerably: "a gentleman," he claimed, "a different man altogether."[70] This youthful killer, who managed to charm some and alarm some others, soon found himself in the thick of the Lincoln County War. Whatever they called him, he would never be forgotten.

～ 7 ～

JOHN H. TUNSTALL
COMES TO LINCOLN

1876–1878

A nother principal player in the period leading up to the Lincoln County War was an Englishman named John Henry Tunstall. His chance meeting with A.A. McSween in late October of 1876 at Santa Fe's Herlow's Hotel would have profound consequences both for the two men who met there and for Lincoln County. McSween, representing the administrators of the Emil Fritz estate, was on his way to St. Louis and New York to attempt to collect the $10,000. due on that troubled life insurance policy activated more than two years before.[1]

Tunstall had arrived in Santa Fe that August in search of land and livestock investments, having made the grand tour in British Columbia and California. Scarcely twenty-three years of age, he was the scion of a moderately well-off British family and a harbinger of the British investors who would play an important role in financing the range cattle industry in the western United States through the next decade. The candid letters between young Tunstall and his family showed a well-honed business sense and ability to weigh investment possibilities. He was frankly looking for the maximum return, the main chance; the struggling McSween was looking to secure his own financial future. The two men undoubtedly saw in one another someone whom the other could use.[2]

J.H. Tunstall, Prospective Entrepreneur and Merchant

McSween persuaded Tunstall to visit Lincoln County, where Tunstall found what he was looking for. As he wrote to his father,

> *Everything* in New Mexico that pays *at all* (you may say) is worked by a "ring." There is the "indian ring," the "army ring," the "political ring," and "legal ring," the "Roman Catholic ring," the "cattle ring" the "horse thieves ring," the "land ring" & half a dozen other rings. Now "to make things stick" to do any good it is necessary to either get into a ring or make one for yourself. I am work[ing] at present making a ring. . . .
>
> I propose to confine my operations to Lincoln County, but I intend to handle it in such a way as to get the half of every dollar that is made in the county by anyone, and with our means we could get things into that shape in three years, if we only used two thirds of our capital in the undertaking.[3]

Tunstall believed that McSween was someone he could manipulate and felt that there was good reason to have confidence in him. With respect to British apprehensions about being in a wild Indian country, Tunstall wrote:

> As regards indians, it is much better to be quite close to an indian reservation than 150 miles off one, as indians never raid near home, as their cattle & horses would then be recognized.[4]

John Henry Tunstall, ca. 1875. His arrival upon the scene precipitated the Lincoln County War. Photo Archives, Museum of New Mexico.

His presumption of safety was delusory, as John Chisum and other local citizens could have told him. By 1877 conditions were changing, if only because outlaws had largely displaced Indians as stock thieves. Tunstall went on to analyze the economic situation:

> Let me tell you that groceries in this country realize a profit of 50 percent on the *return* & they are a cash article; in the second place there are two cash customers for four staple items in this country, viz., the Indian department & the Army, & the articles they buy are corn, hay, flour & beef; . . . produce raised here is protected from foreign produce by a tariff of 1½ cents per pound (for it costs 1½ cents per pound for wagon freight from any other produce market).
>
> Now the question arises, out of the existing circumstances & with these ascertained points, what scheme, if practicable, would catch the ready money of the Indian department, & the Army, & avoid the dangers of too many debtors among a needy & improvident class?
>
> The first part of the question is simple to answer; by having hay, beef, corn or flour raised within the district, Uncle Sam is compelled to patronize you & pour his almighty dollars into your cap. The answer to the second is simple likewise; Don't credit the poor shiftless wretches with what they can't pay, . . . the solution I think you will agree is found in the following problem. T. opens a grocery store, M. applies for groceries; T. supplies him with groceries in return for promissory notes to deliver x lbs. of grain to his store of fair merchantable quality, upon the 20th day of August. T. having ascertained beyond doubt that the crop planted by M. will (when gathered) equal x. The same problem can be solved in the same way on the flour question. By this means T. can acquire a controlling interest in both these articles. The question then arises, is T. sure to get the contracts? perhaps he may not. but whoever *does*, *must* come to T. to buy, or get "bust."[5]

Tunstall then explained how the hay market could be cornered. There were plenty of other opportunities as well:

> That [Stanton] Post Tradership I am sorry to say will be open in January next [1878]. I say sorry because I want it. Have a good show to get it & you don't appear to think you can raise the coin by then. It is worth a cool £1,000 per annum, & could be run on £2,000 like a charm & would afford such a grip on the country that I would make money so fast that you would think I stole it, I believe. But unless you were here you could never understand all these things about the army & Indian contracts, the post tradership, the cattle ranges, and the way one range secures the other & the ranches & the water rights & the mills & the squatters & a thousand other corners that have to be tucked up & worked "& then don't the grist just come in, Stranger?"[6]

In laying out his plans he modestly admitted that "I can't touch the beef contract *yet*,"[7] but in time that would fall into place.

Apparently he had ideas about acquiring property as payment for groceries. Once he had done this,

> There is nothing more profitable than buying *young stock* . . . & this would be more so, & I shall be able to acquire stock by degrees, which I would much rather do, than in one big lump, as I can gain experience more easily that way. . . . & I can acquire the cattle for at least ⅓ less than any other way.
>
> To make all this *work*, I ought to have the *land* & the *stock money* as soon as possible for you see as I acquire cattle I shall reduce the capital I have to run my store with; or else I shall have to turn my acquired property into money again before they shall have had a chance to increase in value.[8]

Actually a stock ranch was the first opportunity presented to him, as McSween described later:

In November 1876 John H. Tunstall came to this county for the purpose as he said of going into the stock raising business, & took steps to secure four thousand acres of land for that purpose and invested about $25,000 in his business of stock raising and in merchandise for a store which he opened at Lincoln. At this time the firm of J.J. Dolan & Co. composed of J.J. Dolan and John H. Riley, seemed to be friends of his, and knowing that he had considerable money to invest, they tried to have him as far away from Lincoln as they could and also to get his money away so that he would be financially crippled and for that purpose tried to have him purchase L.G. Murphy's ranch at Fairview about 35 miles from Lincoln and knowing that I was a friend of Tunstall, they tried to induce me to use my influence with Tunstall to buy it, that they would give me $5,000. I informed Tunstall of this offer and told him that they had no good title to the land and Tunstall refused to buy. This was the beginning of the enmity of Murphy, Dolan & Riley against Tunstall.[9]

In his letters home, Tunstall combined an idealized view of the current operations of L.G. Murphy & Co. with his own plan for the future. While essentially accurate, and reflecting McSween's knowledge of Murphy's business practices, there were things that Tunstall failed to grasp. To make such a system work, the labor force had to be in a condition of near-peonage and the supply of commodities roughly balanced with the demand. The entrepreneur would also need control over the market as well as the means of production. These conditions were slipping away or already lost even by 1870, although the House tried to maintain its control by increasing coercion. And as seen earlier, its unchanging ways were driving the House into bankruptcy.[10] By 1878 most of the Indian and army contracts were going to bidders elsewhere in New Mexico, such as Levi and Willi Spiegelberg, Zadoc and Abraham Staab, and to other local-area merchants.[11] Except for army beef contracts, the House had been reduced to the position of a subcontractor or agent.

Tunstall's and McSween's megalomaniacal vision was of a bygone world. Freight rates were going down, and the coming of the railroad would reduce these even more. Rail transportation came to Las Vegas, New Mexico, in 1879 and within a year the army at Fort Stanton was importing corn and hay from Kansas for less than it cost to buy locally.[12] In another decade the costs had reversed again, but by that time both prices and demand were even lower.[13] The competition that would lead to the Lincoln County War involved issues no longer susceptible to local control and which were partly a myth anyway. The Lincoln County War was about money, and it needn't have happened at all. But given the personalities and their intentions, and the entrance of John Henry Tunstall to the Lincoln County scene, the stage was set.

Tunstall was not a bad sort or even untypical with respect to what he hoped to accomplish. He did represent something quite unfamiliar and therefore perceived as a threat: foreign capital. By himself Tunstall might have gone on to accomplish part of his program with conditions becoming no more volatile than they were already. Lincoln did have other merchants— Juan Patron, Isaac Ellis, and José Montaño.[14] The lethal ingredient was McSween, who saw in Tunstall the means for making Lincoln his El Dorado at last.

An unexpected bonus came with the passage of the Desert Land Act in March of 1877. This was a speculator's delight and soon recognized as such, although General Land Office administration of the act was somewhat uncertain during its first year. Basically the act provided that a settler might purchase up to 640 acres of land if he would irrigate it within three years, paying 25¢ per acre at the time of filing a claim. The claim was perfected by actually conducting water to the land anytime within the three years and paying an additional sum of $1. per acre. Residence upon the land was not required nor, until 1908, was the right of entry restricted to surveyed land. Non-citizens could file if they had declared an intention to become a citizen.[15]

In effect, a person could hold a section of land for three years under the Desert Land Act merely by paying $160. to the land office, with no further investment. From a rancher's standpoint this was an improvement over either a homestead or a preemption claim. Tunstall had six persons file on lands under the act, thereby reducing his capital needs considerably for the first year or two. Originally he seems to have filed on 640 acres along the Rio Peñasco and another 3,200 acres on the upper Rio Felix. After his death in February 1878, McSween tried to persuade Tunstall's father in England that the titles could be made secure with another $3,840. invested.[16] A year later an attorney retained by Mrs. McSween reported that Tunstall had entered 2,300 acres under the Desert Land Act, all in the names of other men.[17] With his death these claims evaporated.

Tunstall and McSween Team Up

John Henry had no ready money to invest as of 1876. Initially he asked his father for £6,000.[18] The family fortunes could not bear this much and by April 1877 he had scaled the request down to £3,200.[19] At the then-current exchange rate of $4.81 this still came to almost $15,400. McSween may have tried to hurry up the remittances by fueling Tunstall's apprehensions; a letter from Tunstall's father alluded to this in his son's previous letter: "written under nervous depression from McSween coming in while you were writing and telling you there were more settlers going in upon the spot your mind has been set upon, the last few months."[20]

How much Tunstall did invest has been a subject of speculation. McSween said about $25,000., and it seems clear from the correspondence between father and son that at least £3,000 was sent. An undated letter from J.P. Tunstall probably written in February 1878 mentioned the possibility of sending £1,400 more.[21] Evidently a substantial remittance arrived after J.H. Tunstall's death and someone pocketed the money.[22] Much later, in November 1879, Tunstall told the British Foreign Secretary that his son's invested capital was £5,000 sterling.[23] This would nearly match McSween's figure. All but a few hundred dollars disappeared in the estate settlement.

As for McSween, he may have been keeping busy in Lincoln but he wasn't making much money. Between the $2,000 draft from R.D. Hunter in March 1876 and a $1,000 credit on October 30, the only deposit to the lawyer's account was a $42.83 check. The $1,000 credit looked suspiciously like a loan.[23a] By February 1877 McSween was in no better financial shape. His legal services for L.G. Murphy & Co. probably brought in no cash since the House settled accounts by allowing credit wherever possible. Murphy's deeding of 5.94 acres in Lincoln to McSween on February 9, 1877, may well have been a settlement of their account.[23b] This soon became an important tract—the site of a new dwelling and law office for the McSweens, the Lincoln County Bank, and John H. Tunstall's new store.

Although McSween had no money of his own he was not idle. By August 1877 he had received more than $7,000. (all that was realized) in settlement of the Fritz insurance policy. He kept the money for himself, using it to construct the McSween home and stock the Tunstall store in Lincoln, as testimony later made clear.[24]

August of 1877 saw the smallpox epidemic that had been sweeping Lincoln County nearly played out and recriminations over the recent Pecos War dying down. The Jessie Evans gang was running off horses from the Mescalero Agency and Frank Freeman had just shot up the town of Lincoln. An area newspaper meanwhile reported on other newsworthy activities:

> A.A. McSween Esq., has built a new dwelling house; also a building for business purposes, in which he will have one of the nicest and best furnished law offices in

JOHN S. CHISUM, *Pres't.*   ALEX. A. McSWEEN, *Vice-Pres't.*   JOHN H. TUNSTALL, *Cashier.*

LINCOLN COUNTY BANK,

———o———

Lincoln, N. M., ... *187*

In August of 1877 the Lincoln County Bank and Tunstall Store (later Dolan-owned) opened for busi-
ness, both built by McSween. Top, Courtesy Special Collections, University of Arizona Library; bottom,
Courtesy Western History Collections, University of Oklahoma.

the Territory, also a bank—The Lincoln county bank—and store. The proprietors of the bank are Col. R.D. Hunter, St. Louis, John S. Chisum of Bosque Grande and A.A. McSween of Lincoln.[25]

Plans for these enterprises had been under way for some time; Tunstall had ordered goods from St. Louis forwarded through Otero Sellars & Co. of El Moro, Colorado, back in January. Tunstall Sr. referred to his son's plans for banking and storekeeping in a letter dated at London on March 21, 1877.[26] J.H. Tunstall was in St. Louis on a buying trip during August that year, about the time that the bank and store opened for business. One Mesilla newspaper reported,

> We received a check this week drawn on the "Lincoln County Bank". . . . we had heard that something of the kind was contemplated but this is the first intimation we have received that the Bank was really in existence. We are informed that John S. Chisum and A.A. McSween are the principal managers.[27]

According to the bank's letterhead, Tunstall was the cashier, a position roughly the same as a business manager.

That fall a newspaper correspondent painted conditions at Lincoln in very rosy colors:

> The town of Lincoln, the County Seat, shows considerable enterprise and prosperity in the rapid and substantial improvement seen on every side. A number of good business houses and handsome residences have been recently erected, notably among which are the banking house, offices and residence of A.A. McSween, Esq., who has not only established a reputation as a good lawyer, but has shown himself to be "at home," as a banker and business man generally. . . .
>
> Speaking of these "prominent citizens" [he meant desperadoes] reminds me that the authorities of Lincoln county have just completed a substantial jail. The cells are entirely under ground, and are lined with heavy squared timber substantially put together. I was shown through its "dungeons" (no rays of daylight reaches its lower precincts) by Sheriff Brady, and from a hasty inspection I should judge those who are unfortunate to become its inmates will find it a rather difficult undertaking to "go through" it without the consent of those in charge.[28]

This last structure was the famous $3,000. jail, otherwise described as "a horribly dismal hole, unfit for a dog-kennel." The door to one cell supposedly bore the penciled legend:

> William Bonney was incarcerated first time, December, 22, 1878; Second time, March, 21, 1879, and hope I never will be again.
>
> W.H. Bonney.[29]

Jessie Evans and three of the Boys were among the first to enjoy the dungeon's dubious hospitality. They had returned to Lincoln County in early October and were known to be at Beckwith's Ranch on the Pecos. Tunstall and McSween prodded Sheriff Brady into accompanying a posse that captured Evans and gang members Frank Baker, Tom Hill, and George Davis on October 17 after a gun battle. The four were brought back to Lincoln and duly incarcerated, only to be rescued in late November by some of their associates. According to the newspapers, they paused on their way south to Texas to relieve rancher Dick Brewer of eight horses and shoot up his ranch. Later, at the Beckwith ranch, they announced that McSween's, Patron's, and Montaño's death warrants had been signed and related the tale of their escape from Lincoln.[30] For the next few weeks this contingent occupied itself in the El Paso area.

According to later testimony by both Jessie Evans and Andy Boyle, who aided in the escape, this story was a fraud. McSween had actually assisted the gang by having horses,

Jessie Evans and the Boys. Fifth from left, standing with violin, was thought to be the Kid. Photo Archives, Museum of New Mexico.

saddles, and arms brought to Brewer's ranch the night before.[31] The Boys were grateful, according to Tunstall, and said they would never touch another hoof of his stock.[32] The whole affair sounded like it might have been a scheme to enlist the Evans gang as rustlers on behalf of Tunstall and McSween.

During 1877 Tunstall had become a rancher in fact as well as in name. In the spring, Sheriff Brady had attached some 209 head of cattle, mostly yearlings, from the widow of Robert Casey to settle a judgment against her. When sold at auction in May they brought between $4. and $5. per head, roughly half of the current market value, with A.A. McSween the highest bidder.[33] These became the core of Tunstall's herd of around 400 animals. When the Caseys left for Texas that fall, they attempted to take most of these cattle with them, prompting Tunstall's ranch foreman, Dick Brewer, to lead an outfit in pursuit and recover the livestock.[34] Tunstall was to continue having problems with his ranch operations.[35]

His system of securing promissory notes from farmers to deliver corn, hay, or other types of produce against their accounts in Tunstall's store was also running into trouble. How popular these notes were and the accuracy of the claim that "Tunstall's prices were much fairer than those of Murphy-Dolan-Riley" are debatable.[36] A bitter and obviously biased letter dated just before Christmas 1877 claimed that "McSween went back on his word in nearly every particular" in an agreement to haul hay from the Casey ranch, while Tunstall may have attempted to seize a hay delivery intended for J.J. Dolan & Co.[37]

The actual prices offered by Tunstall through his grain notes, as they were called, would be the best guide as to whether his prices were any fairer than those of the Dolan firm. The Tunstall estate documents provide an inventory of grain notes that gives a dollar value for each, plus a separate list of promissory notes with the type and quantity of produce for every note. To some extent these can be matched and Tunstall's actual prices learned.[38] For corn and wheat he offered 2¢ per pound, though one wheat note was for only 1⅓¢ per pound; for hay the price was 1¢ per pound. These, of course, were 1877 prices, and although newspapers that fall spoke of crop damage due to early frosts, the contract prices for corn at both Fort Stanton and the Mescalero Agency were relatively low; close to 2½¢ per pound.[39] Hay prices varied by up to 100 percent depending upon whether it was bottom or grama hay. The list of Tunstall hay notes did not specify which type was meant. A surviving note dated February 2, 1878, payable in wheat or money, carried an annual interest rate of 25 percent.[40]

All in all, John H. Tunstall probably offered no better values on produce than did Murphy's successor, J.J. Dolan & Co., and it's hard to see why farmers would have been any better off dealing with one merchant than the other. If Tunstall's prices for merchandise were lower, then that might provide an answer. Unfortunately, we have no information on this point. Since Tunstall had no contracts with the army or anyone else, there is also a question as to what he would have done with the produce he received, other than store it or hope to become a contractor's agent. He indeed was carrying through the plans outlined to his parents earlier that year, but in 1878 he would have had to face the economic realities of no market and problematic storage. His advantage at the end of 1877 was that while *he* recognized the shaky financial condition of J.J. Dolan & Co., *they* were left to speculate about his own resources. If they went under, then John H. Tunstall, merchant, was ready to step into the vacancy and supply the local market with both grain and cattle.

Marketable cattle, as we've seen, generally meant beef steers, and in this regard Tunstall was no better off than Dolan and Riley—less so, perhaps, because of his lack of experience. However, there were rustlers ready and willing to serve either or both parties, which may explain General Sheridan's comment that

> it is said that one of these parties is made up of cattle and horse-thieves, and the other party of persons who have retired from that business.[41]

Tunstall and McSween, while seeking to use one another to their personal advantage, were also perfectly capable of banding together and employing still others for their joint purposes. As early as April 1877, Tunstall announced to his father that "my ring is forming itself as fast & faster than I had ever hoped & in such a way that I will get the finest plum of the lot."[42]

Eight months later, Tunstall and McSween launched an orchestrated campaign to take over the economic reins in Lincoln County from Dolan and Riley. They seem to have been able to work on a number of fronts at once, with Tunstall more the strategist and McSween the plotter who spread doubt and discord, writing to newspapers and seeking to twist whatever opportunities came along to his and Tunstall's advantage. Their ethics were right at the same level as those of Dolan and Riley, who in every way were the successors to L.G. Murphy.[43]

James Dolan knew exactly what the game was about, and he explained it later to the U.S. Indian Inspector sent to investigate the Mescalero Agency:

> Mr. A.A. McSween, John S. Chisum and others have during the past year endeavoured to have Agent Godfroy removed from his present position; from my knowledge of the character of these two men and their tools I do not hesitate to declare that they would be guilty of any crime, even murder, to accomplish their ends. It is further known to me that they intended to bid on Indian contracts and as Agent Godfroy could not be manipulated by them, they desired to have him removed. Men have been killed by the hired assassins of these men, McSween & Chisum, in order to remove all evidence of their guilt, and others have been murdered because their interests conflicted.[44]

Although a certain bias was evident, Dolan spoke the truth as he saw it, and there is enough

J.J. Dolan.

Sheriff William Brady. Original caption read, ". . . killed by 'Billy the Kid' and his gang April 1, 1878, by 16 bullets in the back." Courtesy Special Collections, University of Arizona Library.

John H. Riley.

Thomas B. Catron. Top and left, Photo Archives, Museum of New Mexico.

evidence to support the intentions that he spelled out. For example, early in February of 1878 McSween wrote to the secretary of the interior charging "fearful villany on the part of all concerned," particularly by Dolan, Riley, and the Mescalero agent Godfroy, and recommending one Robert A. Widenmann as a temporary replacement for Godfroy. Later in the same month, following Tunstall's murder, he wrote to the Secretary of the Board of Home Missions with a similar blast against the same parties, but now pushing for Rev. Taylor F. Ealy, a Presbyterian medical missionary just arrived in Lincoln, as Godfroy's successor.[45] Meanwhile, the clerk at the Mescalero Agency had been sounded out as to how he felt about joining the Tunstall-McSween team. He declined and later told Inspector Watkins:

> Some time in November last [1877] Robert A. Weidenman stayed over night at the Agency and informed me that McSween & Tunstall had opened or were going to open a store at Lincoln, that they intended to bid for future Indian Contracts, that it was not their intention to have Riley & Dolan run the County referring to Government contracts and the purchase of grain and he offered me an interest in the contracts if they should obtain them, that there was lots of money in them and I could not afford to work for the salary I was getting. . . . Weidenman's reputation here and at Santa Fe was that of a "dead beat." He left Santa Fe without paying his board or wash bill and I believe him to be a confounded rascal.[46]

Tunstall had imported Robert Widenmann from Santa Fe to Lincoln County in February 1877 and employed him in a variety of ways, although claiming that he paid him only board and clothing. Tunstall thought highly of him and wrote in glowing terms about Widenmann in his letters back to England. Others on the Lincoln scene, less impressed, were inclined to share the clerk's opinion.

The Indian Inspector also took a sworn deposition from McSween, whose accusations had launched this investigation, and came away more than a little disgusted. Under oath, McSween backed all over the place excusing himself; in connection with his earlier charges, he knew nothing of his own knowledge and "of my own personal knowledge I know nothing against the character of Major Godfroy or reflecting upon his management of the Indian Agency."[47] Watkins, in his own report to the secretary of the interior, barely disguised his contempt for McSween "who was himself the head, and moving spirit of a Banditti, at the time."[48]

Tunstall's plans were simply the old Murphy formula repackaged and, it was hoped, shorn of economic liabilities. Even the effort to have an Indian agent appointed who would have a favorable attitude fit the Murphy pattern from the early 1870s. What this might have accomplished in the face of competitive bidding for supplies is questionable. It was one of the fronts on which Tunstall, McSween, and their "ring" moved.

The House Insolvent

The House's weak financial situation and declining power offered possibilities for economic warfare. Merchant Juan Patron said that since the time of the Horrell War

> there has been although not concentrated opposition, but there has been enough of individuality among some of the people that Murphy, Dolan and Riley have been opposed in their schemes and plots.[49]

Florencio Gonzales painted a thoroughly black picture of life in the Lincoln country under Murphy, but recognized

> the power of said L.G. Murphy & Co. was visibly declining. Strangers were settling

in the County and the oppression of L.G. Murphy & Co. had become so fearfully oppressive that people for the past two or three years began to show a disposition to withstand the tyranny of L.G. Murphy & Co.[50]

There were plenty of skeletons for an adroit and ambitious competitor to rattle here, especially if half-truths were employed. McSween's inside knowledge about the House's financial condition, from his work on the Emil Fritz estate, made the lawyer a special threat.

A week after Dolan spoke with Inspector Watkins, he gave another deposition to Special Agent Frank Warner Angel from the Departments of Justice and the Interior, who had a more sweeping responsibility to investigate the conduct of U.S. officials in New Mexico. To Angel, Dolan said that the Tunstall-McSween combine had spread reports that Dolan & Co. checks had been protested, telling commercial firms at Denver and St. Louis that they were not credit worthy. Dolan had countered this. When the story cropped up again, T.B. Catron of Santa Fe, U.S. Attorney for New Mexico and a land baron of considerable wealth, said that he would endorse Dolan's and Riley's notes for $10,000. This was back in June of 1877 when Catron had already co-signed to the tune of $6,000. He continued to endorse notes and advance them money to a total of more than $20,000.[51] Dolan even borrowed $1,000. from Tunstall.[52] Their bank records confirmed that by September 1877 J.J. Dolan & Co. was in a mess, with chronic overdrafts and borrowings.[53] McSween's charges had a basis in fact.

There was also the story of a $1,545.13 check written by McSween to Sheriff Brady in payment of taxes, and the diversion of this check to John H. Riley. The governor's annual report had pointed out the absence of tax receipts from Lincoln County, and one source had it that Catron covered this discrepancy almost immediately by diverting vouchers due to Riley. The claim was plausible enough, and Tunstall aired it publicly. Brady boiled with resentment; although the territorial treasurer absolved him of any impropriety, to Brady this was a personal humiliation.[54]

As of January 19, 1878, J.J. Dolan & Co. was insolvent. That day the partners mortgaged their property, real and personal, to T.B. Catron as security for the notes he had already endorsed plus a new one for $25,000. Catron sent his brother-in-law down to Lincoln to manage the business and wind up affairs. That summer Dolan and Riley executed a second mortgage with the Second National Bank of Santa Fe to secure another large debt. By then their partnership had been dissolved.[55]

Seeds of War: The House vs. Tunstall and McSween

Instead of giving up and walking out when they mortgaged everything to Catron, Dolan and Riley turned on their tormentors with the old Murphy ploy of legal harassment. McSween had returned to Lincoln early in January 1878, in the custody of a deputy sheriff from San Miguel County, to appear in district court at Mesilla on the charge of embezzling insurance money from the Fritz estate. He entered a plea of not guilty. Posting bail required property bonds, which were subject to approval by the district attorney, one William L. Rynerson. Rynerson refused to give his approval. McSween was allowed to continue technically in arrest while effectively at liberty, accompanied all the time by the deputy, until the Lincoln County grand jury freed him of the criminal charge of embezzlement in April.

While McSween was in Mesilla awaiting the outcome of the criminal case, the administrators of the Fritz estate, strongly encouraged by Dolan, filed a civil suit against McSween. Two days later the district judge issued a writ of attachment "as will be sufficient to make $8,000 to answer the complaint," the money owed to the family on Emil Fritz's insurance.

Dolan happily took this writ in charge and set off for Lincoln to deliver it to Sheriff Brady for service.[56]

All of this legal web-spinning affected McSween directly, but was aimed at Tunstall as well. While Dolan and his party hastened towards Lincoln, they passed McSween and Tunstall by the eastern foot of the Organ Mountains and nearly settled their differences with a Winchester carbine then and there. Tunstall refused to be baited and the incident passed.[57]

By February 9, Sheriff Brady had the writ and was proceeding to attach the goods and chattels, lands and tenements, etc. of Alexander A. McSween to satisfy the sum of $8,000. plus damages and costs. He levied on everything in sight including McSween's home and furnishings and the Tunstall store with its contents; McSween later claimed that the attached property was worth over $40,000. Robert Widenmann, then in charge at the store, protested that it belonged to Tunstall, but Brady went ahead anyway on the basis of alleged testimony that McSween and Tunstall were partners.

When these two "partners" (that question was never finally settled) arrived at Lincoln on the evening of February 10, they had quite a homecoming. Brady was still taking inventory when Tunstall began to protest in vain about his property being taken for a debt of McSween's. As for the lawyer, he later told Special Agent Angel

> that when he [McSween] arrived at the Town of Lincoln he was informed that a courier had preceded me from Mesilla with a writ of attachment—That Riley, Dolan and Murphy and Sheriff Brady were in ecstasy over deponent's prospective confinement in the County jail and I was informed that Sheriff Brady was making the occasion a subject of merriment by making contracts to grind corn in the mexican mills to make gruel for my maintenance; that said Riley had swept out the jail in order that he might in future have it to say that he swept out the room in which I was incarcerated.[58]

Neither this one-sided euphoria nor Mac's contemplation of humble pie lasted long. When Tunstall and Widenmann strode into the store the next day, their armed escort stopped in the doorway with Winchesters and pistols ready. That day passed with hard words and threats.

At this point Lincoln County was poised on the brink; another week and it would go over the edge. Although it's clearer in retrospect what happened, a few people did know at the time. The Silver City newspaper reported that "the whole fight was because McSween and Tunstall wanted to run Murphy and Dolan out." Others more or less agreed.[59] With some justice the *Mesilla Valley Independent* consistently claimed that the Lincoln County troubles "were inaugurated and almost entirely carried on by outlaws driven out of Texas," encouraged and aided by a few bad men in the county.[60] Inspector Watkins went so far as to accuse McSween of being the head of one group of Banditti. The outlaws, including Jessie Evans and his gang, certainly played a prominent role. The Boys, joined with men from Lincoln and the Pecos, worked for Dolan and Riley part of the time, while Tunstall employed an equally hard core, not the least of whom was the Kid, and had his own adherents among the local population.

Why Did the Lincoln County War Happen?

Until early February of 1878 the competition between the two sides had been in political, business, and economic realms, accompanied by lies, halftruths, backstabbing, attempts at character assassination and intimidation, and manipulations of the legal system. No one had been shot or probably even shot at; economic warfare was not the same as actual warfare. Was there anything inevitable about what happened next? How had conditions in Lincoln County reached such a tense state?

One element was the lack of economic opportunities. Farming and stock raising were the only avenues for making a living. As of the 1870s John Chisum virtually monopolized the national market for livestock from New Mexico, supplying both the commission buyer R.D. Hunter in the Midwest and the Indian reservations in Arizona. For other local producers there were markets at Fort Stanton and the Mescalero Apache Reservation. After 1879, when the railroad reached Las Vegas, New Mexico, eastern and foreign capital entered the cattle business and all of this changed. Mining began at the end of 1879 at White Oaks, less than thirty miles from Lincoln.[61]

As of 1878 Lincoln still had its horizons where they had been for the past ten years. By 1880, or at the latest 1882, it was a different world altogether. The conditions that led to a violent upheaval in 1878 were a part of the past.

Personalities had a part in what happened, possibly even a decisive role. Here McSween was the most important figure—the lawyer who came to Lincoln to make his fortune, but abandoned his counselor's role to turn knowledge gained from one client to the advantage of another and against the first. McSween's tactics were bad enough, but the financial ineptness of L.G. Murphy & Co. and its successor, J.J. Dolan & Co., laid the firm open to any number of charges. Meanwhile their guarantors in Santa Fe had a direct monetary interest in keeping Dolan & Co. from drowning in a sea of debts, for which Catron and others would be responsible. In the end the business failed and it was probably an expensive lesson. Tunstall and McSween saw this coming and tried to turn the situation to their personal advantage, but they were ultimately unsuccessful.

There were some unusual elements that by themselves might not have been decisive. One was the increasing dependence upon cattle rustlers for supplying the local markets. By raiding Chisum's herds these banditti could peddle their stolen steers at a price no legitimate source could match. This introduced a number of very tough outlaws and would-be badmen into Lincoln County, who in turn attracted more of their kind. The available legal mechanisms could not cope with this development.

Self-deception no doubt also played a part. Dolan and his party, as a result of their legal maneuverings in Las Vegas and Mesilla, finally saw the tables turning and things going their way. Tunstall and McSween foresaw a bonanza of contracts at the end of their rainbow once the present difficulties had been cleared away. Neither side was right. What was about to happen was that by early February 1878 the kind of competition that led up to conditions as they were then wouldn't matter in one more week. The balancing of interests was so unstable that the outcome might have gone in several directions, depending upon which prop collapsed first.

Finally there were the personal humiliations to Sheriff Brady; first in the escape of Jessie Evans and several of his gang from jail, and then in the disappearance of tax monies—both whipped up or misrepresented to benefit Tunstall and McSween. This, with McSween's existing liabilities, blocked what little recourse the two might have had to the principal law enforcement office in Lincoln County. In any frontier community it was not a good idea to alienate the man who wore the star.

PART III

"The war is raging now as fiercely as ever. The county is overrun by horse & cattle thieves, & there is no law in force...."
                              Godfrey Gauss writing to J. P. Tunstall,
                              August 22, 1878.

Winchester Model, ca. 1876; caliber 45/60; designed for large game.

～ 8 ～

THE LINCOLN COUNTY
WAR I
February–March 1878

On February 10, 1878, Sheriff William Brady deputized J.B. "Billy" Mathews to lead a posse to the Rio Felix and attach the cattle and horses held there by A.A. McSween or J.H. Tunstall & Co. The posse started out with five men and was joined en route by A.L. "Buckshot" Roberts, Jessie Evans, Frank Baker, and Tom Hill. Waiting for it at the Tunstall ranch on the morning of the 13th were Robert Widenmann, Dick Brewer, John Middleton, Fred Waite, William Bonney, and several others.[1] A few months later, the Kid told Special Agent Frank Angel what happened:

> Before the arrival of said J.B. Mathews, deputy Sheriff, and his posse, having been informed that said deputy sheriff and posse were going to round up all the cattle and drive them off and kill the persons at the ranch, the persons at the ranch cut portholes into the walls of the house and filled sacks with earth, so that they, the persons at the ranch, should they be attacked or their murder attempted, could defend themselves. This course being thought necessary as the sheriff's posse was composed of murderers, outlaws and desperate caracters none of whom had any interest at stake in the County, nor being residents of said County.
>
> That said Mathews when within about 50 yards of the house was called to to stop and advance alone and state his business, that said Mathews after arriving at the ranch said that he had come to attach the cattle and property of A.A. McSween, that said Mathews was informed that A.A. McSween had no cattle or property there, but that if he had he, said Mathews, couldn't take it. That said Mathews said, that he thought some of the cattle belonging to R.M. Brewer, whose cattle were also at the ranch of J.H. Tunstall, belonged to A. A. McSween, that said Mathews was told by said Brewer that he, Mathews, could round up the cattle and that he, Brewer, would help him. That said Mathews said that he would go back to Lincoln to get new instructions and if he came back to the ranch he would come back with one man. That said Mathews and his posse were then invited by R.M. Brewer to come to the house and get something to eat.
>
> Deponent further says that Robert A. Widenmann told R.M. Brewer and the others at the ranch, that he was going to arrest Frank Baker, Jesse Evans and Tom Hill, said Widenmann having warrants for them. That said Widenmann was told by Brewer and the others at the ranch that the arrest could not be made because if it was made they, all the persons at the ranch would be killed and murdered by J.J. Dolan & Co. and their party. That Jesse Evans advanced upon said Widenmann, said Evans swinging his gun and catching it cocked and pointed directly at said Widenmann. That said Jesse Evans asked said Widenmann whether he Widenmann was hunting for him, Evans, to which Widenmann answered that if he was looking for him, he, Evans would find it out.
>
> Evans also asked Widenmann whether he had a warrant for him. Widenmann answered that that was his (Widenmann's) business. Evans told Widenmann, that if he ever came to arrest him (Evans) he, Evans would pick Widenmann as the first

Chisum's South Spring Ranch, where McSween and others took refuge after Tunstall's murder. Photo Archives, Museum of New Mexico.

From left: Rancher Dick Brewer, ca. 1870; deputy Billy Mathews and family; Robert A. Widenmann. Left and center, Photo Archives, Museum of New Mexico; right, University of Arizona Library, Special Collections.

man to shoot at, to which Widenmann answered that that was all right, that two could play at that game. That during the talking Frank Baker stood near said Widenmann, swinging his pistol on his finger, catching it full cocked at said Widenmann.[2]

About this time Widenmann overheard Baker say to Roberts, "what the hell's the use of talking? pitch in and fight and kill the sons of b——s."[3] Instead they all had breakfast and Mathews set off back to Lincoln with the posse to get further instructions.

The Murder of Tunstall

Brady sent the deputy back again, this time with twenty-four possemen "among whom were the most desperate out-laws of the Territory" according to Angel's report. The Special Agent continued:

> In the mean-time Mr. Tunstall had been informed of the action of the Sheriff, and believing that the real purpose was to murder and not to attach left his ranch, taking with him all the horses and started for Lincoln, the County seat.[4]

According to Widenmann, he and Tunstall, along with Brewer, Middleton, Waite, and Bonney, started for Lincoln about 8 a.m. on the 18th. They rode all day. Angel fleshed out what happened late that afternoon from testimony later:

> Directly after Tunstall had left his ranch, the Deputy Sheriff and said posse arrived there, and finding that Tunstall had left with the horses, deputized W. Morton who selected eighteen men and started out ostensibly to capture the horses. After riding about thirty miles, they came up to Tunstall and his party with the horses, and commenced firing on them. Immediately Tunstall and his party left the horses and attempted to escape—were pursued and Tunstall was killed some hundred yards or more from the horses.
>   Who shot Tunstall will never be known. But there is no doubt that Wm. S. Morton, Jesse Evans and Hill were the only persons present and saw the shooting, and that two of these persons murdered him. For Tunstall was shot in two places—in the head and breast. Of these persons Morton and Hill were afterwards killed, and the only survivor is Jesse Evans a notorious outlaw, murderer and horse-thief. Of these persons Evans and Hill had been arrested at the instigation of Tunstall.
>   They were at enmity with Tunstall, and enmity with them meant murder.
>   There was no object for following after Tunstall, except to murder him, for they had the horses which they desired to attach before they commenced to pursue him and his party. These facts, together with the bitter feeling existing against Tunstall, by certain persons to whom he had become obnoxious, and the deputy allowing these notorious out-laws to accompany him lead me to the conclusion that John H. Tunstall was murdered in cold blood and was not shot in attempting to resist an officer of the law.[5]

The agent completed his report in late November 1878 and it remains as accurate in essentials as anyone can reconstruct. Within a month of the murder, Jessie Evans was the only living witness; though he denied even being there. Tunstall's companions had scattered at the first shots and none of them actually saw what happened; the whole affair was over in a few minutes. Bonney and the others assumed that Tunstall had been killed and made their way to Lincoln that night. Morton, the deputy who led the pursuit, was the foreman of Dolan's cow camp on the Pecos.[6]

Tunstall's body was brought to Lincoln the next day. Justice of the Peace John B. "Green" Wilson impaneled a coroner's jury, which found that Tunstall came to his death "by means of divers bullets shot and sent forth out of and from deadly weapons" and named various of the persons in Morton's posse. The Rev. Taylor Ealy, a Presbyterian medical missionary, arrived at Lincoln the same day with his family and found himself in charge of the funeral arrangements. His wife later recalled:

> I was asked to play two or three hymns. Beside the organ on which I played stood Billy the Kid and his cowboy friends, armed to the teeth. Billy's voice was a sweet tenor, and he sang with all his might.

Tunstall was laid to rest on February 22 in a lot on the east side of his store. Of the thirty funerals the Reverend Ealy conducted during his five months in Lincoln, only one resulted from a death by natural causes.[7]

Lincoln Slides into Anarchy

During this period a parallel judicial and law enforcement system existed in Lincoln whereby arrest warrants could be issued by a justice of the peace and arrests made by the constable for the same precinct. McSween immediately sought to use this system to have Sheriff Brady brought up on larceny charges involving hay taken from the Tunstall store. The sheriff was released on bond. The arresting party, Constable Atencio Martinez, backed by Bonney and Waite, later went to either the Dolan or the Tunstall store with a new warrant for the arrest of eighteen men in the sheriff's posse charged with Tunstall's murder. Brady supposedly refused to allow the constable to serve this warrant and instead arrested all three, later releasing Martinez but keeping the Kid and Waite in custody until the evening of February 21. If this incident did happen, Brady's attitude no doubt heightened the Kid's hostility toward the sheriff.[8]

Efforts such as this to manipulate the legal system through the cross-serving of warrants issued by the district judge and by local justices of the peace continued into the summer. The situation became even more complex since Judge Warren Bristol was both the territorial and the federal judge for the Third Judicial District, and it was he who had issued the federal warrants for the arrests of Baker, Evans, and Hill that so nearly brought about a shootout at the Tunstall ranch scarcely a week before. Tunstall's erstwhile aide Robert Widenmann still held these warrants as a deputy U.S. Marshal and on February 20 he applied for troops at Fort Stanton to arrest the three, said to be at the Dolan store. Under cover of the soldiers, Widenmann and people with him ransacked the store, found no one, and continued on to the Tunstall store. The dozen or so gunmen with Widenmann outnumbered Brady's deputies, whom Constable Martinez promptly arrested on the Wilson warrants. None happened to be the men charged with Tunstall's murder and all were released the next day. Brady never tried to retake the store.[9]

Lincoln's slide into anarchy began before Tunstall was in the ground. By the day of the funeral, bands of armed men were roaming the town and Sheriff Brady told Capt. George Purington at Fort Stanton that a state of lawlessness beyond his control existed in Lincoln. The captain sent a detachment to protect life and property, and wrote for instructions: "I have the honor to report that the usual Lincoln County war has broken out and a terrible state of affairs exists."[10]

John Henry Tunstall's death triggered a wave of plottings and counterplottings that involved almost everyone. For awhile it was paper flying about, rather than bullets, and no one else was shot during February. Widenmann, McSween, an all-around meddlesome Englishman named Montague Leverson, and others sent reports to Secretary of the Interior Carl Schurz and also to President Hayes. These soon stirred things up on the Washington level. Since Tunstall was a British subject, the British minister Sir Edward Thornton

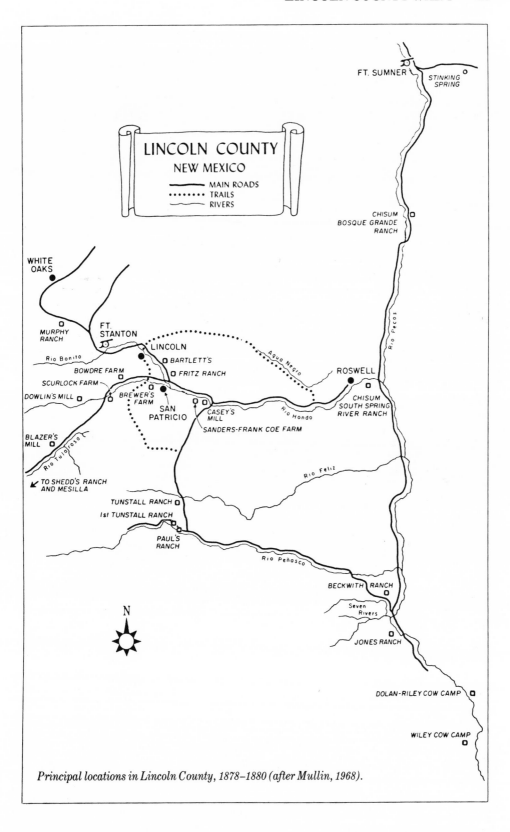

Principal locations in Lincoln County, 1878–1880 (after Mullin, 1968).

received all of the details and used these to make his own inquiries through the U.S. State Department. Tunstall's father was sent the bad news by letters from Widenmann and McSween written the same day, in which these two showed that they were already maneuvering to gain control of his son's assets.[11]

One of the more curious bits of paper was a letter addressed to "Friends Riley and Dolan" and signed Wm. L. Rynerson. In this the district attorney alleged that the McSween outfit was a bunch of scoundrels that should be shaken out of Lincoln. Although supposedly dropped by Riley and well-publicized at the time, the original letter is probably in McSween's own handwriting. It also has an internal reference to John Wilson as alcalde, i.e. justice of the peace, something that Rynerson could hardly have known since this letter from Las Cruces bore the same date, February 14, 1878, as Wilson's appointment made at Lincoln.[12] A fraud was suspected at the time, but the Dolan-Riley faction had come to realize that McSween's rather inept scheming could be defeated by simply keeping quiet and letting the man hang himself. From their standpoint they were right; Mac was not a good general. His gunslingers were another matter.

Two things happened to mark McSween's abdication of leadership. About February 25 he learned that Dolan had gone off to Mesilla to obtain a new warrant for his arrest, whereupon Mac wrote a few more letters and made his will. Perhaps this is when he arranged for a $10,000. insurance policy on his life. Two days later, still accompanied by the faithful deputy from San Miguel County, he headed for the mountains. They stayed at one place or another until March 9.[13] During all this time, Sue McSween was visiting in the East and did not return to New Mexico until late March.

Rise of the Regulators

Captain Purington had seen thirty-five to fifty armed men gathered around McSween's house a day or so after Tunstall's death. Most of them were employed by McSween, some for as much as four dollars a day.[14] They were the beginnings of the "Regulators," the group of men who fought on McSween's side following the murder of John Henry Tunstall. Justice Wilson's warrant for the accused murderers had been returned unserved, so he appointed Dick Brewer as special constable and issued an alias warrant for the men charged. The Regulators needed some exercise and Brewer left Lincoln with ten of them on March 4, after hearing that some of the wanted men were at Dolan's and Riley's cow camp on the Pecos. The posse "jumped" William Morton and Frank Baker, and after a running fight of five or six miles ran them to the ground. Brewer confessed that he was sorry they gave up as he hadn't wished to take them alive.[15]

Morton, the deputy who had led the posse that killed Tunstall, perhaps saw that he was already a dead man. On the way back the party stayed at Chisum's South Spring Ranch the night of March 8. From there Morton wrote a letter to an acquaintance or relative in Virginia. In this he described the events just past and named the posse members. Late the next afternoon as they rode along, Morton supposedly snatched the pistol of a posse member, McClosky, and shot him dead, then tried to escape followed closely by Baker. Both "were speedily overtaken and killed" as the newspaper reported it, with Morton's body supposedly containing nine bullet holes in the back. The possemen then split up and headed towards San Patricio, while Brewer rode on to Lincoln.[16]

Death of Tom Hill and Wounding of Jessie Evans

Two of the men involved in Tunstall's murder were now dead. In an unrelated incident, a sheep drover wounded Jessie Evans and killed Tom Hill, the third member of the trio accused of shooting Tunstall, when the two tried to rob his wagon:[17]

> Evans and Hill went on over to the west side of the mountains. An old German from California was camping over there with a large herd of sheep he was taking over to Texas. It was reported he had a large sum of money at his camp in the mouth of the Alamo Canyon. So Evans and Hill concluded they would pay the old man a visit. They thought it would be an easy job for the old man was not supposed to know anything about handling a gun.
>
> When Evans and Hill got to the camp, the old man simply gave up, and they proceeded to hunt for the money he had with him. Hill investigated the wagon. He leaned his gun against the wagon wheel and then stepped on the brake and on into the bed of the wagon. There he saw a trunk, which he thought might have the old man's money. He stomped on the lid with his boot heel and broke it open. The first thing he seen was a looking glass, and he could not resist picking it up and looking at himself. He called out to Jesse Evans, "Here's a looking glass. I didn't know I was such a fine looking robber, but I'm a daisy."
>
> Then Jesse, he had to have a look, too. "I want to see myself," he said, and went over to the wagon. The Dutchman saw his chance while they were looking at themselves in the glass. He picked up Tom's gun, and killed him with it, literally blowing his spine to pieces. He could have killed Jesse Evans, too, had it not been for the fact that the old man did not know how to reload. When he did finally get a cartridge in place, he took a shot at Jesse, but only managed to wound him in the wrist.[18]

Jessie was forced to surrender at Fort Stanton to get medical aid. He was arrested there and remained in jail until early July.

J.J. Dolan and John Riley had been looking to their own interests, aided by Wm. L. Rynerson and by T.B. Catron. As a result, Governor Samuel B. Axtell visited Lincoln for three hours on March 9, leaving there before McSween returned to town later the same day. While in Lincoln, Axtell issued a proclamation that effectively undid McSween's cause, declaring Wilson's appointment as a justice of the peace illegal and naming Judge Bristol as the only proper source of legal processes, with Sheriff Brady and his deputies as the enforcement officials. These actions ignited a new storm of controversy, but in the meantime McSween had to flee Lincoln a second time because of possible repercussions over the three shootings by Brewer's posse.[19] Two weeks later the army clarified its instructions to Captain Purington with respect to the conflicts between civil authorities in Lincoln County. The captain would render assistance to the sheriff when required.[20]

Calm Before the Storm

The latter half of March saw Mac lying low at Chisum's South Spring Ranch and conditions at Lincoln unusually tranquil. On March 29 Captain Purington wrote that affairs were now running smoothly and he anticipated no further trouble in civil matters. Sheriff Brady was preparing for the upcoming term of court.[21]

On another front things were very active. The two great American letter-writers, Robert Widenmann and Montague Leverson, began firing off their earnest, if unsolicited, demands for justice to the Tunstall family and their friends, as well as to Sir Edward Thornton, President Hayes, and the newspapers. This last provoked the Santa Fe *New Mexican*, a staunch defender of Catron-Dolan-Riley interests. In a kinder moment the newspaper had called Leverson "a crazy Englishman" even as they published his letter. Investigator Frank Angel assessed Leverson simply as knowing "6 times more than he can prove and 6 times more than anyone else."[22]

With respect to Widenmann the *New Mexican* worked itself into a real dither:

Widerman [*sic*] is believed by all who know him to be liar, a coward, and a hypocrite. When Tunstall was killed, he ran and bellowed like a calf, and never stopped running until he got into Fort Stanton and told Colonel Purington that he was afraid that Tunstall was killed, for he heard some shots fired, saw Tunstall ride down into a ravine and did not see him come back; he did not know whether there was one or five men pursuing him, or eighteen as he says in his lying letter. Oh! Falstaff's guts! nor did he turn in his saddle to look.[23]

And on and on. To all of this the *News and Press* from Cimarron, New Mexico, replied in full measure, with somewhat more restrained language.[24] The issue was that the April term of the district court for Lincoln County was coming up. It promised to be a showdown.

THE LINCOLN COUNTY
WAR II

April–July 1878

A few days before the end of March 1878, while some of the boys were loosening up with a little target practice in Lincoln, Sheriff Brady showed up at Chisum's South Spring Ranch with a troop of cavalry in tow. He came to summon jurymen and by a clerical mistake the writ had been made returnable for the first Monday in April (April 1) rather than the legally prescribed second Monday. McSween was at Chisum's then and so was his just returned wife. Brady attempted no arrests and a considerable amount of discussion was held on issues such as guarantees for McSween's life. In the end the cavalry lieutenant accompanying Brady convinced Sue McSween to persuade her husband to return and stay at Fort Stanton until the court met.[1]

Another meeting at Chisum's about that time involved McSween and a dozen or more men, including members of the Regulators. According to Francisco Trujillo, who was present and recalled what happened in an interview fifty-nine years later, McSween offered a reward for Brady's assassination. Or perhaps this was a conclusion that the men drew themselves. In any event a mixed party of Hispanics and Anglos, the latter including Jim French, John Middleton, and Billy the Kid, set off towards Lincoln. At Agua Negra Spring they split up and only the Anglos continued on to Lincoln, evidently reluctant to see the Hispanic men involved because of Brady's wife being a native New Mexican.[2]

The Murder of Sheriff Brady

Sometime during the night of March 31 Billy the Kid, French, Middleton, Fred Waite, Henry Brown, and Frank McNab slipped into Lincoln and hid themselves behind the adobe wall of a corral that extended east from the rear of the Tunstall store. About 9 a.m. the next morning Sheriff Brady and deputies Mathews, George Hindman, George Peppin, and Jack Long started down the street from the Dolan store to the building used as the courthouse, the one now known as the "convento," to give notice that the court would actually convene on the second Monday of April. As they passed the corral, the men concealed there let loose a volley of rifle fire. Brady fell in his tracks, his body riddled with bullets. Hindman was hit by one shot and mortally wounded; he staggered back a few steps and moaned for water, dying as someone helped him towards a nearby saloon. Ex-justice Wilson happened to be hoeing onions at the time and caught a stray bullet across the back of his thighs.

The deputies scattered and ran for cover. Billy the Kid dashed out from the corral to seize Brady's rifle; Mathews snapped a shot as the Kid stooped over and hit him in the thigh. The wound was not serious and Billy ran back to the corral; later his buddies made their way out of town, while he turned up at Dr. Ealy's back door to have his wound dressed. The Murphy-Dolan people soon came looking for a wounded man, but by then Sam Corbet (formerly Tunstall's clerk) had sawed a hole through the floor under a bed and concealed the Kid there with a revolver in either hand.[3] Later he made his escape.

Left: Fred Waite, an associate of the Kid and the McSween-Tunstall faction. Courtesy Special Collections, University of Arizona Library.

Above: Lt. Col. N.A.M. Dudley, Fort Stanton's commander during the Lincoln County War. Photo Archives, Museum of New Mexico. (pho-

It turned out that Robert Widenmann had also been in the corral at the time Brady was shot, but he insisted that he had gone there only to feed his dog. Asked why he had a rifle and two pistols, he replied that the dog was vicious and he was afraid it might bite him.[4] When the newspapers learned of this they began to allude to Widenmann as "the dog-feeder." According to John P. Meadows, an otherwise anonymous figure in Lincoln who first met the Kid about two years later and left an interesting manuscript detailing his observations,

> Billy the Kid and several others of his party waylaid Major Brady, the sheriff, in Lincoln and killed him and his deputy Hindman. Kid told me all about that affair. He said, "There was three or four of us shooting at Brady, and I don't know which of us killed him. But I am the one who seems to be blamed for it. Just why I should be picked out I don't know."[5]

The shooting of Brady was a turning point in the Lincoln County War and a major blunder on the part of the Regulators. They damaged their cause irreparably by ambushing the lawmen as they were peaceably going about their business.

That same day, perhaps around noon, the McSweens rode into Lincoln with John Chisum and Leverson. The town was in an uproar and Leverson promptly responded with pen to paper, firing off a new round of letters, with McSween scarcely lagging. Captain Purington rode in at the head of twenty-five cavalrymen that afternoon. He recognized George Peppin as the acting sheriff and stood by while Peppin's men made arrests and searched houses without warrants. McSween protested and the excitable Leverson got into a sharp verbal exchange with Purington, which concluded with the exasperated officer calling Leverson an ass and telling him to shut up. Peppin arrested McSween, also his brother-in-law David Shield, Widenmann, and McSween's two servants. At their own insistence the McSween group was taken off to Fort Stanton for safe-keeping until the district court should meet.[6]

It was quiet in Lincoln for a couple of days, but as Dr. Taylor Ealy noted on April 4, "It was quiet all day, very quiet, but like an earthquake, quiet then war! war! war!"[7] That same day Lt. Col. N.A.M. Dudley, Ninth Cavalry, arrived at Fort Stanton and as of noon on April 5 he relieved Captain Purington in command. For the next year, Dudley would have a prominent and controversial role in the Lincoln County violence. He released McSween and the others from confinement, but allowed them to make application for military protection and to remain on the post.[8]

The Battle at Blazer's Mill

Thirty-five miles from Lincoln at Blazer's Mill, on the upper Rio Tularosa, one of the classic gun battles of the old West was fought out on April 4 when Dick Brewer and fourteen men, some of them Regulators, came by and stopped at the mill for dinner. While they were eating, "Buckshot" Roberts rode up. He was a member of the Mathews' posse that had gone to Tunstall's ranch on February 18. An attempt to seize Roberts ended with Charlie Bowdre shooting him through the body. Roberts fired at the same time and cut off Bowdre's gunbelt, the bullet also mangling George Coe's trigger finger. Roberts then forted up in the mill and sent another shot through John Middleton's chest before he blew off the top of Brewer's head at long range. With their leader gone, the rest of the Regulators withdrew. Roberts' own wound was mortal and he died a little before noon the next day.[9]

McSween's Vindication

The district court began its deliberations at Lincoln on April 8 with the military affording protection. It remained in session until the 24th, with Judge Bristol and the jurors hearing both territorial and federal cases. Since there was no officer authorized to serve warrants, the judge appointed John Copeland to do so. The county commissioners quickly confirmed him as sheriff. Copeland inclined towards the McSween side and thereby angered Dolan's followers. Seven weeks later Governor Axtell replaced Copeland with George Peppin.[10]

As the court met, Judge Bristol lectured the grand jury on McSween's business activities, especially covering the accusations stemming from the Fritz insurance policy and the attempted attachment writ.[11] The jurors ignored the judge's anti-McSween bias and refused to indict the lawyer for embezzlement or anything else. Mac took this as a vindication.

There were plenty of murder charges, on the other hand, and the grand jury handed down indictments against Jessie Evans and three others as principals in Tunstall's death, with Dolan and Mathews as accessories. True bills were found against the Kid, Henry Brown, and John Middleton for the Brady and Hindman slayings. Buckshot Roberts' death was made a federal case and the three last named along with George Coe, Fred Waite, "Doc" Scurlock, and several others were charged with aiding Charlie Bowdre, who was named as the killer. Most of these people had skipped, but Sheriff Copeland was able to bring Billy the Kid in on the Brady and Hindman indictments. He pleaded not guilty and was long gone by the time a warrant for his arrest was issued on April 22. For the rest of his short life William Bonney was dodging the law.[12]

Although McSween still faced the civil suit over the insurance money, he considered his victory complete and acted accordingly. A citizens' meeting held the same night the court adjourned thanked Lieutenant Colonel Dudley, condemned Governor Axtell, and generally expressed optimism for the county's future. At the same time a petition in circulation asked Messrs. Murphy, Dolan, and Riley to leave the county and charged them with being the cause of all the troubles during the past six years. In a buoyant letter to the *News and Press* at Cimarron, New Mexico, Mac replied to a variety of accusations printed in the Santa Fe *New Mexican* and lodged a few new ones of his own. He wrote to Wm. Rynerson, who had fared badly as district attorney at the recent term of court, and demanded that warrants for the arrest of parties indicted for the Tunstall murder be issued. Rynerson sent back a sarcastic note telling McSween to mind his own business. In fact, warrants apparently were never written. Mac himself lacked any sense of grace or diplomacy and seemed bent upon running his enemies into the ground. They, in turn, remained implacably hostile. The newspaper wars began again, and there was no humor in such expressions as "McSween's band of assassins."[13]

The Gangs Roam the Countryside

During the next two months gangs of armed bravos roamed the countryside looking for a scrap, while Sheriff Copeland dithered until he was pushed into action by a posse of soldiers. Leadership was weak and confused, so that little of what the bands did appeared to have any purpose. Jessie Evans languished in jail. Lawrence G. Murphy, "so besotted with liquor he was almost a negative quantity," moved to Santa Fe early in May and died there in October. J.J. Dolan also vacated the field during May, leaving John H. Riley to watch over whatever livestock and property the House retained and to work with the Seven Rivers men who enlisted on the Dolan side. McSween remained in residence at Lincoln until about the middle of June. Frank McNab, with a commission as deputy constable, assumed leadership of the Regulators until twenty or more of the Pecos men, led by a couple of ex-Brady deputies, riddled him with bullets on April 29.[14] Doc Scurlock then succeeded McNab with the Regulators.

Monitoring all of this from Fort Stanton, and as often as not adding to the problems, was Lieutenant Colonel Dudley. Fresh from a bruising court martial at Fort Union, thin-skinned and contentious, vindictive and possessing both a weak intellect and bad judgment, he was not the man for the job of post commander. (The fourteen charges brought against him at Fort Union included two counts each of disobedience to the lawful commands of a superior and conduct unbecoming an officer and a gentleman, six counts of conduct to the prejudice of good order and military discipline, and two counts of drunkenness on duty.)[15] One non-admirer called him "a whiskey barrel in the morning and a barrel of whiskey at night."[16] Even the departmental commander admitted, after he finally removed Dudley from command at Fort Stanton,

> I am under the impression if Dudley had not been so constantly under the influence of liquor while at Stanton when he first went there he might have managed matters very well. Attribute the most of his trouble to drink.[17]

In eleven months at Fort Stanton, Dudley also showed that as a military bureaucrat he had few peers. He sent frequent reports, made sure that every action was covered, and saved every piece of paper.

J.J. Dolan & Co. announced a suspension of business on April 17 and dissolution of the partnership as of May 1, 1878. At that time the partners were subcontractors for the delivery of both flour and beef at the Mescalero Agency, while Riley held the contracts for fresh beef and beef cattle at Fort Bayard, Fort Bliss, and Fort Stanton. By May, Dolan and Riley were defaulting on deliveries for the Indians, which forced Agent Godfroy to make purchases in the open market. The 1,500 head of cattle, yearlings, and two-year-olds mortgaged to T.B. Catron in January were Catron's now, leaving Riley with a problem of finding cattle to meet his contracts. The military required beef steers or dry cows, so the Catron herd probably wouldn't have been of much help. Since the army paid more than twice as much for beef as did the Rosenthal contract with the Indian Bureau, Riley no doubt followed his own interests and tried to meet the army's demands while he neglected or ignored the Mescalero Agency. Riley's high visibility during May and June came about because he was trying to buy livestock as well as to round up the Catron cattle, rather than from any desire to involve himself in the war.[18]

The Regulators may or may not have understood these things when Scurlock led eighteen or twenty of them in a raid on Dolan's and Riley's cow camp in mid-May. Scurlock was a deputy sheriff under Copeland, and the raid had a legal guise in either the recovery of stolen horses or the arrest of parties implicated in the McNab killing some two weeks earlier. It also led to Catron's cattle being mixed with the vast Chisum herd. If the raid was intended as harassment then it backfired badly since Catron now had a perfect reason to complain to the governor about what "seems to be an utter disregard of the law in the county, as well as of life and private rights."[19] He did so and Governor Axtell acted immediately, replacing John Copeland as sheriff of Lincoln County with a confirmed Dolan follower, George W. Peppin.

Investigators from Washington

In the meantime all of the letters to the British ambassador about the death of one of Her Majesty's subjects in Lincoln County had borne fruit. The same correspondents—McSween, Widenmann, Leverson—had written to the secretary of the interior, a senator from Rhode Island, President Hayes, and to others as well, but it was the international complications that prompted the secretary of state to request the acting attorney general to make a thorough inquiry. Within a month a young attorney named Frank Warner Angel arrived in Santa Fe as special agent for the Department of Justice. He came on to Lincoln May 14 and remained in the county for almost two months, taking affidavits and witnessing for himself the chaotic conditions there.[20]

Angel was charged with investigating the cause and circumstances of Tunstall's death, but also the lawlessness in Lincoln and Colfax counties, allegations of misconduct by U.S. officials, and irregularities at the Mescalero Apache Agency. He had been an attorney for nine years and gained valuable experience through other inquiries done for the government. When his report, with over 300 pages of testimony, landed on official Washington, it proved devastating to members of the Santa Fe Ring, as will be seen later. The agent's timing was fortunate in that he took a lengthy deposition from McSween before Mac was killed, and sworn statements from others who either died or fled the country before Angel finished his field investigations.[21]

One month after Angel's arrival another federal investigator showed up. E.C. Watkins, U.S. Indian Inspector, had been sent to inspect the Mescalero Agency and the charges made against Agent Frederick Godfroy by McSween and Widenmann. Watkins' probe took two weeks and was just as thorough as Angel's; indeed, the two investigators talked with some of the same people and exchanged copies of affidavits. Both seem to have allowed witnesses to talk about what was on their minds although the questioning had some direction.[22]

Curiously the two agents came away with quite different impressions. Angel firmly believed that McSween and Tunstall acted conscientiously, while Murphy & Co. plundered the country for private gain and revenge. Watkins, on the other hand, scarcely bothered to disguise his contempt for McSween, whose allegations had turned out to be hearsay. Enough irregularities did exist to warrant a change of Indian agents, which happened the following spring. At the time, Watkins' report had considerably less impact than Angel's; today the two sets of testimony form one of the most valuable sources on the Lincoln County War.

Lieutenant Colonel Dudley, under orders to send a weekly report on affairs in Lincoln County to the district headquarters, began with a very long account on May 4. In many of his later communications there was nothing to report, but for the first month or two it was the calm before the storm broke again. Others began compiling statistics, too. Colonel Edward Hatch wrote on June 1, 1878, that twenty-five men had already been killed, that all business in Lincoln County had stopped, and it was impossible to supply the Indians with beef or flour. Later that month Inspector Watkins reiterated that the assassin's hand had already claimed at least a score of men.[23] Who all of these people were isn't clear, but through mid-June Dudley's reports indicated that the lid remained on the caldron at Lincoln.

McSween Flees Lincoln—Again

Perhaps just barely so. When the Indian inspector and his escort came in sight of Lincoln about June 14 or 15, McSween and his party assumed that they were Sheriff Peppin's posse and took to the mountains.[24] Considering that Mac had no warrants outstanding for his arrest, he was certainly jumpy. Mrs. McSween sent a note and her husband returned to make a deposition and bring in a few witnesses. Many men were gone right at the time, since they had been summoned to appear before the district court in Mesilla, where the sessions began on June 17. Among those absent was Robert Widenmann, who never returned to Lincoln.

On the night of June 18 Sheriff Peppin rode into Lincoln with a posse of twenty citizens, escorted by twenty-seven soldiers and two officers. This formidable group caused a general exodus out of the town—not just of the McSween crowd, who moved over to San Patricio, but of others who simply wanted to avoid being shot by either side whenever the violence broke out again. Peppin also carried a deputy U.S. Marshal's commission and federal warrants for most of the Regulators, issued in connection with the shooting of "Buckshot" Roberts.[25] Dr. Ealy had a laconic diary entry that day:

> June 18. Peppin in town—came in the night; soldiers with him. All the men left town.[26]

For the first week or so following Peppin's arrival the principal excitement was probably the rooster pull on San Juan's Day, June 24. The *News and Press*, however, referred to "the murderous band of horse thieves and cutthroats whom Axtell's bush-whacking sheriff had imported," and they did have a point in that John Kinney and his band of outlaws had joined Peppin, hoping to take part in the expected fray and share in the spoils. The army refused to have anything to do with Kinney's outfit, whose reputation for murder, mayhem, robbery, and rustling had been building for a couple of years, mostly in Doña Ana County and the El Paso area. When Frank Warner Angel later asked Governor Axtell to explain the association between Peppin and Kinney, the governor waffled.[27]

Peppin bestirred himself enough to send out Deputy John Long with six men to find and arrest the McSween party. About dawn on June 27, Long's posse, which included Kinney, found McSween and ten or so of the Regulators near San Patricio. They started a running fight and quickly lost two of their own horses but ran the McSween crowd up a mountain. Long sent a courier to Peppin and Peppin asked Fort Stanton for troops; Dudley dispatched two officers and thirty-five men. As these came into view, the McSween contingent withdrew towards the Pecos. The troopers started to follow but were suddenly recalled to the fort by an order from the post commander. Dudley himself had just received new orders from the War Department that virtually prohibited the use of troops to aid a civil officer in making arrests or in enforcing the laws.[28] These new orders would have a profound impact in Lincoln County.

The army had long looked upon Lincoln County as a place where lawlessness and murder ran riot. After the Tunstall shooting in February, Governor Axtell had asked for and been granted the use of troops to support civil territorial authorities. This was soon clarified to mean supporting the sheriff in maintaining order and enforcing legal process. A section of the army appropriation act approved June 18, 1878, made it unlawful to employ the army as a *posse comitatus*, or otherwise, for executing the laws except in such cases and under circumstances where authorized by the Constitution or by an act of Congress. This effectively prohibited the military from aiding civil authorities.[29]

The Fort Stanton garrison perhaps saw the new orders as a mixed blessing. Dudley received them on June 28 and immediately wrote out an order of his own recalling the cavalry unit that had trailed McSween's band as far as Coe's ranch on the upper Rio Hondo while aiding the deputy sheriff's posse. From McSween's viewpoint the order may have seemed like a positive development since it probably saved his people from capture and meant that Peppin could no longer call upon the army for a posse. To Peppin it meant that he was on his own resources. Perhaps more importantly, it denied the army any moderating influence in Lincoln County. In another month or so, desperadoes worse than any yet seen began to appreciate the opportunities that a strife-torn country offered and flocked to it.

The Gangs Skirmish

There were several incidents early in July. When Deputy Sheriff José Chaves y Baca entered San Patricio the morning of July 3, apparently with a small posse, McSween and ten or so of the Regulators were there and fired on them. Chaves called for reinforcements and Peppin sent a dozen men, evidently with Dolan and Kinney. McSween's gang pulled out and a running gun battle developed as the Regulators rode off towards the Pecos, pausing for about an hour to fort up on a high ridge. One posse member caught a bullet in the arm. They did capture one of McSween's horses, by the name of Pet.

When a posseman rode Pet back to Lincoln the next day, Sue McSween incorrectly assumed that Mac had been killed. She flew into a rage and headed for the House and Dolan with blood in her eye and shotgun in hand. Sheriff Peppin and about forty men were waiting and tried to calm her down, evidently with little success. Dolan was in a back room listening to all of this and finally he stepped out to brave her wrath. The correspondent who sent this story in to the newspaper ended it by saying "Guess what happened then" and promised to tell the rest of the story "next time I see you."[30]

The day of the San Patricio fight the sheriff's posse was very rough on people and property both there and in the nearby Ruidoso and Bonito valleys. Under Deputy Chaves y Baca and Dolan's direction they tore an upper story room off of Elisha Dow's house, broke into and searched a number of other houses without warrants, and roundly insulted the citizens. An investigation by the army confirmed these claims even as the women of San Patricio pleaded with Dudley for protection. This put Dudley into a quandary since the civil authorities, which he couldn't aid anyway, had been acting the part of bandits. In the end he asked the district headquarters in Santa Fe to request the governor to take action. He also foresaw that no matter which side won, the hired desperadoes would compensate themselves with whatever property was available.[31]

While Sue McSween waved her shotgun at the Peppin and Dolan crew, Mac and his boys rode back to Chisum's ranch. Another deputy sheriff and a dozen possemen laid siege to the ranch house on July 4; McSween and his Regulators stood them off all day and through the night. The posse then raised the siege and, with a dozen or fifteen reinforcements, followed the lawyer and his band as they struck off towards Lincoln. When McSween's forces came back through San Patricio about July 10 they evidently numbered forty men. For the next four or five days they kept to the mountains, adding to their strength, while Sheriff Peppin stayed in Lincoln recruiting more gunmen for his side.[32]

Then the fugitives stopped running. Just after dark on Sunday, July 14, McSween led his private army into Lincoln, convinced that he had to stand his ground and fight.[33]

⌒ 10 ⌒

THE LINCOLN COUNTY WAR III

July–September 1878

The Five-Days Battle, July 15–19, 1878

For five days, July 15–19, 1878, a pitched battle raged between the two sides in the town of Lincoln. McSween's partisans numbered about forty-five men, although some estimates claimed more than sixty. Their return to Lincoln caught the sheriff by surprise; he had only a dozen men with him initially. Within a day Peppin called his posse back from San Patricio while the addition of John Kinney's outlaws, Jessie Evans, and the Seven Rivers men raised the total on that side to thirty or forty.[1] During the fighting Lieutenant Colonel Dudley said that the town was in a perfect state of war, with about one hundred men equally divided holding the several prominent buildings.[2] Most of the residents had fled, and those who lingered stayed indoors.

In Lincoln the buildings lay along either side of a single main street. Peppin's headquarters was the Wortley Hotel across from the Murphy-Dolan store near the west end of town. He also had a half-dozen men in the old torreon. McSween's house and the Tunstall store were roughly in the center of the village. The post surgeon from Fort Stanton found McSween and his wife alone in their house on July 15, but fifteen men subsequently defended the place. Most of the McSween supporters occupied the Montaño store and Juan Patron's house and store some 300 yards east of the Tunstall-McSween property. Another dozen or so warriors garrisoned the Isaac Ellis place at the eastern edge of town. Finally, three men were barricaded in the warehouse behind the Tunstall store.[3] Dr. Taylor Ealy's family lived in part of this store.

Although McSween enjoyed an advantage of strength, he dispersed his forces to positions where they could not support one another and scarcely even communicate. By taking a defensive stance rather than attacking the sheriff's party, McSween lost the initiative. Other incidents during the Five-Days Battle showed that the defense was not properly organized.[4] Whether he actually had any strategy seems doubtful; at the most he could have scattered Peppin's posse temporarily and perhaps killed a few people. By simply occupying several buildings and letting Peppin decide the course of events, Mac threw away his initial advantages. His return to Lincoln turned into another bumble; one that this time would cost him his life.

The torreon, with its small garrison of Peppin-Dolan supporters, stood midway between the McSween house and the Montaño store. Both the torreon and the house next to it, occupied by Captain Saturnino Baca, stood on property owned by McSween. Baca himself was a Dolan man. On July 15 McSween ordered Baca to vacate the premises, which sent him into something of a panic. Baca appealed to Dudley; Dudley sent the assistant surgeon from Fort Stanton to investigate and this in turn led to an effort, ultimately unsuccessful, to have soldiers replace the possemen in the torreon. The post doctor returned to the fort about dusk and met the returning sheriff's posse on his way out of town. Ealy recalled later

95

The Wortley Hotel, on the west side of town, where Peppin's posse headquartered. Photo Archives, Museum of New Mexico.

Juan Patron's house and store, on the east side of town, where McSween supporters took cover. Courtesy Special Collections, University of Arizona Library.

that they rode in at full gallop, hallooing, and began shooting up McSween's house before getting off of their horses.[5]

Sheriff Peppin held a number of arrest warrants, including two each on Billy the Kid, Doc Scurlock, and Charlie Bowdre for murder, and one for McSween on a charge of assault with intent to kill. He sent a deputy to Mac's house to make the gesture of attempting to serve these, but that worthy was greeted with gunfire and beat a hasty retreat. Perhaps the hundred or so shots Ealy heard that evening were fired when a party of McSween men left the Montaño store to go over to McSween's house. The only casualties that first day were a horse and a mule.[6]

The next day shooting went on intermittently into the night. McSween's sharpshooters, particularly those on the roof of the Montaño store, had made themselves troublesome to Peppin's men. As a countermove Peppin sent several of his best shots to the hillsides south of town to drive the McSween men from the roof. This they finally did without a loss on either side.[7]

That same day Peppin, who was also a deputy U.S. Marshal, sent a note to Dudley asking to borrow one of his howitzers to intimidate the persons for whom he held U.S. warrants into surrendering. Dudley regretted that he could not comply with the request, but he threw off any pretense to neutrality in his answer to Peppin:

> Were I not so circumscribed by laws and orders, I would most gladly give you every man and material at my post to sustain you in your present position, believing it to be strictly legal.[8]

Dudley's courier, a black soldier named Berry Robinson, rode back to Lincoln late that afternoon. As he approached the Wortley Hotel, men shot at him from the roof of the McSween house, startling his horse but missing the trooper. Peppin capitalized on the incident in a second note to Dudley that claimed the sheriff's men had tried their best to cover the courier, who would explain the circumstances. In effect this was a veiled invitation for the army to intervene. The next day Dudley did send a board of officers to investigate the shooting.[9]

That evening, as firing continued, Ealy made arrangements for McSween's two black servants to dig a grave alongside Tunstall's and bury a man named Daniel Huff, who had died of poisoning before daylight that same day. About the time they were lowering the body into the grave, the riflemen in the torreon opened fire and so scared the men that they dropped the body and ran for their lives.[10] Apart from Huff, the second day ended without casualties.

The third day was fairly quiet until after dark. The Ealys barricaded the windows in the Tunstall store with their trunks and rolled out their beds on the floor. The Ealy children kept their dolls on the floor under the windows so that they wouldn't be shot. That morning, as some of the Peppin men were making their way across the hills just south of town, a marksman in the Montaño store dropped Charlie Crawford, alias "Lallacooler," with a severe wound that left him unable to crawl away. When the board of officers from Fort Stanton came around to investigate the shooting of the day before, they rescued Crawford but were also shot at by McSween's men. This shooting at U.S. soldiers only intensified the army's hostility towards Mac's side.[11] Crawford died at Fort Stanton a week later.

That night Ben Ellis, the son of Isaac Ellis, was shot in the neck while in his corral feeding his mules. A couple of the McSween men, who had forted up at Ellis' place, ran a gauntlet of gunfire to summon aid from Dr. Ealy. Ealy tried to return with them but he had to visit the wounded man the next morning instead.[12]

Dudley wrote to military headquarters in Santa Fe about the state of affairs in Lincoln

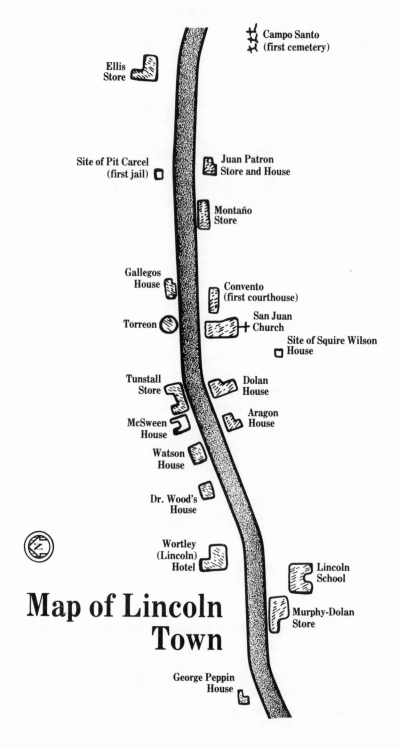

Campo Santo
(first cemetery)

Ellis
Store

Site of Pit Carcel
(first jail)

Juan Patron
Store and House

Montaño
Store

Gallegos
House

Convento
(first courthouse)

Torreon

San Juan
Church

Site of Squire Wilson
House

Tunstall
Store

Dolan
House

McSween
House

Aragon
House

Watson
House

Dr. Wood's
House

Wortley
(Lincoln)
Hotel

Lincoln
School

Murphy-Dolan
Store

Map of Lincoln
Town

George Peppin
House

Map of Lincoln showing prominent locations of Lincoln County War. Courtesy New Mexico State Monuments.

as of noon on July 18, his report mixing description, opinion, rumors, and predictions. He virtually demanded action either by the governor or through orders from the district commander. Chisum was supposed to be on his way to McSween with a six-pounder and thirty-five men. Both parties were reported as being determined to fight to the last round. Dudley's troops had been fired upon. People up and down the Rio Bonito as well as the citizens in Lincoln had holed up, the shooting being almost continual during the day.[13] To all of this he received no reply.

Several of Peppin's possemen had been wounded and received treatment at the post hospital. At McSween's house, a Regulator named Thomas Cullins was killed and buried in the cellar, while another fighter had a serious wound. The fight itself was a stalemate; the McSween forces held all of their positions and Peppin's men were reportedly becoming discouraged. Dudley claimed that he had received numerous appeals to protect the lives of women and children, although the only one on record appears to be a letter that Saturnino Baca sent on the evening of the 18th, saying that McSween had told him to vacate his house or he would be burned out. Whether there was just one appeal or many, Dudley conferred with his officers that evening and they decided to march for Lincoln the next morning to preserve the lives of women and children and any non-combatants.[14] Sometime that night a messenger warned McSween that "they" were coming to kill him.[15] This could scarcely have lightened his load.

The morning of the fifth day found the mood among the Regulators still upbeat, as an oft-reprinted letter by one Joseph Smith showed.[16] Smith himself was one of the defenders at the McSween house. Within a few hours the situation changed drastically. About 11 a.m. Dudley arrived in Lincoln at the head of a column that included four other officers, thirty-five soldiers, a twelve-pound mountain howitzer, and a Gatling gun. Long-range shooting between the McSween house and the Wortley hotel stopped momentarily and Dudley announced to Peppin that he had come to town simply to protect women and children, not to assist the sheriff's posse. He intended to camp near the town and if attacked would demand that the parties who did the firing be turned over to him. Otherwise he would ask women and children to leave and would then open fire with his howitzer. The column marched on and went into camp about three hundred yards beyond McSween's house, opposite Montaño's store.[17] Even as they did so, some of Peppin's men moved into buildings much closer to the McSween house.

Dudley repeated his ultimatum to the people in the Montaño store and trained his howitzer on its door; in short order the nine defenders left there, their heads covered by blankets, and hastened down the street to the Ellis place. Shortly afterwards the whole group at Ellis', numbering at least thirty men, left and headed up a canyon into the hills. The sheriff and five possemen started after the fleeing party and there was a brief exchange of gunfire, but no one was hurt.[18]

About this time McSween sent a note that Dudley sanctimoniously called "probably the last letter he ever wrote," asking why soldiers surrounded his house. Dudley replied that no soldiers surrounded his house and he desired to hold no communication with McSween.[19] The claim about the soldiers is debatable and, from the viewpoint of people inside the house, may have had merit. At the Court of Inquiry held later to look into allegations of misconduct by Dudley, William Bonney testified as to where he was and what he saw on July 19:

> I was in Mr. McSween's house in Lincoln, and I seen the Soldiers come down from the Fort with the Sheriff's party, that is the Sheriff's posse joined them a short distance above there, McSween's house. Soldiers passed on by the men dropped right off, and surrounded the house. The Sheriff party. Shortly after three soldiers came back with Peppin, passed the house twice afterward. Three soldiers came down and

"Billy the Kid Escaping the Burning McSween House," a mural by Peter Rogers, 1984 (132" x 114").
Courtesy Lincoln County Heritage Trust, Lincoln, N.M.

stood in front of the house in front of the windows. Mr. McSween wrote a note to the officer in charge. . . . I read the note myself.[20]

Sue McSween said much the same in her testimony at the Court of Inquiry, except that she had not read the note. Under cross-examination the Kid added that Peppin, with an escort of three soldiers, passed the McSween house twice that day. Dudley denied that a mounted patrol sent out by him had been within 200 yards of the place.[21] The testimony as to what happened that day was marked by many such disagreements, denials, significant omissions, and efforts to cover exposed official backsides.

After Dudley had replied to Mac's note, Sue McSween came down and confronted the officer in what must have been an acrimonious exchange. She was trying to save her husband's life and stop the sheriff's men from burning her house, while Dudley maintained that he could not interfere with civil authorities. Dudley reported that she was in a very excited condition; reconstructions of their conversation suggest that she may have baited him considerably. It ended with Sue more bitter than ever and Dudley's mind even more firmly set against McSween. Any claim at neutrality had been swept away when Dudley threatened the local justice, a McSween supporter, with double irons if he didn't issue new warrants for the arrest of McSween and others. Intimidated, the man complied.[22]

Gunfire between the posse members and the defenders inside the McSween house increased to such an extent that Dudley had his men take shelter beside an unfinished adobe building. About 2 p.m. a couple of the possemen succeeded in getting a fire started in a pile of shavings against the back door of the kitchen at the northwest end of the house. During the afternoon the fire burned down the west side, across the front and back up the east wing, the defenders abandoning one room after another while continuing to blaze away at the posse. About 5:30 p.m. the Ealys asked Dudley for protection. He sent a wagon and escort to evacuate them from the Tunstall store. At the same time Sue McSween with her sister Mrs. Shield and the latter's five children left the McSween house and were sheltered in the Patron home.[23]

McSween's home was a torch by now, with all of the men crowded into the last remaining room, the northeast kitchen. No one chose to surrender, recognizing that this was suicide. The seriously wounded man could not be moved and he preferred to die in the burning building. The others held out until dusk when they had some hope of making a break for it. Billy the Kid evidently proposed the desperate escape strategy; he would lead a small group in a dash through a gate on the east side of the yard, drawing the attention of the attackers, whereupon McSween and the others would make their getaway through another gate just north of the house.

The second group delayed too long and were trapped at the back side of the yard. Someone called out "We want to surrender." When four of the possemen came forward a shot rang out, killing Deputy Robert Beckwith. Firing broke out again and McSween fell riddled with five bullets, while two of those with him—Francisco Zamora and Vicente Romero—died at the same time. Yginio Salazar lay on the ground badly wounded, but he managed to crawl away during the night to a house where his sister-in-law was staying. Harvey Morris, a young man who had come to Lincoln to read law with McSween, was shot down and killed just as the first group reached the east gate.[24] Dudley estimated that over 2,000 shots were fired that evening.

Several days later, in the relative calm of Fort Stanton, Dudley sought to evaluate what he had witnessed. He seemed almost stunned:

Men who have the reckless courage to attack a building in bright mid-day, its walls forming a perfect protection against any modern musketry to its inmates, pierced as this castle of McSween's was with scores of loop holes for rifles on every side and angle, to say nothing of the flat roof, protected by a perfect wall of defence, and for hours hugging the walls, exposed to the fire of not only from the loop holes, but from the roof and adjacent buildings held by McSween's men, charging this position across a space perfectly exposed to the fire of McSween's men for a distance of nearly three hundred yards, are not of a character to be easily induced to abandon a course they believe is only half completed. A similar remark can be made of the party holding this structure, who held the same fortification for five days, the last nine hours gradually retreating from one room to another, as the heat compelled them to do what no amount of leaden missles from the rifles of the attacking party could do, and for an hour finally, all huddled in one room, nearly surrounded by the flames, some as it is claimed, preferred to being burnt, rather than surrender to the Sheriff's posse.

More desperate action than was exhibited on this unfortunate day by both sides is rarely witnessed.

He also anticipated correctly that worse was to come.

If troops of some character, are not sent to patrol the country between Lincoln and the Pecos, I fear that we shall hear of some wholesale thieving, cattle stealing, and inhuman murders, and ill treatment of women and children.[25]

McSween and Harvey Morris were placed in boxes and laid to rest near Tunstall, without ceremony. Posse members broke into the Tunstall store and looted the place, followed the next day by a mob of local Hispanics. T.B. Catron's local business agents helped Sam Corbet, nominally in charge of the store, to nail up the doors and windows and save what remained. The Ealy and Shield families went off to Fort Stanton and then on to Las Vegas, New Mexico. Sue McSween, made of stouter stuff than almost anyone, stayed in Lincoln to salvage what she could of her husband's property. This proved to be little enough. Dudley left town about 4 p.m. in the afternoon of July 20 and returned to Fort Stanton with his soldiers, leaving three men to guard Saturnino Baca's family.[26] Ten months later Dudley would be called to account for his part in the five days of battle.

Lincoln itself remained quiet for awhile, partly because people stayed away from the town.[27] The sheriff's posse was down towards the Pecos pursuing the remnants of McSween's partisans in the vicinity of Chisum's ranch. On August 5 the clerk at the Mescalero Agency was shot by a group of the old Regulators in an unplanned, almost accidental encounter. Dudley went into high dudgeon over this, partly because he had a detachment stationed just over the hill at the agency headquarters.[28]

Hardly had the dust settled in Lincoln when Sue McSween, Robert Widenmann (then in Mesilla), and other former Tunstall employees began a series of wheedling letters to Tunstall Sr. that bore news of the most recent happenings but managed to include claims for alleged debts and back wages owed by his son's estate. Montague Leverson resumed his letter-writing crusade.[29] More importantly Frank Angel, the special agent for the Department of Justice, abruptly reversed his judgment about Governor Axtell as a result of the agent's Colfax County investigations and startled Axtell with a series of heavily critical interrogatories. Axtell's replies were evasive. By the end of August it no longer mattered; the secretary of the interior had heard Angel's verbal report and decided that a change in the New Mexico governorship was needed, the sooner the better. Axtell was suspended on September 4, in part because of the Lincoln County War.[30]

The Reign of Terror

The relative calm in Lincoln was deceptive. August and September of 1878 would be a time of worse terror, if possible, than anything since the Horrell War. There were no sensational newspaper headlines, but letters and reports gave the story.

When news of the Five-Days Battle reached John Chisum, he began to close out the ranch and move his herd north to the Canadian River country in eastern New Mexico, with the probable return date a moot question. Drovers, or trail bosses, had been moving large trail herds of Pecos livestock to distant points in Kansas and Texas since the spring of 1878. By mid-August the newspapers reported that all of the big cattlemen, with their stock, were leaving the "infected" district of Lincoln.[31] The thieves and rustlers began to prey on the small ranchers, as Dudley had predicted.

Late in July Sam Corbet, caretaker at the Tunstall store, wrote to both Widenmann and to John P. Tunstall that he expected every day to hear that the Tunstall estate cattle on the Rio Felix had been stolen.[32] This finally happened on August 18:

> Mr. Gauss got back last night but brought no cattle. The 9 men that was here went out there and taken every thing, even old Gauss'er clothes.[33]

Godfrey Gauss had been staying on at Tunstall's ranch on the Felix as custodian. Gauss himself described the circumstances in more detail:

> The war is raging now as fiercely as ever. The county is overrun by horse & cattle thieves, & there is no law in force. . . . The thieves took last Sunday the herd of cows about 200 in number worth perhaps $2,500.00 the last of the property belonging to your son's estate, which could have been at present turned into ready money. . . .[34]

According to Lieutenant Colonel Dudley, the nine referred to by Corbet was a party headed by an ex-member of John Kinney's outlaws, now "just going it free" and without opposition.[35] Later an investigator hired by Sue McSween found the Tunstall cattle at Seven Rivers, in the hands of one of John Selman's "scouts."[36] More will be said later about this murderous crew.

The same day the Tunstall cattle disappeared, a rancher at Seven Rivers wrote to Dudley to plead for help from the army. This was most unusual since Seven Rivers people were notably able to take care of themselves. Now the country was in a deplorable condition, full of men of the worst class with rumors of a party organizing to the north to plunder and murder, and civil law powerless:

> All of us helpless to protect ourselves and property against armed parties who are traveling through this Section of the Country.[37]

Charles Fritz rode in from the Spring Ranch, seven miles below Lincoln, on the morning of September 7 and told Dudley that the day before two men had captured his herd of fifteen horses plus the horses his two boys were riding on. Dudley advised the district headquarters in Santa Fe that the sheriff had no legal posse to pursue the thieves; that there were "undoubtedly many unprincipled Mexicans in the Country who are coalescing with these bands of outlaws" to steal stock and drive it into other sections, and that this class of people would increase "while it is well known throughout the Country that there is a perfect absence of all law or power to resist them."[38]

Whatever had happened to Sheriff George Peppin and the posse that shot it out with McSween's defenders? Peppin felt that Governor Axtell had promised him support from the army that was not forthcoming, without which it was impossible to restore peace and order.[39] Neither did he receive support from the county commissioners. By the end of August the sheriff had disbanded his posse and suspended all official action, in effect handing Lincoln County over to the outlaws:

There is no questioning the fact that the County is thoroughly raided over by Bands of armed men, belonging to the various factions. Are stealing Stock and such property as they may lay their hands on, regardless of law, if it existed, or the taking of life if opposition is offered to their depredations.[40]

One curious result was that the Kid, Scurlock, Charlie Bowdre, Jim French, and others of the old McSween ring now held the town of Lincoln, while the sheriff was holed up at Fort Stanton, not daring to go home.

Agent Angel's report to the U.S. Attorney General on the Lincoln County troubles pertained especially to conditions there during August and September 1878. He first reviewed the growth of L.G. Murphy & Co. and the formation of a second party headed by McSween, now deceased:

Bands of desperate characters who are ever found on the frontier, particularly along the Texas border, who have no interest in Lincoln County, men who live by plunder, and who only flourish where they can evade the law, have naturally gravitated to one or the other of these parties, and are now in their pay, being hired for so much a day to fight their battles.

Peppin came into Lincoln accompanied by John Kinney and his band of outlaws and murderers; McSween then collected an equally distinguished lot:

A battle is fought—for five days it rages—more desperate action than was seen on these unfortunate days, by both sides, is rarely witnessed. Both parties desire revenge, and they are now reorganizing, and collecting more desperate characters, (if it were possible), than they previously had. Before I left Santa Fe, it was reported that there were two hundred armed men in the field.

Men were shot down on sight simply because they belonged to one party or the other:

When these men were not engaged in battles, and when the County seemingly was at peace, they were employed to steal cattle, either from the farmers or the indians—a ready market and no questions asked, was found in the persons who held government contracts.

Law-abiding citizens had been reduced to poverty and laws could not be enforced since the law was either all Murphy or all McSween, depending upon who was in power. As a result,

The leaders of these parties have created a storm that they cannot control, and it has reached such proportions that the whole Territory cannot put it down. Lands go uncultivated; ranches are abandoned; merchants have closed their stores; citizens have left the homes they have occupied for years; business has ceased, and lawlessness and murder are the order of the day.

These outlaws who prowl the County with the avowed purpose of murder; who have no interests in the County or wrongs of their own to redress, no matter on which side they belong, should be hunted down, and made to answer for their crimes.

The Territory has no militia, and the County being in the hands of these armed out-laws, the laws and mandates of the Courts cannot be enforced or respected, nor lives or property protected. It is impossible for even the Courts to be held.[41]

Who were these outlaws pillaging the countryside? The question brought some interesting answers. John Kinney seems to have left after the Five-Days Battle in July, although members of his gang evidently stayed around. The doings of Jessie Evans and the Boys are difficult to track, but they may have been involved in the banditry. By the early fall of 1878 Billy the Kid had his own gang, all Lincoln County War veterans. Their concern was mainly with collecting horses in New Mexico to sell in the Texas Panhandle.[42]

The new post surgeon at Fort Stanton observed that

> the war is no longer the faction war of Dolan vs. McSween, but seems almost altogether confined to depredation and murder by a band of miscreants who have probably been attracted from all parts of the Country by the Knowledge of the utter inability of the authorities, Civil or military, to afford protection. Of course the feeling between the survivors in the original disturbance is still very bitter.[43]

Peppin, during the time when he was pursuing desperadoes, came across three or four bands of men who defied him to arrest them. So far as he knew he had no warrants, as these were bands of unknown men; one party of ten armed men were all perfect strangers both to himself and to all of his posse members. The intentions of this group were clear enough: robbery and horse and cattle stealing.[44]

Several Lincoln County officials petitioned Governor Axtell for relief from the preying bands, "some from Mexico some from Texas some from one place or other and more daily arriving,"[45] who were doing nothing but raiding and committing every kind of violence and destruction. Axtell, during his last month in office, asked the president for assistance. Most of his information evidently came from Peppin and Dudley, but he added that one gang, when asked who they were, replied "We are Devils just come from Hell." When the sheriff ordered them to disband and return to their homes and ordinary avocations, they told him "We have no homes" and "we are at our ordinary avocations." The governor added that several women and young girls, mere children, had been ravished.[46]

There was worse to come. John Selman, also known as John Gunter and John Gross, has been called "a particularly vicious specimen of border scum."[47] He drifted in from Texas and took over the leadership of some ruffians known variously as "The Wrestlers," "the Rustlers," or "the Scouts." During the last few days of September they swept through Lincoln County, stealing everything of value at the Coe Ranch on the Rio Hondo and firing the haystacks, wrecking Will Hudgen's saloon in the old Murphy brewery and insulting Hudgens' wife and sister, then passing on towards Lincoln.

There they broke open the houses and took what they wanted, except where the defenders at Isaac Ellis' store stood them off. Continuing down the Rio Bonito, they killed three members of a hay-cutting party at the ranch of José Chaves y Sanches without the least provocation, two of the victims being Chaves' sons. The same day, September 28, they rode past Martin Sanchez' house on the Rio Hondo and put three bullets into his young son, mortally wounding the boy. They rounded out the evening at Bartlett's ranch, a few miles below Lincoln, where the Wrestlers took the wives of two of his employees into the bush, stripped them naked, and raped them. One of the women made it back to Bartlett's house by 2 a.m. and told her story; both survived.[48]

This wholesale mayhem left the population terror-stricken and the commander at Fort Stanton considerably unnerved. The people at Lincoln apparently recovered first; there is an apocryphal story about a running gunfight between the Scouts and volunteers led by Juan Patron through every village between Fritz' Spring Ranch and the Martin Sanchez ranch, a distance of about thirty-five miles. The outlaws were routed and left to seek easier prospects. A few days later two of them were found dead near the Pecos, perhaps killed by their own gang.[49]

Dudley, for his part, sent reports almost daily from Fort Stanton to district headquarters in Santa Fe. He was not deaf to the frantic appeals for protection and begged to be allowed to use his soldiers:

> I respectfully and earnestly ask in the Name of God and humanity, that I may be allowed to use the forces at my command, to drive these murderers, horse-thieves,

and escaped convicts out of the Country.

As before, he was turned down.[50]

All of this was about to hit the desk of General Lew. Wallace when he took the oath as governor of New Mexico on September 30, 1878.

~ 11 ~

GOVERNOR LEW. WALLACE
NEW HOPE FOR
NEW MEXICO

October–December 1878

L ewis Wallace, or Lew., as he signed his name, had been hoping for a presidential appointment ever since the election of Rutherford B. Hayes in 1876. At age fifty-one Wallace was a successful Civil War general, reluctant lawyer, Indiana political figure, and budding literary lion. He was at home in Crawfordsville, Indiana, when the news came on September 4, 1878, that he had been appointed territorial governor of New Mexico. He was already a national figure, and the territory felt honored by having such a man become its governor. The territorial politicians, however, who had considered ex-Governor Axtell one of their own, were cool towards Wallace.

His reasons for accepting the appointment were probably pragmatic; he needed money. The annual salary of $2,500. would meet expenses, but by investing in a successful gold or silver mine he might make his fortune. The new governor toured the Los Cerrillos area near Santa Fe during his first month in New Mexico and subsequently bought interests in claims at Shakespeare and the San Simon mining district in southwestern New Mexico. As his term in office was ending he wrote to his son Henry that

> I have held the office until I have accomplished what I wanted—the acquirement of what I consider as good mining property as there is in the Territory.[1]

After Wallace received the notice of his appointment, he traveled to Washington to be briefed on the existing difficulties in the territory. There was no want of information. Dudley's reports from Fort Stanton had been forwarded (unbeknownst to Dudley) to the secretary of war, while both the secretary of the interior and President Hayes had collections of unsolicited and somewhat biased correspondence. More importantly, Special Agent Frank Angel was completing his report for the Department of Justice. Angel produced a small, red leather notebook with his assessments of the personalities the new governor would meet. Wallace received this and undoubtedly studied it while on his way west. In a general way he was familiar with the acute problems in the territory and possible actions for their solution before he left for New Mexico.[2]

He found Lincoln County given over completely to bandit rule—"Devils from Hell" indeed—with no semblance of civil order. News of the Wrestlers' rampage of pillage, rape, and murder was about to shock Santa Fe. Dudley greeted Wallace by saying that ten murders had been reported within the past fifteen days and no man, woman, or child was safe in the county outside the shadow of the military. The U.S. Marshal stayed away from Lincoln County; Judge Warren Bristol refused to hold court there; the sheriff had taken refuge at Fort Stanton and the county officials were impotent. Orders stemming from the *posse comitatus* act kept U.S. troops at the fort. New Mexico lacked an organized militia or any arms for one, and most of the good people had fled, leaving the county overrun by outlaws. Cattlemen's associations were unknown in New Mexico. In short, every institution designed for the maintenance of law and order that existed in the territory had failed.[3]

On October 5, Wallace telegraphed the situation to the secretary of the interior together with his recommendations. He wanted the president to place Lincoln County under martial law, suspend the writ of habeas corpus and appoint a military commission to try offenders. Cooperation by the Texas Rangers should be sought, on their side of the line. "The great need is a few rugged examples."[4]

President Hayes' Proclamation

Two days later Wallace received the text of a presidential proclamation that fell far short of meeting his requests, but which followed closely a precedent set during August of the same year. A legal opinion then held that the president had authority to employ the land and naval forces of the U.S. to enforce the laws if it became impracticable, in his judgment, to enforce these by the ordinary course of judicial proceedings.[5] The text of the October 7 proclamation referred to this authority, applied it to the situation in Lincoln County, and ordered everybody engaged in obstructing the laws to disperse and return to their homes on or before October 13, 1878. Wallace telegraphed the proclamation to Judge Bristol, who had copies printed at Mesilla and distributed through Doña Ana and Lincoln counties.

The practical effect of this edict was that the army had authority to enforce the laws of the United States while the civil judicial machinery remained in place. The day following the president's action, the secretary of war issued instructions for the army to aid the governor and authorities of New Mexico Territory in keeping the peace and enforcing the laws. This order put teeth in the proclamation, and Dudley may have had a copy of both by mid-October. By October 27 district headquarters at Santa Fe had compiled a lengthy set of instructions that gave the Fort Stanton commander everything he had been asking for. Thenceforth he could use troops to assist the U.S. Marshal and the sheriffs and their deputies, also to break up armed bands and to recover stolen property. Additionally, he was to protect the U.S. mails and establish a cavalry camp near Roswell, New Mexico. In a complete reversal from previous restrictions, the troops were now free to pursue criminals without waiting for a civil officer.[6]

By Dudley's own reports, Lincoln County was completely quiet during late October. Actually a Mexican family that had left Seven Rivers for Texas became the victims of a brutal mass murder when the Jones boys and others from Seven Rivers followed the family and caught up with it below Pope's Crossing on the Pecos River, in western Texas. The army didn't hear about this until later, but next February Captain Henry Carroll

> crossed the River in company with Mr. Pierce and Olinger, and moved down the River 2 miles and found the Skeleton of a Mexican Boy, 18 years old, shot by the Jones Boys and Collins about the 20" of October 1878. The ball entered above the right ear and came out in front of the left ear. 4 miles further on the cart was burned, and about 2 miles still further, fragments of womans clothing was found. This was the remains of a family of nine Mexicans reported killed. They started from Seven Rivers, and were followed by Collins or Hall, John Jones, Jim Jones, Tom Jones and Billy Jones. The Mexicans had a wagon and 2 Horses, also a cart. The men were arrested on a charge of killing an American named Hunt, taken back some miles on the road and killed, it is said while the prisoners were attempting to escape, but what became of the women is as yet unknown. The cart was burned, their clothing was scattered along the road, and the wagon having been taken back to Seven Riv-

ers, the women were killed or allowed to walk to the nearest settlement, about seventy-five miles. One named Fales said to have escaped to Stockton could perhaps throw some light on this Tragedy.[7]

When Governor Wallace compiled a wanted list for Captain Carroll he included four of the five alleged murderers. They were subsequently charged with the killings, but never indicted or prosecuted.[8]

When a courier rode into Fort Stanton on the evening of November 2, 1878, with the new instructions from district headquarters, things started to happen. Dudley immediately informed Sheriff Peppin, who in turn furnished the post commander with a list of persons for whom he held legal warrants. Ten individuals, all of them members of the old Regulators as it happened, were charged with murder on U.S. warrants. Seven other people were mostly charged with larceny on territorial warrants. Peppin requested twenty-five cavalrymen for a posse. Dudley provided these and on November 5 they started to ride.

That same day was general election day, and Lincoln County managed to participate in spite of all its problems. The voters elected a new sheriff, George Kimbrell, who was issued his commission on December 14 and assumed office on or after January 1, 1879.[9] Until then Peppin and his posse chased bandits, apparently with little success since many of the outlaws had gone elsewhere.

Whether due to the president's proclamation, to Governor Wallace's actions, or to the sight of army patrols, people who had fled the violence began returning to Lincoln County. By the middle of November, Dudley could write that

quite a number of the old residents, who fled the country Several months since, taking with them everything they possessed, except houses and lands, have returned with their families and stock to their former homes at Seven Rivers, among the number are the Beckwiths, Powell, Pierces and Paxton, and many of the residents of Lincoln and vicinity are also back again at their houses, and on their Ranches.[10]

Saturnino Baca and his family had gone home after three months living under the protection of the garrison at Fort Stanton. One newspaper thought that a rest or a lull in the disturbances was a more accurate claim than to say that peace had been restored. None of the malefactors in the recent war had yet been arrested.[11]

Stirring the Fires: Sue McSween vs. Lieutenant Colonel Dudley

Sue McSween, disheartened by the law and order breakdown and the threats made against her, had packed her few belongings and departed from Lincoln on September 17. She went to Las Vegas, New Mexico, where she harbored ideas about bringing her late husband's murderers to justice and suing everyone involved with her losses. In Las Vegas she met and employed Huston I. Chapman, an attorney recently arrived from Portland, Oregon.[12]

This was an unfortunate choice, as Chapman turned out to be quite a firebrand. He first wrote to Governor Wallace on October 24, charging among other things that

I am in possession of facts which make Col. Dudley criminally responsible for the killing of McSween and he has threatened that in case martial law was declared that he would arrest Mrs. McSween and her friends immediately. Through fear of his threat Mrs. McSween left Lincoln and is now residing here, until such time as she may with safety return to her home. She has no fears of harm only from Col. Dudley and in case he has the power he will do all in his power to annoy and arrest her.[13]

Yginio Salazar survived Lincoln's violent era to become one of its old timers. Courtesy Special Collections, University of Arizona Library.

Francisco Gomez, who was victimized by Sue McSween's alleged promiscuity and lived to tell the tale. Photo Archives, University of Arizona Library.

Sue McSween was administratrix for the estates of her late husband *and* John H. Tunstall. The probate court in Lincoln County was due to meet in November and she had business there. Chapman asked if the governor would prevent Dudley from exercising any authority to interfere with Mrs. McSween.

Wallace found Chapman's accusations against Dudley "incredible" and forwarded a copy of this letter to Gen. Edward Hatch, commander of the Military District of New Mexico and Dudley's superior officer. Wallace's own choice of words was infelicitous in that he requested "a special safeguard" for Mrs. McSween while implying Dudley's unfitness for such duty, requesting at the same time that the district commander call Dudley's attention to the Chapman letter.[14]

Hatch had been in New Mexico since the fall of 1875 and he was no stranger to Lincoln County's problems. Nor was any love lost between himself and Dudley; the differences between them spanned almost a decade.[15] In forwarding the two letters he must have anticipated an explosion when they arrived. Dudley had a tendency to become increasingly worked up in the course of a letter anyway and responded true to form when he wrote back directly to Wallace and ended the letter by saying

> I am not here, quietly to submit to, and allow such allegations against myself, as your Excellency has seen proper to forward to District Headquarters, without making an unqualified denial, and I defy proof to the contrary.[16]

In his reply at the same time to district headquarters, Dudley struck back viciously against Sue McSween. He declined to comment other than by enclosing eight affidavits for the governor's perusal, adding gratuitously that he didn't have to go off of his parade ground to obtain these and any number of a similar kind could be forwarded if these did not satisfy. Then he commented anyway, dipping his pen in vitriol:

> If His Excellency the Governor desires a "safe guard" for a woman bearing the character represented by these Affidavits, I most sincerely hope his wishes will be gratified. He need have no fears of my molesting or interfering with the class of women to which these Affidavits show Mrs. McSween to belong.[17]

The affidavits in question must have pulled both Hatch and Wallace upright in their chairs. The deponents all lived at Lincoln or Fort Stanton and were mostly recognizable anti-McSween partisans. Nonetheless, they may have known whereof they spoke in making specific allegations about Sue McSween's sexual promiscuity. Young Francisco Gomez freely admitted his role, while George Peppin had been a reluctant peeping Tom:

> Deponent [Peppin] further states that he has known young Francisco Gomez the last twelve years and considers him a truthful honest and reliable man. Affiant further deposes that he was forced to witness the said Mrs. McSween's lascivious conduct towards Francisco Gomez and that the same was to disgusting to relate.[18]

Francisco Gomez survived the experience for almost seventy years, living in Lincoln until his death in 1946. He told a WPA interviewer in 1938 that he was about eighteen when he went to work for the McSweens, staying with them for some two years.[19] Dudley's interest in Sue McSween's personal life dated back to at least the late summer of 1878 when he mentioned her nocturnal visitors in two of his weekly reports.

Whatever the substance to the allegations, Huston Chapman, Sue McSween, and her attorney brother-in-law D.P. Shield all tried to get their hands on these depositions. Hatch denied Chapman access to Dudley's reports—or affidavits—unless the secretary of war should so direct.[20] Wallace was evasive. He wrote back to Dudley and termed the latter's letters "perfectly satisfactory," but then put his foot in it again when the conciliatory tone of his own letter turned slightly patronizing. He also enclosed a copy of a proclamation he had just issued and asked that it be passed on to Sheriff Peppin.[21]

Governor Wallace Issues His Own Proclamation

Lew. Wallace's proclamation of November 13, 1878, invited people to return to Lincoln County and declared a general pardon for misdemeanors and offenses against territorial laws committed in that county since February 1, 1878.[22] In part this action reflected his tendency to declare a success and then walk away from the problem. He also wanted to claim all of the credit that he could for peace in Lincoln County, since Wallace was still waiting for the Senate to confirm him as governor. They finally did so on December 16.[23]

The governor claimed that his action was intended to curb the vendetta spirit among the people, but in reality it was only half thought out. All but one of the territorial warrants held by Sheriff Peppin were for larceny, meaning theft of cattle or horses. The U.S. warrants, which were not affected by the amnesty, were all for murder. Newspaper editors failed to make a distinction and instead pointed out that the governor's amnesty subverted the principle of justice.

One effect of the pardon was to invite back into the country some of the outlaws who had previously left. This was the very opposite of what Wallace claimed had been accomplished through ordering the army into action.[24] Finally, the language of the proclamation antagonized still further that thin-skinned and contentious Dudley who had just gone to such lengths to demonstrate how ill-advised the governor had been in requesting that Sue McSween receive some measure of protection.

Dudley found the inclusion of himself and fellow officers under the provisions of the pardon offensive. Although Wallace had apparently intended to exempt army officers from legal harassment, Dudley construed the phrasing to mean that the governor classed them with the outlaws who had been pillaging and murdering through the countryside. Convinced as ever that his actions were above criticism, Dudley reacted with a long, insulting, and not very lucid open letter to Governor Wallace, first published in the Santa Fe *Weekly New Mexican* on December 14, 1878.

Wallace, who was unaware of Dudley's frame of mind, had written another conciliatory letter to him on November 30 and included with this the November 28, 1878, *Rocky Mountain Sentinel*, a Santa Fe newspaper that supported Wallace. The governor said that Dudley would "doubtless be interested" in the paper, which contained some curious correspondence about Dudley's seeming indifference to a herd of stolen cattle that wound up with livestock furnished by the beef contractor to the Mescalero Apache Agency. The *News and Press* at Cimarron smelled a rat and pointed out that such thefts to the benefit of government contractors were what had led to the Lincoln County War.[25]

Just as Wallace's amnesty drew criticism, so did his failure to visit Lincoln. He had been promising since his arrival in the territory to go there forthwith.[26] By late November this had worn thin and the critics were becoming less than kind about his neglect.[27] Perhaps Wallace felt that peace could be restored by waving proclamations, with no need for his personal presence. Wallace eventually offered some lame excuses:[28]

> It is my opinion that if the present status continues thirty days, or sixty at the furthest, affairs in Lincoln county will settle down and go on in peace. The trouble is ended now, so that I have only to prevent its renewal, and help the people back to quiet control.[29]

This prognosis only showed his talent for misjudging a situation, as events were to demonstrate. Just one month later Dudley wrote that "if his Excellency Governor Wallace thinks peace and order prevails in Lincoln County he is the worst fooled Official I ever saw."[30]

If Wallace had gone to Lincoln while he still held the initiative in October, or if he had refrained from his amnesty proclamation, the town might have escaped some of the renewed violence.

Huston Chapman: A Lawyer vs. the Army

Sue McSween came back to Lincoln on November 23, accompanied by her attorney Huston Chapman, and took up residence in the house formerly occupied by Saturnino Baca's family. Chapman began to bombard Wallace with allegations against the military in general and Dudley in particular; he also managed to insult Wallace, but his main target was Dudley. The message was clear: the Fort Stanton commander enjoyed his whiskey but not public confidence.[31] These claims, coupled with his leanings toward the old Dolan faction and his ability to antagonize everybody, probably spurred the governor's request to Colonel Hatch that Lieutenant Colonel Dudley be relieved of his command.[32]

Hatch bucked this hot potato up the army's chain of command, pointing out that no charges had been made. Within a month the answer came back that Dudley would not be deprived of his command and any charges that the governor preferred would be thoroughly examined.[33] There the matter rested for awhile.

The presence of Dudley, Sue McSween, her fiery young lawyer, Billy the Kid, members of the old Regulators, and the Dolan partisans set the stew to bubbling once again at Lincoln. Soon there was another incident of the kind that kept people in a murderous frame of mind. One night in mid-December, 2d Lt. J.H. French and two soldiers invited themselves into the house where Sue McSween and Huston Chapman were staying. French then got into a violent argument with Chapman. The soldiers waved guns and threats, to the point where Mrs. McSween swooned away. In the end French departed and no one was hurt. Dudley promptly charged a board of officers with investigating the lieutenant's conduct and wrote to district headquarters that he regretted the incident exceedingly. The board took testimony at length, one of the low points being French's own sarcastic remarks about Lincoln and the people there. The recommendation was that no further action be taken.[34]

This mass of evidence said quite a lot about the situation in Lincoln as of mid-December 1878. The Regulators were back in control, one of their rendezvous being the house of Maximiano de Guebara in the lower (eastern) part of town. George Peppin, still the sheriff, had warrants for some of them but was afraid to go into Lincoln without a military escort, much less try to make arrests. Lieutenant French commanded his escort and volunteered to make the arrests. By all accounts French went about this aggressively, though failing to find the wanted men.

In sorting through the contradictory testimony, this whole affair looked a little like it was staged, with Huston Chapman as the target. Dudley, on the other hand, displayed a bit of his own paranoia: "I begin to believe with others that it is a conspiracy on the part of Chapman, the notorious Mrs. McSween, and others to blackmail Lieut. French."[35] Whatever the case, Chapman's inflammatory rhetoric about Dudley—"a whiskey barrel in the morning and a barrel of whiskey at night"—as well as other officers at the fort had a nightmare ring to it. Dudley had seen Chapman's letters to Governor Wallace beginning with the one on October 24. In these, Chapman sounded like McSween reincarnated.[36] Mac's old gunmen had returned and people were being murdered again; Lincoln might be heading back into the worst days of the summer.[37] No one wanted to see that.

Just before Christmas, Dudley banned the Kid, Jim French, Scurlock, Henry Brown, and other "notorious murderers, horse and cattle thieves, escaped convicts and desperadoes" from the Fort Stanton reservation except during daylight hours to pick up their mail. He thoughtfully included lawyer Chapman in the proscribed list.[38] On December 27 Dudley issued a special order granting J.J. Dolan, J.B. Mathews, and John Long permission to remain on the post at Fort Stanton in view of reliable information that a band of twenty-two outlaws was in Lincoln.[39]

In Lincoln, George Kimbrell was about to succeed George Peppin as Sheriff of Lincoln County, much to Peppin's relief. The McSween-Bonney-Chapman crowd was riding high and the Dolan outfit was on the run again during the last few days of 1878. There is nothing to confirm that William Bonney was incarcerated in the pit-jail on December 22, 1878.[40]

The year ended with an embittered Dolan writing to Governor Wallace, his letter including this ominous passage:

> Your friend [Chapman] appears to be the only man in this County who is trying to Continue the old feud. I and many of our Citizens feel Confident that if this man was silenced, the trouble would end.[41]

∽ 12 ∽

THE LINCOLN COUNTY
WAR IV

January–July 1879

Peaceful Interlude

J anuary 1879 was the longest period of peace and quiet at Lincoln in more than a year. John B. Wilson, the old justice of the peace, had been returned to office in the November election along with a generally new slate of county officials. Wilson was a known McSween supporter and an irritant to Dudley and Peppin since he released the outlaws that the sheriff's posses brought in.

Now Judge Wilson turned peacemaker. He wrote to both Governor Wallace and the *Mesilla Valley Independent* on January 11 to say that the county was enjoying peace and plenty, that the new Board of County Commissioners was determined to put matters into proper shape, and many persons from the two parties had been getting together and settling their old difficulties.[1]

A person who signed himself as "A.H.B." wrote something even more startling to the *Mesilla News*:

> Mrs. A.A. McSween and James J. Dolan have met and concluded a treaty of peace, the exact terms have not as yet been made known only in diplomatic circles, but it is presumed that it is based on the Berlin "Articles." Hurrah for Lincoln County.[2]

Skeptics remained, and a week and a half later "H.A.Y." used lightly disguised names in a mock account of a citizens' committee meeting at Lincoln concerning the newly found peace:

> Resolved, that the thanks of our people be sincerely tendered to the two high contracting parties who through their love for their fellow man—and woman—have at last concluded to bury the hatchet and smoke the pipe of peace.[3]

People probably did feel that any peace was preferable to what they had endured.

Attorney Chapman and Sue McSween were busy trying to settle the estates of both her late husband and John H. Tunstall. Perhaps in this connection Chapman traveled to Santa Fe, only to be refused access to Dudley's reports, orders, and affidavits on file there. On the way back to Lincoln he wrote to Tunstall's father about bringing his son's murderers to justice and conserving what was left of the estate.[4]

Sue McSween vs. Lieutenant Colonel Dudley—Again

Meanwhile Mrs. McSween was going ahead to recover what she could of the cows stolen from Tunstall's ranch back on August 18. This led to a rather fascinating exchange in which Sue McSween wrote to her arch-enemy, Dudley, and informed him that 275 cattle, branded "X.S.K.C." and belonging to the Tunstall estate, were in the hands of Robert Speakes and others at Seven Rivers. Speakes was a tough customer, one of John Selman's Wrestlers, and she asked for Dudley's aid in protecting the interests of the estate.[5] Dudley replied just as politely that if she would make the necessary legal representations and the sheriff made a requisition for troops to form a posse, every assistance would be given.[6]

Underneath this surface politeness, Dudley seethed. He reported the request to district headquarters in a way that exposed all of his old bitterness, right back to the Five-Days Battle. The request was a reasonable one and he couldn't decline it, but he could still harbor dark suspicions as to whether there was any real desire to recover the cattle or just to raise a complaint against Dudley *if* he should decline to help. In his mind this wasn't all, but "the other reason does not effect the Public interest."[7] With an attitude like this, Dudley was clearly nearing the end of his usefulness at Fort Stanton.

Captain Carroll's Ride Down the Pecos

A bizarre episode was also being acted out along the banks of the Pecos. Captain Henry Carroll and a detachment of the Ninth Cavalry were garrisoning a temporary camp near Roswell, New Mexico. On February 1, special constable Emil Powers rode up and made a requisition for a posse to go after stolen livestock. Carroll referred this to Dudley for instructions. Dudley denied permission, saying that the use of troops was authorized only to aid the sheriff and his deputies and the U.S. Marshal and his deputies.[8] Carroll was not there to receive the answer, since he had already furnished a posse on February 5 and joined it himself the next day, while neglecting to inform his commander of these actions.

For nearly three weeks, Carroll and his men simply disappeared. Dudley's concern grew when he heard second-hand that this troop had gone off with a special constable to recover the Tunstall cattle. Was Sue McSween presenting him with a fait accompli? Dudley didn't know, and the sheriff knew nothing about this. The constable himself had been deputized to recover cattle stolen from the firm of Hunter and Evans.

This posse swept down the Pecos valley into Texas and returned to Roswell in late February, driving some 294 head of stock. Various owners sorted out their own animals, 140 of which were claimed for the Tunstall estate. Dudley's reaction was remarkably mild—he ordered Carroll to turn the cattle over to the sheriff—when he got all of this unscrambled.[9] By this time the Fort Stanton commander had much more pressing concerns.

The Gunslingers Make Peace

William Bonney and Yginio Salazar returned to Lincoln the morning of February 18. They sent the Dolan faction a proposal that the two sides either make peace or fight. Bonney had evidently assumed leadership of the old McSween gunfighters, many of whom were charged with murders going back to the Brady killing. That evening the two parties got together and worked out a compact. An area newspaper reported,

> They met; Dolan, Jesse Evans and Campbell were the high contracting parties on one side; Kid, O'Fallord and some one else on the other. Evans thought it impossible to treat with such a man as Kid, and informed that worthy individual that he would have to kill him then and there. Kid said they met for the purpose of making peace, and he didn't care to open the negotiations with a fight, and after some further talk "peace" was declared, a grand hand-shaking was indulged in, and all hands started around town to celebrate the event.[10]

Campbell was a new face in the Dolan crowd and apparently equal to the worst. Dudley's informers soon had the terms of this outlaw peace pact:

I am informed by three of the parties to the compact that the agreement entered into by the Dolan party and Bonney alias "Kidd" and his party is, in substance, as follows. Neither party will kill any member of the other party, without first giving notice of having withdrawn from the agreement; all persons who have acted as friends to either party are included in this agreement and are not to be molested; that neither officer nor soldier are to be killed for any act previous to this date; that neither party shall appear or give evidence against the other in any civil prosecution; that each party will give the individual members of the other party every aid in their power to resist arrests on civil warrants, and if arrested they will try and secure their releases; any member of either faction, failing to carry out this compact, which they informed me had been sworn to by their respective leaders, should be killed by either party on sight.[11]

The third clause must have given Dudley cold comfort, since he would have been the prime target.

Murder of Huston Chapman

Sheriff George Kimbrell had ridden into the plaza that evening and found Bonney and his pals there. The Kid told Kimbrell that he would not be taken alive on a murder charge. The sheriff thereupon headed for Fort Stanton and asked Dudley for a military posse. Dudley provided him with one officer and twenty cavalrymen, which may or may not say something about the Kid's reputation at that time.[12] First Lieutenant Byron Dawson and his men left the post at 10:40 p.m. and were in Lincoln fifty minutes later. They found none of the men they had come to arrest but they had a rude surprise nonetheless:

In our search through the town, we came across the dead body of H.I. Chapman, late a resident of Lincoln, who had evidently been killed a few hours previous to our arrival in the town; the body was very badly burned and most of the clothing, off the upper portion of the body, was burned.

They helped Justice of the Peace Wilson remove the deceased to the courthouse and then returned to the fort.[13]

Huston Chapman had left Las Vegas on February 12 after completing his business there. Just before leaving, Chapman said that he did fear his life was in danger but only from Dudley and Lieutenant French.[14] He traveled back in company with Juan Patron and they arrived in Lincoln on the evening of the 18th. Patron went to his own home, where Campbell and others soon made an uninvited visit. As reported in the media,

hardly had they entered the house before Campbell drew his pistol, and was only prevented from murdering Patron by the latter jumping behind other persons who protected him.[15]

Patron was lucky. Chapman's fate was described in a letter by a correspondent at Fort Stanton:

That evening early Chapman arrived from Las Vegas and put his horses in Mrs. McSween's corral. Then they went to a neighbor's to get some bread to make a poultice for his face. He was suffering from a severe attack of neuralgia. He was returning about 10 o'clock and met Dolan, Jesse Evans and Billy Campbell with Billy Bonny (the "Kid") and Tom O'Follard of the McSween party. Dolan and his party had insisted on their accompanying them and they had consented to do so rather than show any unfriendliness.

When they met, one of the Dolan party asked "who are you and where are you going?" Chapman answered and told them he was attending to his business. He was told to talk differently or they would make him. He answered, raising a bandage from his face, "You cannot scare me, boys. I know you and it's no use. You have tried that before." "Then" said Campbell "I'll settle you," and fired his pistol, the ball going in at the breast and coming out at the back. As he fell Dolan shot him with his Winchester. They then soaked his clothes with whiskey to make them burn.

When they first met, "Kid" tried to get away and ran around an angle in the lane wall, but Evans held the other fast and made him look on during the whole affair. Next day a coroner's jury was held, but the Dolan party was in town armed and the people were so bulldozed no evidence could be brought out.[16]

With the deed done, the assassins then walked on up the street to Cullum's eating house and had an oyster supper.[17] There was hardly a doubt about the murder being premeditated; Dolan's letter the previous December had made a clear threat against Chapman's life.[18]

The next day the male citizens of Lincoln all signed a petition asking Dudley to station troops in the county seat, while Sheriff Kimbrell asked for another military posse. As a result, 2d Lieutenant M.I. Goodwin with twenty men plus the Gatling gun were in town by 9 p.m. The day following, Dudley himself came to Lincoln for the first time in seven months. He told the people that it was time they got organized and they had no right to expect a military posse always to be tagging along after the sheriff. In the next few days he did withdraw most of the troops. In both Dudley's and Kimbrell's correspondence the old animosity against the McSween faction showed as strongly as ever. Kimbrell asked for a detachment to go to San Patricio to arrest the Kid and a Mexican (Salazar), but remarkably, no one even mentioned trying to arrest anyone for Chapman's murder.[19]

Governor Wallace Comes to Lincoln

The Chapman murder shook Governor Wallace out of his lethargy. He dashed a note off to Colonel Hatch, commander of the military district, saying that an "instant" proclamation of martial law might be necessary in Lincoln County. To the secretary of the interior, Wallace was bitter or perhaps just embarrassed that his earlier judgments about the peaceful state of affairs had been shown up as so much wishful thinking. So he spread some more oil on troubled waters, saying "the morale of the community will restore itself" and so forth.[20] Fortunately he also responded to appeals that he come to Lincoln and see for himself. On March 5 the governor arrived there while Colonel Hatch, who came at the same time, continued on to Fort Stanton.[21]

Several things then happened in very short order. Up in Las Vegas, attorney Ira Leonard preferred charges and specifications against Dudley to the secretary of war, alleging misconduct back to the time of the Five-Days Battle. Governor Wallace had no hand in Leonard's action.[22] In Lincoln itself, the governor made his headquarters at Montaño's store and met with the local citizens. Immediately he asked Hatch to send a force to arrest three of the men accused of killing Huston Chapman. This was done and the next day all three—Jessie Evans, William Campbell, and J.B. Mathews—were in custody.

The rest wasn't so easy. While a certain number of federal warrants for past crimes were still outstanding, people had been so terrorized by the murder of Chapman and intimidated by Dudley that they refused to make new affidavits, without which arrest warrants for more recent crimes could not be issued. Wallace decided to bend the law; he asked the military to make arrests without warrants and hold the parties until their cases could be investigated by the grand jury during the April session of court in Lincoln County. Within a week his wanted list grew to thirty-six names, all but two of whom were suspected of murder.[23]

Wallace perceived that neither his clean-up campaign nor the restoration of public confidence would go anywhere so long as Dudley commanded at Fort Stanton. The governor renewed his request that the post commander be relieved, and this time Colonel Hatch promptly obliged, removing Dudley and ordering him to Fort Union as of March 8. Hatch and Wallace were apprehensive about what Dudley's unseen friends in Washington might do, particularly as to whether the man had sent a telegram over Hatch's head. Such a telegram was sent and on March 18 Dudley also wrote directly to General Sherman, but he was smart enough not to disobey orders. The secretary of war reviewed the accumulated orders, charges, and reports, then ordered the appointment of a Court of Inquiry to investigate Dudley's conduct.[24]

The governor moved rapidly on other fronts, though the sometimes cryptic notes in his papers give us only a glimpse as to what was going on. Capt. Henry Carroll, back from his trip down the Pecos, succeeded Dudley in command at Fort Stanton and proved obliging to Wallace's requests. Carroll arrested J.J. Dolan and held him for the murder of Chapman, along with the three already in confinement for that crime. Wallace sent Carroll a list of the registered cattle brands in Lincoln County and instructions to bring any unbranded cattle to Lincoln, arresting anyone in possession of stock for which they could not produce a bill of sale. The object was twofold: to break up the cattle camps where outlaws were holding stolen livestock; and to give honest citizens a chance to reclaim their property.[25]

Wallace's Clean-Up Campaign: The Governor Meets the Kid

The blizzard of orders and reports issued on March 13 marked the launching of Wallace's dragnet; military posses rode off with deputy sheriffs to round up the murderers and cattle rustlers named in the governor's lists. That same day the first break came in the dilemma of how to prosecute criminals when witnesses were too intimidated to testify. William Bonney offered to testify in court if the indictments against him could be annulled. Wallace jumped at the opportunity.[26]

The Governor and the Kid met at 9 p.m. on the night of March 17 in the house of John B. "Squire" Wilson. Bonney walked in with a Winchester in his right hand and a revolver in his left. He lowered them when assured of no trap, and they sat down. Wallace outlined his plan. If the Kid would testify in court as to what he knew about the killing of Chapman, Wallace would pardon him for his past misdeeds. Bonney thought it over for a few days and then agreed. One very important detail was that the Kid would have to submit to a staged arrest and stay a prisoner until the court met so that his partners wouldn't realize that he was going to turn state's evidence in order to save his own skin.[27]

Word of this secret meeting soon leaked out. Campbell and Evans, then in the guardhouse at Fort Stanton, realized that Bonney had been an eyewitness to the Chapman killing and his testimony alone would probably see them indicted for first-degree murder. As noted in a Mesilla newspaper, they quickly made arrangements to be elsewhere.

> Campbell and Jessie Evans, who were held prisoners at this post for the murder of H.J. Chapman at Lincoln, got up and dusted on the night of the 19th [in fact, the 18th]. "Texas Jack," a member of Capt. Carroll's Co. who was a sentinel over those prisoners at the time left with Campbell and Evans, taking his arms with him. Nothing has been heard of these Knights of the Winchester and spur since their departure and they are probably breathing the free air of Mexico.[28]

Lew Wallace, territorial governor of New Mexico during the Lincoln County War. Photo Archives, Museum of New Mexico.

An alleged portrait of Billy the Kid, published in Life *magazine in 1936. Photo Archives, Museum of New Mexico.*

With these two outlaws free and willing to kill him on sight, the Kid was duly apprehensive. He also worried over how the escape might affect his deal with the governor. On March 20 he sent Squire Wilson a note:

> Please tell you know who that I do not know what to do now as those Prisoners have escaped, to send word by bearer, a note through you it may be that he has made different arrangements. . . . Send a note telling me what to do.[29]

Wallace replied immediately; the escape made no difference in their arrangements. To remove all suspicion of a deal between them he thought it better to have Sheriff Kimbrell use an arresting party of citizens, duly instructed to see that no violence was used. The "capture" was set for 3 p.m. the next day at the junction.[30]

The Kid digested all of this and then wrote again, this time displaying fear of an ambush by his former buddies and changing the rendezvous to a house a mile below San Patricio:

> I will keep the appointment I made but be sure and have men come that You can depend on. I am not afraid to die like a man fighting but I would not like to be killed like a dog unarmed. tell Kimbal to let his men be placed around the house and for him to come in alone; and he can arrest us. . . . Tell the Commanding Officer to Watch Lt. Goodwin he would not hesitate to do anything there Will be danger on the road of Somebody Waylaying us to kill us on the road to the Fort.[31]

Apparently everything went according to schedule. Since the posse was composed of civilians no report was made and the details of this voluntary capture are lost. A note from Wallace to Colonel Purington at Fort Stanton established that the sheriff and a posse had just brought in the Kid and Tom O'Folliard, captured about a mile below San Patricio. Wallace proposed to keep them under guard for a couple of days and then send them on to the fort.[32]

For Bonney it was back to the pit-jail, that "horribly dismal hole." Things might have been worse; Wallace cited an incident at just this time to illustrate his lack of faith in the impartiality of Lincoln County jurors:

> A precious specimen nick-named "The Kid," whom the Sheriff is holding here in the Plaza, as it is called, is an object of tender regard. I heard singing and music the other night; going to the door, I found the minstrels of the village actually serenading the fellow in his prison. So, speaking generally, the prisoners are good brave boys according to the code on which they have been fighting.[33]

At that moment the army was holding twelve prisoners in custody, but with the prevailing attitudes how could convictions be obtained under civil processes? Better martial law, thought the governor, and a military commission to mete out punishment.

Wallace walked over to the jail at least once to talk with the Kid. Fortunately he also made notes when the young bandit began to name off John Selman's Rustlers and the trails and places frequented by cattle and horse thieves. Bonney said nothing self-incriminating, but the point in this exercise for Wallace was to learn what he could tell a jury that might lead to indictments.[34]

The Lincoln County Rifles

Practically from the moment Lew. Wallace became governor of New Mexico he had sought arms and ammunition from the federal government to equip a territorial militia. This had run into all sorts of red tape, partly because there was no organized militia. Not only that, but Wallace had been led to believe that he had no authority to raise volunteer companies.

Actually there were two laws granting such authority, passed in 1851 and in 1855, but in the spring of 1879 no one knew this.[35] The governor considered that he would have to bend legalities once again and he did so on March 15 when he instructed Juan Patron to organize a company of mounted riflemen—the Lincoln County Rifles—to protect citizens from outlaw bands. This marked the beginnings of an organized territorial militia.

Captain Patron quickly enrolled two more officers along with fifty privates and non-coms. The men came from various precincts around the county; many were Hispanic and there was a notable lack of Dolan supporters.[36] They mustered on March 19; the same day the governor ordered Patron to turn out his men and join in the hunt for Jessie Evans and William Campbell. When Wallace sent a request for Captain Purington at Fort Stanton to furnish nine of these militiamen with rations and cartridges, the officer balked, believing that he had no authority. Patron's men rode and watched and scouted nonetheless, collecting a good deal of incidental intelligence for the governor and wearing down their horses in the process. While they failed to recapture Evans and Campbell, one party led by Patron brought in Doc Scurlock and another one arrested an accused murderer named Dan Dedrick. Wallace authorized Sheriff Kimbrell to call upon the Rifles, but for the most part they were not taken seriously. John B. Wilson wrote that "they call your milicia Heel Flys & make fun of them generaly when they meet them."[37]

Lincoln County stayed fairly calm that spring to the opening of district court on April 14. Wallace had eighteen prisoners "to occupy its time and attention," charged variously with murder and grand larceny. The governor himself left four days after court opened to return to Santa Fe, following a six-week stay in Lincoln County.[38] His request for a declaration of martial law had been quietly pigeonholed.

The territorial newspapers generally supported Wallace's clean-up campaign, the major exception being the *Mesilla News*. The *News* tried to smear the governor with charges that he had attempted to bribe Judge Warren Bristol; had stolen 500 head of cattle from a Texas cattle-drover named John Slaughter (one of those arrested for murder); and was on "intimate terms" with Mrs. McSween.[39] Wallace refuted these in the *Rocky Mountain Sentinel*, saying that he didn't own so much as one head of cattle and was not on intimate terms with Mrs. McSween. His answers seem to have satisfied the reading public and the episode blew over.[40]

The Outlaws Indicted—and Plead Immunity

Governor Wallace had pinned his hopes for suppressing outlawry on a restoration of the judicial process and particularly on the April term of district court at Lincoln. That session started off well enough; Judge Bristol delivered a lengthy charge to the grand jury as he had done one year earlier, only now he admonished citizens to step forth and testify and the jurors to put aside bias and partisan feelings.[41] The reports that Wallace received from his correspondents as the court moved along gave little comfort, especially with regard to William L. Rynerson, the district attorney. As Ira Leonard wrote:

> Court is moving on . . . have tried no more habeas corpus cases. . . . I stave them off. I tell you Gov. that the prosecuting officer of this Dist. is no friend to the enforcement of the law. He is bent on going for the Kid & notwithstanding he knows how it is proposed to destroy his testimony & influence he is bent on pushing him to the wall. He is a Dolan man and is defending him by his conduct all he can.[42]

John Wilson sent Wallace this assessment:

> They are all devising some means to help Dolans party out of their troubles. Dolan

was brought down on Friday & plead in the Tunstall murder & was required to give a bond in $2000. You can begin to see what they mean & his attys moved for venue to another county. It is also said that the troops are to be taken from us. I think if there is not a new commander got here & Bristol sent to the devil out of office & Rinerson also this trouble will keep taking root more & more as the time pases as they are all going to help the thieves & murderers escape the law.[43]

The session was given over almost entirely to grand jury proceedings. The jury reported and was discharged on May 1. Billy the Kid kept his promise and appeared as the star witness on the Chapman killing. Rynerson was the prosecuting attorney, but he also bore the reputation of being a Dolan partisan. By refusing to let the Kid plead the governor's pardon after turning state's evidence, he benefitted Dolan at Wallace's expense. When arraigned on indictments for murdering Sheriff Brady and his deputy, Bonney pleaded not guilty.[44]

Despite pessimistic forecasts the session was a qualified victory for Wallace, even if he was the only one to proclaim it so. A Las Cruces newspaper gave a good summary of the proceedings:

> At the recent term of court in Lincoln about 200 indictments were found. Among them Gen. Dudley and Pepin for burning McSween's house; Dolan and Campbell for the Chapman murder, in which the Kid is the principal witness; about 25 persons for the murder of McNab; Tom O'Folliard for stealing Frietze's horses. But two criminal cases were tried—that of Lucas Gallegos for murder of his nephew, found guilty and sentenced to one year, and a case of assault in which the accused was acquitted. No civil case was tried. In nearly all of them one or the other party was dead. O'Folliard, Jack Long, Marion Turner, Mathews, Buck Powell and others plead the Governor's pardon and were discharged. Pepin, Dolan and Mathews took change of venue to Socorro and Dudley to this county. The District Attorney would not consent to the release of Kid for turning State's evidence. His case comes to this county. The greater portion of persons indicted and not yet arrested will probably come forward and plead the Governor's pardon. Dolan and Mathews, indicted at last term for the Tunstall murder, also go to Socorro. Opinion is divided as to what the result will be. Some think a fresh outbreak is imminent, and others that the trouble is over. The two opposing factions have about exhausted themselves and future troubles will probably only arise from bands passing thro' and plundering. Evans and Campbell have not yet been rearrested.[45]

The victory turned hollow when many of those indicted pleaded immunity from prosecution under the governor's proclamation of November 13, 1878. Others had left the country. Those who were granted changes of venue or continuances, including Dudley and Dolan, later had their cases dismissed or were tried and found not guilty.

By offering a pardon to criminals, Wallace had indeed undercut justice, and of all the persons indicted only one—Billy the Kid—was ever tried and found guilty.[46] This came two years later. After the April 1879 court session ended, the Kid remained in custody until the time came for his transfer to Doña Ana County and trial. Then on the night of June 17, Bonney and Doc Scurlock slipped out of Lincoln and disappeared.[47]

The Dudley Court of Inquiry

The final act in the Lincoln County War was played out in May and June of 1879 when a court of inquiry met at Fort Stanton to investigate the charges that attorney Ira Leonard and Governor Wallace had lodged against Lieutenant Colonel Dudley. Dudley stood accused of allowing the McSween house to be burned, failing to protect women and children, permitting the pillage of the Tunstall store, slandering Sue McSween, and other charges mostly growing out of the Five-Days Battle. The court convened on May 9 and held sessions for almost two months, adjourning finally at 4:10 p.m. on July 5.

During this time sixty-four witnesses filled almost 1,000 pages of the court record with their direct testimony, cross-examinations, and re-direct statements. The hundreds of documents introduced as exhibits constitute one of our most valuable historical resources for this period. Dudley's witnesses were well prepared; Wallace's less so. Ira Leonard assisted the recorder, who in a court of inquiry was equivalent to a prosecutor. Leonard's letters to Wallace showed an early optimism about sustaining the charges and specifications. As spring wore into summer, his optimism turned to gloom.[48]

Finally, Dudley's defense counsel delivered his lengthy closing argument and the recorder made his own summary. On the forty-ninth day of hearings the court delivered its opinion. This held that none of the allegations against Dudley had been sustained and that proceedings before a Court Martial were therefore unnecessary. Gen. John Pope, commander of the Department of the Missouri, received the opinion and disapproved it. He offered another set of charges and specifications against Dudley. Pope, in turn, was overridden and the secretary of war eventually decided that all proceedings against Dudley would cease.[49] The charges against him in civilian courts were cleared as well, but he did not win a hoped-for reassignment to Fort Stanton. With this episode the Lincoln County War ground to a halt.

If Governor Wallace had gone to Lincoln and shown decisive leadership when he first came to New Mexico, the fighting might have been ended then. Instead he procrastinated and let things drift following the president's proclamation, compounding the difficulties by announcing his own amnesty. In the end, the old factions dissolved and the problems simply dissipated when many of the outlaws either were killed or departed for other places. Violence continued with incidents as brutal as any in the past, but these became more scattered. At White Oaks, the mining boom brought in a new breed of people who would not tolerate such lawlessness, as the Kid and his followers soon found out.[50]

About the time the Dudley court of inquiry began its hearings, the governor and the military establishment turned their attention from Lincoln towards a major Indian war that was just beginning to heat up. During the remainder of 1879 and through much of 1880 the Apache chief Victorio and his followers ravaged southern New Mexico. In roughly the same length of time, they left from five to ten times the number of casualties of the Lincoln County War—estimated at fifty men.[51] Victorio's raids scarcely touched Lincoln County other than to draw support from the Mescalero Apache Reservation and to see the Apaches charged with livestock raids along the Pecos.

PART IV

Double Barrel Shotgun, ca. 1880, caliber 10 gauge; break action; 31½ inch twist barrels.

⌁ 13 ⌁

LINCOLN IN TRANSITION

1879–1884

Lincoln and Lincoln County were witnessing changes even as the last echoes of the Lincoln County War died away. Edgar Walz ran the old Murphy-Dolan store for about a year on behalf of his brother-in-law, T.B. Catron. Catron sold the property to Will Dowlin & Co. on January 5, 1879, after which Dowlin and his partner John C. Delaney kept a general mercantile operation there until it went bankrupt in December of 1880. On December 15 the Lincoln County Board of Commissioners purchased the building for a Lincoln County Courthouse.[1]

As administratrix for both the McSween and the Tunstall estates, Sue McSween had plenty of business to keep her in Lincoln. Early in 1880 Sam Corbet wrote that

> Mrs. McSween is still here she is living at the Baca house, has had it fixed up real nice round house torn down and also the rock wall and plank fence in place. She seems to be getting along very well.[2]

The $10,000. from her late husband's life insurance policy would have enabled her to live very well indeed.[3] The Tunstall store had been fixed up and rented to J.A. LaRue, a merchant from Las Vegas, who kept a store there until December of 1882 when Charles Fritz bought the property as part of the Tunstall estate settlement. James J. Dolan, Fritz' son-in-law, then became the proprietor of his old enemy's store.[4]

In another ironic twist of fate, Dolan, in partnership with Wm. L. Rynerson, acquired Tunstall's ranch on the Rio Felix, later known as the Flying H Ranch. J.B. Mathews asserted his earlier claim to the Tunstall holdings on the Rio Peñasco and took possession there.[5] Mathews had led the posse that killed the young Englishman. Still another ranch changed hands in October 1882 when an English syndicate represented by J.A. Alcock acquired Murphy's old Carrizozo Ranch from T.B. Catron.[6]

Sue McSween employed Ira Leonard as her lawyer to aid with the estate settlements. Leonard moved his law office from Las Vegas to White Oaks, then to Lincoln, before finally settling at Socorro in 1882. During the court of inquiry, Dudley and Leonard developed a contempt for one another that carried on afterwards. In a generous moment, Leonard said of Dudley that

> he is impetuous, vindictive, overbearing, self-conceited and meddlesome. His normal condition is to be in a constant turmoil and jangle with some one, and he is the promoter of strife and discord. His life in the army has been one of luxurious expense to the government. His only excuse for interference in the difficulty that has made that county a pandemonium, was that he was acting in a humanitarian capacity; that he went to Lincoln to protect women and children, and the protection he gave was the same kind that the wolf would naturally give to the lamb.[7]

Dudley, never one to let an insult pass unremarked, characterized Leonard more succinctly as ". . . one of the most crafty, low down, unscrupulous men I ever came in contact with in my life."[8] Thus did the Lincoln County War continue in spirit.

Not all of the bandits left the Lincoln area. One who should have, but didn't, was William Bonney. In early July a newspaper reported that "the latest news from Lincoln is that the Kid and Scurlock party are still in the country and are getting a crowd together again and that no effort is being made to arrest them."[9] A little later one of the weekly summaries out of Fort Stanton reported that

> Captain L.H. Rucker 9th Cav. with 15 mounted men of C. F H and M 9' Cav. was ordered to proceed to Lincoln N.M. and report to the Sheriff as a Posse to assist in the capture of "Kid", who has been seen in Lincoln and vicinity during the past week. "Kid" was tracked to a cabin about 6 miles below Lincoln and the house surrounded but effected his escape through the chimney, on account of the darkness of the night, leaving his arms behind him.[10]

Some time after this, Bonney moved to the Fort Sumner area and resumed rustling cattle and horses for a livelihood, occasionally depredating as far south as White Oaks and the Mescalero Reservation.[11]

But new economic opportunities began opening up that were less subject to control by a few hands than in the past. Railroads would have a major impact. The first train pulled into Las Vegas, New Mexico, on April 4, 1879. Within Lincoln County, the White Oaks mining district was organized in December 1879. The town of White Oaks was platted the following May, and within a few years the mines there, only twenty-eight miles and an easy day's ride from Lincoln, became major gold producers. By the summer of 1880 additional gold discoveries had been made and camps started at Vera Cruz, Nogal, and Rio Bonito, in the Nogal district west of Lincoln.[12] Before 1879 no one had thought seriously about mining; by 1881, mining dominated the local news. The new people who flocked in on the mining surge would show little patience with range wars, feuds, and lawlessness, such as Lincoln featured in its past.

Lincoln didn't share in the new wealth right away and instead continued in many of its old ways, including a quick resort to the six-gun for settling differences. One night in late November 1879, for example, twenty men entered a room in Lincoln where a prisoner named Dick Hardeman was confined. They fired five shots into him, killing him instantly.[13] The next Fourth of July, three men died by mob violence in three nights at Lincoln. The first night a mob riddled a young man named Harriman with bullets while he lay bound in jail; the next night a deputy sheriff was overcome and killed outright at the same jail; and on the night of July 5 another mob took a prisoner from the jail and lynched him from a nearby tree. The reporter added that Lincoln was maintaining its reputation for lawlessness; down there people "seemed to think it was all right."[14] Governor Wallace, moved to comment on a somewhat unsettled condition of affairs, as he put it, gave the reason as a failure of the district court in Lincoln County to meet for two successive terms.[15] He recommended the appointment of Ira Leonard to the judgeship, then walked away from the problem and turned to something else.

Lincoln in the 1880 Census

During the first week of June 1880, Sheriff George Kimbrell put on his hat as a U.S. Census enumerator and took the 1880 Census for the Town of Lincoln. As always the census unit was the entire precinct (No. 1). His figures showed a community of 638 persons, nearly all of whom were Hispanic and born in New Mexico, living in 157 dwelling houses. By comparison the 1870 Census had recorded 223 residents in 88 houses.[16] Lincoln had almost tripled its population in ten years, despite the violence of that decade.

Other statistics from the 1880 Census showed Lincoln as a very different community from what it had been ten years earlier. Not one of the 167 heads of households in 1880 gave his or her occupation as rancher, stock raiser, or working in cattle, and only 7 identified themselves as farmers. Aside from a scattering of professional people—2 merchants (José Montaño, J.A. LaRue), 3 lawyers, 1 blacksmith, 1 hotel-keeper—a solid seventy percent (89) of the male heads of households listed their occupation as laborer. This was a tremendous change from 1870, when more than seventy-five percent (65 of 85) of the male heads of households had said that they were farmers (52) or farmhands (13).[17] At what did the citizens of Lincoln labor as of 1880?

Perhaps a few were employed in the mines or as cowboys, although the only person with more than a few hundred animals was James Chisum down on the Pecos, who claimed 6,000 head of cattle. The answer is that most of the men who claimed to be laborers were *farm laborers*. Lincoln in 1880 had a total of twelve full and part-time farmers, or fifteen if one included three persons along the lower Rio Bonito and Rio Hondo above the Casey ranch. In 1870 the same stretch of valley below Fort Stanton and above the Caseys had supported fifty-two farmers. Yet while the number of farmers had decreased by more than seventy percent, from fifty-two to fifteen, the tilled acreage increased almost one-quarter—from 1,695 acres of improved land in 1870 to 2,111 acres in 1880. On the Bonito and Hondo rivers the farmlands principally grew corn and wheat, while tilled lands along the Pecos evidently consisted of irrigated pastures.[18]

In ten years' time, more than seventy percent of the farm holdings had been acquired by a few large owners who now employed people to work the lands. The agricultural lands were tightly held as of 1880; three persons each farmed between 300 and 400 acres, representing almost fifty percent of the total arable land. Six other farmers owned 850 acres among them.[19] Seven of the fifteen farmers paid laborers year-round and four of the others hired people for at least twenty-six weeks out of the year.

Such a concentration of resources in the hands of very few people is reminiscent of the charges against L.G. Murphy during his heyday—that he took the farmers' lands, monopolizing the sources of wealth, etc. Murphy never really had this kind of power as has been seen, but other people now did and none of them were very well known. Merchant Montaño, Francisco Valencia, and Charles Fritz, owner of the Spring Ranch below Lincoln, were the three principal landholders. Others included Bonifacia Brady (widow of William Brady), Charles Bartlett, and Antonio Torres; even Sue McSween had 50 acres of her 160-acre homestead in corn as of 1879.[20] Old John B. Wilson evidently handled his 7 acres by himself, as did the Brady family with their much larger 200 acres.

Wealth, or at least well-being, followed in the train of the land holdings. The amount of corn raised on the fifteen farms in 1879 was 21,116 bushels or 1,182,496 pounds, scarcely 2,000 bushels less than the amount that fifty-two farmers had reported for the crop year ending June 1, 1870. Where all of this corn was going as of 1879 is anyone's guess, and the Lincoln farmers may have been substantially overproducing. Montaño did have one good corn contract at Fort Stanton that year, but for only 150,000 pounds.

By the following year, Kansas contractors were winning bids at cut-rate prices and bringing in their own produce via the new railroad, thereby reducing or eliminating the market for local crops at least for a time. Given that situation, it's probable that people soon began searching for other uses for their land than raising the traditional corn and wheat. They may have cut down on the cultivated acreage altogether. This last trend, coupled with more diversified land ownership, was indeed shown by the 1885 territorial census. The major switch to new fruit and forage crops, especially alfalfa, already under way in the territory impacted Lincoln County mainly after 1890.[21]

Apart from the tight holdings of farm lands, the 1880 Census showed another peculiar condition at Lincoln. A high proportion of the households—39 of 167 or twenty percent —were headed by women. This by itself would have distinguished Lincoln from any other town in New Mexico, but even more remarkable, some 33 of these 39 family heads were widows. The possibility of their having been divorcees can be ruled out, since all but one (Sue McSween) were Hispanic. Perhaps some had been abandoned by their spouses, while others likely became widows through the death of their elderly partners. But more than half of these women were relatively young, in their twenties through their forties, and all but one (again, Sue McSween) had children.

The overall impression is that Lincoln in the aftermath of the Lincoln County War was a town of war widows. Census figures of the time document a higher mortality among Hispanic men from the Lincoln County violence than popular reports, mainly focusing on Anglo outlaws, have suggested. By 1885 the incidence of widows at Lincoln had dropped to 15 in a total of 180 families.[22]

Sue McSween didn't remain a widow for very long. She married George B. Barber on June 20, 1880. Barber came to Lincoln County in 1877 and worked as a surveyor, taking no part in the Lincoln County War. He bought A.A. McSween's extensive law library in the estate settlement and read law under Ira Leonard's tutelage, soon gaining admission to the New Mexico Bar. The Barbers began acquiring land at Three Rivers, starting with a Desert Land Claim, and by 1888 Sue claimed ownership of 1,158 acres at what was being called the Three Rivers Land & Cattle Company. She managed that while George Barber built a law practice in White Oaks and Lincoln. They divorced in 1892, and she continued to operate the ranch until 1902, when she sold it and moved to White Oaks.[23]

Pat Garrett and Billy the Kid

Pat F. Garrett also came to New Mexico during the Lincoln County War and stayed away from the fighting. He lived first at Fort Sumner; by the summer of 1880 he had moved to Roswell. With the support of John Chisum and other prominent Lincoln County citizens, Garrett won the Democratic nomination for sheriff as a law and order candidate in the 1880 elections. This no doubt reflected upon Sheriff Kimbrell's absence or inaction during the murderous spree in Lincoln over the Fourth of July. Garrett won the election on November 2, 1880, for a two-year term. Nine days later Governor Wallace issued commissions to all of the newly elected Lincoln County officials, but the sheriff-elect remained a deputy until he formally assumed office on January 1, 1881.[24] Concurrently he held appointment as a Deputy U.S. Marshal.

By November of 1880 Billy the Kid was heading a gang of desperadoes that ran stolen livestock between the Texas Panhandle, the Pecos country, and White Oaks, "equalizing the herds, but in true middlemen style they always make heavily by the transaction," as one newspaper put it.[25] The new sheriff-elect of Lincoln County caught up with these fugitives from justice at a place called Stinking Springs, east of Fort Sumner, where the Kid and three cohorts surrendered after a day-long siege that left Charles Bowdre dead. Their capture on December 23, 1880, received wide publicity, as did Bonney's subsequent incarceration and trial. By now he was being called Billy the Kid and his exploits had made him the most notorious outlaw in New Mexico.

Two things that the Kid lacked were friends and money. A slightly macabre sense of humor he did have. When he was brought to Mesilla for trial, few knew him by sight and someone asked, when the coach arrived at Las Cruces, which was Billy the Kid. Bonney answered by placing his hand on Ira Leonard's shoulder and saying "This is the man!" Leonard's response was not recorded but he must have taken it in stride since Judge Bristol

Sheriff Pat Garrett, the man who brought Billy down. President Theodore Roosevelt credited Garrett with introducing law and order to Lincoln. Photo Archives, Museum of New Mexico.

appointed him to defend the Kid on the charge of murdering "Buckshot" Roberts.[26]

Leonard gained an acquittal in that case, but with different court-appointed attorneys Bonney was tried and convicted of first-degree murder for killing Sheriff Brady. Judge Warren Bristol, who had an intimate familiarity with violence in Lincoln County, sentenced the Kid to be hanged by the neck until dead on May 13, 1881, in Lincoln County. The possemen who escorted him back to Lincoln for his hanging included J.B. Mathews, chief deputy of the posse that had killed Tunstall, and ex-outlaw John Kinney, who had fought on Sheriff Peppin's side during the Five-Days Battle. The entourage delivered their prisoner to Pat Garrett on April 21, 1881.[27]

Bonney's subsequent escape from the Lincoln County Courthouse, the so-called "Last Escape of Billy the Kid," is one of the most widely known escapades of the American West. The county had no proper jail, but did own a newly acquired courthouse, the old Murphy-Dolan store. After the Kid's return from Mesilla, Garrett confined him on the second story, in a room at the northeast corner. Deputy Sheriff J.W. Bell and Deputy U.S. Marshal Robert Olinger were assigned as guards. Bell apparently bore no grudge against the Kid, but Bonney and Olinger had a reciprocal hatred from fighting on opposite sides over the past years.

On the evening of April 28, Olinger escorted the other prisoners across the street to Wortley's Hotel for supper, leaving Bell with Billy the Kid. Garrett at the time was off in White Oaks collecting taxes, one of a sheriff's principal duties then. At the Kid's request, Bell accompanied him to a privy behind the courthouse. There are several versions as to what happened on the way back. Billy either concealed a pistol hidden for him in the outhouse or he raced up the stairs ahead of Bell and broke into the armory, snatching a gun there. Whichever the case, Bonney fired as Bell reached the landing partway up the staircase. One shot struck the deputy and he ran downstairs, out the door, and into the arms of the courthouse custodian, Godfrey Gauss, where he died.

The Kid meanwhile slipped his handcuffs, ran into Garrett's office and picked up a loaded double-barreled shotgun, then dashed to the east window of his guard-room. Olinger had come out of the hotel and started across the street when Gauss yelled that the Kid had killed Bell. Billy then shouted "Hello, old boy" from the window. Olinger glanced up and said "Yes, and he's killed me, too," just before the shotgun roared. The deputy died instantly, with eighteen buckshot in his chest and side.

The Kid, armed with two pistols and a Winchester, worked for an hour to loosen his leg shackles, eventually freeing only one. The townspeople were paralyzed. Gauss saddled a horse for him, and on the way from the courthouse Billy gave Olinger's body a tip of his boot, saying "You are not going to round me up again." He mounted and galloped west out of Lincoln, then turned north towards the community of Las Tablas. No one tried to follow.[28]

Bonney's spectacular escape captured the popular imagination and won him at least grudging respect from those who feared and disparaged him. He never returned to Lincoln and stayed on the run until Pat Garrett tracked him to Fort Sumner and shot him dead in Pete Maxwell's bedroom the night of July 14, 1881.[29] The abundant legends surrounding the life and times of Billy the Kid, already in the making when he was shot down, have continued to build ever since.

A New Scandal in Old Lincoln

Attorney Ira Leonard stayed busy in the aftermath of the Lincoln County War. He generally picked the losing side in any contest. During the summer of 1881 his conduct on behalf of one client kept the citizens intrigued for some months. A Mrs. Ella F. Murphy, employed

Deputy U.S. Marshall Robert Olinger, ill-fated guardian of Billy the Kid. Courtesy Lincoln County Heritage Trust, Lincoln, N.M.

briefly as a teacher at the Mescalero Agency, had been kicked off the Reservation on the grounds that she was incompetent, untruthful, lewd, and had been twice intoxicated while on the job, according to the agent. On August 8, 1881, she showed up in Lincoln and obtained a position teaching the school there for one month. Ira Leonard listened to her woes and then wrote to the Commissioner of Indian Affairs, charging that the Mescalero Agent was a brute and a "white demon . . . devoid of every principle of manhood . . . entirely unfit to occupy a position of trust."[30]

This brought a special agent from the Indian Bureau in Washington. He investigated the affair, then told Leonard that he had been duped by a scheming woman and the agency would have been justified in setting her adrift much sooner. Indeed she was already having an affair with the county clerk, Ben Ellis, that had blossomed into a local social scandal. She lived, at the time, in the same house as Leonard's own family and began to stir up trouble between the attorney and Ellis, who was one of his business associates, by claiming to have bought property owned jointly by the two men and then ordering the counselor to vacate his office in the building. He refused, whereupon, reported one paper,

> an attempt was then made to unroof his [Leonard's] office, but the shotgun argument was persuasive enough to put a stop to the rash proceedings, and Ellis was told that this persecution must cease, or open hostilities would be declared.

The lawyer retaliated anyway by investigating Ellis' handling of accounts of the county clerk. Ellis promptly left for Santa Fe and Leonard waded through the records, finding enough evidence of criminal conduct, so he thought, to send a man to the penitentiary. The news account continued,

> Ellis was found to have forged warrants on the school fund to a large amount, falsified the records and misappropriated funds in his keeping.

At some point Mrs. Murphy skipped out as well. When heard from again, Ben Ellis was somewhere in the southern country.[31] Later that year he returned.

The Economy Expands, Slowly

In the midst of such goings-on, anyone who looked at the Territorial Bureau of Immigration's new ten-page pamphlet on Lincoln County, published in 1881, and had the least acquaintance with the country must have wondered where the pamphlet's writer found this earthly paradise for ranchers, farmers, and miners. The booklet was long on promotion and short on actual descriptions, but it amounted to the first positive statement about Lincoln County in a long time.[32] Everything, whether coal, fish, or vegetable, was "exhaustless" or grew to astonishing size and perfection. That same year a reporter commented favorably on the alfalfa and apples being raised at Charles Fritz' Spring Ranch.[33] These would soon become important new crops in that region of New Mexico.

Ranching rapidly became a corporate business, dependent upon foreign or eastern capital. Among the British-owned ranches in northern Lincoln County were L.G. Murphy's former spread, now the Carrizozo Land and Cattle Co.; the El Capitan Land and Cattle Co., headquartered at Richardson (formerly Las Tablas); and the Angus V.V. Ranch on Little Creek. Charles Fritz was the only person in the Lincoln community with a significant number of cattle; he owned more than 1,500 head. Other large ranchers with at least 3,000 animals were Pat Coghlan at Tularosa, the W.E. Anderson Cattle Co., Holt Cattle Co., Phelps White, Wm. Roberts, and George W. Williams, none of whom had offices at Lincoln. Antonio Torres reported 2,000 sheep in 1885; he may have had the only herd in the

Lincoln area.[34] Elsewhere in Lincoln County, probably on the Pecos slope, the county assessor found over 105,000 sheep and 173,858 head of cattle in 1885.[35]

Mining was slow to develop, mainly due to the twin plagues of speculation and lack of capital. One of the ways to make money in mining was to buy claims, then "boom" or promote the mining district and sell out the claims at a profit, meanwhile doing little or no development work. Shakespeare in southwestern New Mexico was an infamous example of this system at work. The White Oaks district likewise attracted speculators' attentions.[36]

In the early 1880s newspaper articles about Lincoln County mines hailed the prospects of the Vera Cruz District, about halfway between Fort Stanton and White Oaks. Actually very little happened there, due to a lack of capital. As one White Oaks newspaper explained, ownership of the Vera Cruz Mining Co. was controlled by eastern parties "unacquainted with mining, whose timidity has kept it idle for two year[s] and a half."[37]

The situation in White Oaks at that time was not much different; mining languished until 1884 and the first real production came in 1885. The problems were remoteness and a lack of capital. Money that was spent went for equipment and freight. White Oaks had an estimated population of 500 in 1880; after production started it rose to a peak of 2,500 as of 1892. Shortly after the turn of the century, the mines closed and the community slowly faded away. Instead of a rip-roaring, wide-open western boom town, White Oaks had been a staid, orderly place, sometimes with only a single saloon.[38]

Institutions and the Lincoln Community

The appearance of corporate ranching and mining operations helped to tame Lincoln County's frontier image. Even more significant were the institutions established during Governor Wallace's term and in the years immediately following. Juan Patron's Lincoln County Rifles disbanded in July of 1879, but other militia companies soon sprang up around southern New Mexico, notably the Shakespeare Militia Company in August, the Mesilla Independent Cavalry, a company at Las Cruces during November, and a "mutual aid and protection society" at Seven Rivers by March of 1880.[39] A new territorial Militia Law enacted in January 1880 regularized these volunteer companies; within two years southern New Mexico had seven of them. They did good service in scouting against the Apache chief Victorio, ridding the territory of John Kinney's outlaws, and, later, in fighting Geronimo's Apaches.[40]

The idea of livestock owners forming associations to protect their members' mutual interests, such as capturing rustlers, came late to New Mexico. During the Lincoln County War it was every rancher for himself. The cattle thieves pretty much had their own way. When the concept of stock raisers' organizations did arrive, it caught on rapidly. The Southwestern Stockmen's Association effected a permanent organization in Silver City on January 17, 1881; it may have been the first one.[41] In November 1882 the Cattle Protective Association was organized at Socorro to fight an epidemic of rustlers; the following March saw the Doña Ana County Stock Association formed. The Lincoln County Stock Association evidently began in 1882 and by January of 1886 its eighty-seven members claimed ownership of 286,800 head of cattle, horses, and mules.[42] Establishment of a territory-wide stock growers association dates from March of 1884.[43] These well-organized, well-financed organizations made rustling far more hazardous.

Schools also arrived late in Lincoln County. Back in 1871 the territorial legislature had established a common school system supported by tax monies.[44] Whether under this law or as a private subscription system, similar to the school Lily Klasner attended on the Hondo, Lincoln had a school by 1872 with Juan Patron as the schoolmaster. How long it lasted is uncertain, since taxes at times went uncollected while embezzlements of county funds continued periodically.[45]

The 1884 Legislature created a new educational system. Every county had a school superintendent who oversaw the school districts in that county. Each district in turn had its own director, responsible to the superintendent. Districts coincided with the voting precincts, the populous precincts having more than one school, while a few lacked any school. By June of 1885 Lincoln County had twenty-two school districts with 159 students in District No. 1 (Lincoln) and $852.31 apportioned for their education. A schoolhouse was then being built directly east of the courthouse. When school opened on October 12 schoolmaster Lee H. Rudisille had to use the county court room since the new school still wasn't finished.[46]

Churches were another institution. As of 1869 the Diocese of Santa Fe recognized a new parish of Rio Bonito. At some later time, jurisdiction was transferred to the Tucson diocese.[47] No priest was assigned, nor was there as much as a chapel for many years. Protestant services were first conducted by the Reverend Taylor Ealy, whose arrival on February 19, 1878, the reader will recall, had coincided with John H. Tunstall's body being brought into town. Ealy and his family stayed for just over five months and they were only too happy to leave at the end of the Five-Days Battle.[48]

By February of 1884 Lincoln had a subscription campaign under way for a church. Reverend J.M. Garnier, the parish priest at Tularosa, was the moving spirit at Lincoln as well. The building they got was the old courthouse, which, ironically, was also the home of John B. Wilson's saloon. Wilson had mortgaged this building to someone, but Father Garnier paid the mortgage and interest in June of 1884. The following February the property was deeded over to Archbishop Lamy.[49]

As soon as the mortgage was paid, Father Garnier began renovating the saloon as a chapel and residence, with the parishioners contributing labor, materials, and cash. Work continued into the fall, and by the following February it was sufficiently complete for the building to be used:

> Yesterday was the first day of Lent, and the church was well filled at this place at an early hour. Mass will be held every day during the Lenten season, at the church in Lincoln.[50]

Father Garnier liked bells and he ordered one weighing 800 pounds from Henry Stuckstede & Co., Brass and Bell Founders, of St. Louis. It cost $160.00 plus another $41.35 to have J.J. Dolan freight it down from Las Vegas. The bell arrived in Lincoln about the last of March 1885 and was installed in the new chapel.[51] Finally, on June 23 the congregation held their dedication:

> The exercises commenced at 6 o'clock, by six little boys, in costume, entering the church followed by the priest, who made their way to the altar, where a long and beautiful prayer was offered. After a song by the choir, Rev. Garnier, the priest, made the address of the evening. He thanked the people of Lincoln, both Protestants and Catholics, for their liberal contributions, said it showed the good feeling existing between the natives and Americans, and that such united actions would tend to make all more friendly and neighborly. His address was in Spanish, and was said by those who understood the language, to have been beautiful and scholarly.
>
> After prayer and singing, the bell was baptised. Mrs. Capt. Baca, in whose honor the bell was named (Maria Juana), acted as God-mother. The bell was trimmed with beautiful flowers and ribbons and the walls of the room and altar were decorated with cedars, transparencies, and a profusion of American flags, showing splendid taste throughout. During the exercises Prof. Montano's orchestra rendered some very pretty selections suitable for the occasion.

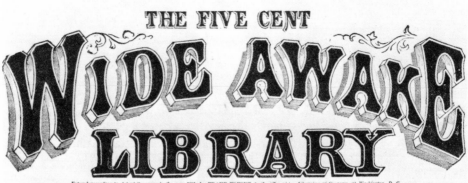

Cover of a popular magazine depicting the Kid. The Five Cent Wide Awake Library, *August 29, 1881.*

The bell is small, weighing only 850 pounds when ready for hanging, but its tone is loud and melodious, and will probably serve the church for a good many years in calling its members together.[52]

The converted building served for about a year and a half. Then on November 22, 1886, the "Catolicos del Rio Bonito" met and set things in motion, again under Father Garnier's direction, for the construction of a new house of worship in Lincoln. Once more the congregation pledged money, livestock, and construction materials. Subscriptions came in so rapidly that a contract for laying the foundation was let on March 14, 1887, and the work completed in less than a month, whereupon the same contractor—Refugio Chavez y Archuleta—also built the walls. The furnishings and bell were moved from the chapel, which then became the priest's residence, or *convento*. The church was dedicated to San Juan on his day, June 25, 1887. Like many early buildings at Lincoln, the San Juan Church is still in use today.[53]

President Theodore Roosevelt credited Sheriff Pat Garrett with introducing law and order to New Mexico, more properly to Lincoln County.[54] Rough spots still lay ahead, but things were never so bad as they had been before Garrett's term. One crying need was for a new jail. The county commissioners awarded Will Dowlin the contract to build a three-cell frame jail on February 18, 1881. This took him almost eleven months to build, at a generous price of $5,500. Even so, the building was evidently in bad shape within a few years.[55]

Pat Garrett chose not to run for sheriff in 1882 and instead he became a candidate for election to the Governor's Council, the territorial equivalent of a state senate. A Las Cruces newspaper made Garrett himself an issue in the election by manufacturing charges that went back to his nomination two years before, also claiming that the "newspaper notoriety" from killing Billy the Kid had upset his brain. Garrett allegedly questioned a Lincoln attorney named W.M. Roberts about the tipoff to the press, but Roberts denied it. Nevertheless, Garrett beat him over the head with a long-barrelled Colt .45, knocking him senseless in the street outside J.A. LaRue's store. This fueled the opposition to Garrett, but on election day he still carried Lincoln County handsomely, while failing to capture the votes in Grant and Doña Ana counties and thereby losing the race.[56]

Garrett's assault might actually have had some other basis; we have only one side of that story. The following summer the press reported an obscure news item that "W.M. Roberts, the Lincoln county forger, has been sentenced to ten years in the penitentiary."[57]

Garrett's successors were two very capable and efficient lawmen, John W. Poe (January 1883 through 1885) and James Brent (January 1886 through 1888), both of whom served three years in consequence of Poe resigning the office as of December 31, 1885.[58] Brent, in fact, was a deputy under Sheriff Poe. Malefactors were assured of either courtroom justice or the more summary kind. When a Texan named Pearl killed a private at Fort Stanton, the post commander barely saved the offender from instant vengeance by the soldier's buddies. Two days later he was taken to Lincoln and clapped into jail. There, however,

> between 12 and 1 o'clock Monday night some thirteen soldiers arrived at Lincoln, and going to the jail broke the door locks, led the murderer forth, conveyed him some half a mile from the prison, in the direction of the Fort, where they hung him to a tree, and then fired into his swinging carcass some nine bullets.[59]

In January of 1884 Nicolas Aragon and another man stole some horses in Lincoln County. Deputy Jim Brent and a posse captured the two and jailed them in Lincoln. On May 28 Aragon broke out of jail and made good his escape. In October, Deputy Sheriff Jasper Corn of Lincoln County learned that Aragon had been seen in his old haunts near Gallinas Springs

Three sheriffs of Lincoln County. Left to right: Pat Garrett, January 1881–December 1882; James Brent, January 1886–December 1888; and John Poe, January 1883–December 1885. Photo Archives, Museum of New Mexico.

in San Miguel County and went after him. The pursuit ended in Corn's death. Three months later, Sheriff Poe rode back to the same neighborhood with Deputy John Hurley and several others after they'd learned of Aragon's return. On January 25, 1885, they caught up with him. After a two-day siege in bitter cold temperatures, the desperado's ammunition ran out and he finally surrendered. Aragon had been wounded at several places but he hit Johnny Hurley with a fatal shot through the bowels. Poe and Deputy Jim Brent took Aragon on to Santa Fe and lodged him in the penitentiary. That summer he was tried in Santa Fe and acquitted on the charge of murdering Hurley. On a change of venue, a Colfax County jury found Aragon guilty of second-degree murder for killing Jasper Corn and gave him a life sentence.[60]

By the mid-1880s Lincoln was leaving its past behind and looking towards the future. Ranching, agriculture, and, especially, mining took hold of peoples' interests. The violence of the years before was virtually forgotten. Within the territory very little about Lincoln's notorious past appeared in print, with the exception of Pat Garrett's biography *The Authentic Life of Billy, the Kid*. Garrett, still Lincoln County sheriff when it appeared, made his reasons for writing it crystal clear as he replied to criticism that his interests were purely mercenary:

> Both of these delectable hermits charge me with intent to publish a life of the Kid, with the nefarious object of making money thereby. O! asinine propellers of Faber's No. 2; O! ludificatory lavishers of Arnold's night-tinted fluid; what the Hades else do you suppose my object could be?[61]

~ 14 ~

1885: BOOM TIMES IN LINCOLN COUNTY

Prosperity finally arrived for Lincoln and the citizens of Lincoln County. Announced an area newspaper,

> The people here have gone to work. Every man who wants work can now readily get it, either in the mines, on the ranches, or in any of the various avocations of busy life best adapted to his talents.[1]

Indeed, by April 1885 the local press reported that there were probably 150 men at work in and close by Lincoln.

> Great as has been the advance in our mining interests, it has not been able to keep pace with the increase in live stock. Three years ago our vast pasture lands were almost destitute of herds; the gangs of rustlers that then infested the country having made legitimate stock-raising a very unprofitable and hazardous business. Now this county ranks second in the Territory in the number and value of her herds.[2]

The boom in the range cattle industry during the 1880s did have a major impact on Lincoln County. The county assessor valued 104,215 head of cattle in July of 1884. A year later the number had increased to 173,858 and by January of 1886 Lincoln County Stock Association members reportedly owned the phenomenal total of 286,800 cattle, horses, and mules.[3] By comparison, the 1982 New Mexico livestock inventory showed 303,000 cattle of all kinds for Lincoln, Chaves, Eddy, and Lea counties, a very rough equivalent in area to Lincoln County in 1885. However, half or more of these cattle were on feed rather than on the range.[4]

We probably know more about Lincoln as a community in 1885 than from any other time. This is because of a territorial census taken that year and the survival of a nearly complete run of the local newspaper, the *Golden Era*, which had an extraordinary content of local area news.

The community profile for 1885 showed 744 people living as 180 families in the Lincoln precinct. Both totals were up slightly from 1880. The great majority of the people were Hispanic and from New Mexico, their names showing a mixture of old residents with newer arrivals. "Laborer" was still the predominant occupation cited, with 80 claiming it, but ranchman and ranch owner rated second (33). Gardener and planter ranked third (27); apparently no one wanted to be called a farmer. However people in agriculture chose to identify themselves, production was higher than ever with 23,645 bushels of corn (= 1,324,120 pounds) reported for 1884 on only 1,112 tilled acres. This acreage was down by almost half from 1880. At the same time, ownership or control of farmlands had become more diffuse and twenty producers now contributed significantly to the corn harvest. Wheat and oats were the other important field or forage crops listed in the census, although the local paper noted many large green fields of alfalfa along the Rio Bonito that spring.[5]

Charles Fritz seems to have been the model farmer. The newspaper visited his Spring Ranch nine miles below Lincoln and found

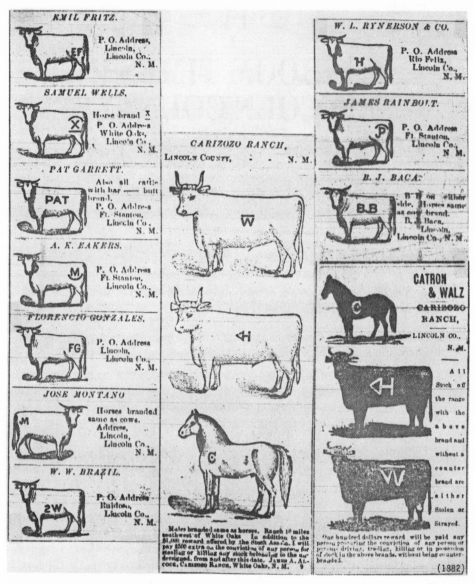

Lincoln County stock brands, 1882–1884. The cattle industry boomed in Lincoln during the 1880s. Printed in White Oaks Golden Era.

it is one of the most desirable places in the territory. Mr. Chas. Fritz, the owner of the ranch, showed us around the same and well he may feel proud of it. His orchard is loaded with fruit, fine apples and pears, and most of the trees are so heavily burdened that braces are required to hold the limbs up. He will have three or four thousand bushels of apples alone. His corn will yield fifty or sixty bushels to the acre, and his alfalfa will run about two tons to the acre. This last crop is about ready to cut again, making the fifth time it has been cut this season. Excellent spring water flows around the front and one side of the house constantly, along side of beautiful cottonwood trees.[6]

Unfortunately Fritz had little time remaining to enjoy this; he had Bright's disease and passed away on December 3, 1885.

Lincoln reported no mines, mills, or other types of industry in 1885 and instead of thirty-three self-proclaimed ranchers, the census statistics revealed that there were really only two—Charles Fritz with 1,565 head of cattle and Antonio Torres with 2,000 sheep. The other ranchmen mostly held no stock while some of them were probably employed by the large individual and corporate ranches elsewhere in Lincoln County. Lincoln was a trading center for the ranchers, with eight merchants competing for their business. Two lawyers, a blacksmith, one tailor, and conceivably the newspaper editor, filled the need for professional services. Mrs. Ben Ellis kept the Lincoln Hotel. The number of households headed by widowed women, one of the singular features of the 1880 Census, was down to fifteen in 1885.

More indicative of community prosperity was the amount of building activity. One of the old-line merchants, Isaac Ellis, laid the foundation for his new store in early March 1884. The following January he sold his stock of dry goods to Rocco Emilio, who renovated Ellis' old quarters in the Lincoln County courthouse and opened his own general grocery and dry goods store there.[7] J.J. Dolan made improvements in the former Tunstall store, putting in new shelving, repainting, installing a fire- and burglar-proof safe besides adding a

> very fine platform and awning along the entire front of his building, which will add greatly to the comfort and appearance of his rooms, as well as affording a pleasant place for a siesta these quiet October evenings.[8]

To stock these emporiums, the paper reported that Dolan was getting in oodles of new goods, hauled in by his own ten-mule teams, while other freight teams unloaded at the warerooms of Montaño & Sais. The dissolution of this partnership was announced on July 2, 1885, scarcely a month after Johnny Whelan made arrangements to go into the grocery business at a location near the court house.[9]

Retail merchants were not the only optimists. By March 1885 Ygnacio Sena had finished a new building directly east of J.J. Dolan's store for Sena's blacksmith and repair shop. Just at this time J.A. Tomlinson got his photographic gallery into running order. Mrs. Ellis added two rooms to her house, duly announced by a new ad for the Lincoln Hotel, of which she was the proprietress. S.A. Johnson leased the hotel from her in November. The boom continued through the end of the year, when the foundation was nearing completion for Judge Tomlinson's new drug store and photograph building, and James H. Carpenter laid the foundation for a furniture store. Whereas most people built with adobe, Carpenter intended to make his establishment of stone, with a deep basement.[10] J.J. Dolan entered the new year by adding to his recently renovated building:

> Dolan is having quite an addition built on the west end of his store. This will give him one of the largest store rooms in the county, and Jimmy knows how to run it too.[11]

Lawrence G. Murphy once had a brewery on the Rio Bonito just off the eastern end of the Fort Stanton Military Reservation.[12] Now, in 1885, Lincoln residents were pleasantly surprised to learn that a new, two-story adobe building for a brewery located *above* Fort Stanton would soon be completed.[13] That fall it was ready for operation:

> The new brewery, above Stanton will commence turning out beer week after next. Messrs. Biederman & Rufley have a brewer direct from Germany to take charge of the work, and promise an article superior to any shipped into the country.[14]

Stores in town began saving their empty beer bottles for recycling to the new plant. Finally, on Christmas Eve the first run was ready:

> Messrs. Biederman & Rufley, the brewers above Stanton, sent down their first installment of beer, Thursday, and left a keg for the sawed-offs on THE ERA to sample. We were a little foolish in sampling the beverage before we finished what work we had on hand, for after drinking the first glass we staid out most of the night and felt bad all the next day. These gentlemen are making an excellent quality of beer, and when it is once thoroughly introduced, bottled beer will be shelved and keg beer will be on tap. Thanks, gentlemen.[15]

Unfortunately the subsequent history of this potent brew and its makers is not known.

New homes were also the order of the day. In 1884 George Peppin built his family "one of the most comfortable residences in Lincoln."[16] By the following April, Saturnino Baca finished adding two rooms to his house while adobes were being made up for the new residence of Rocco Emilio, the merchant who had replaced Isaac Ellis in the court house. By May, both Dolan and attorney George T. Beall had men at work making 20,000 adobes for use in erecting their new homes. Scipio Salazar moved to Lincoln from Las Tablas and promptly laid the foundation for a new dwelling.[17] Johnny Hurley's property also had a new addition. By the third week in October, the Dolan's new house was ready. Mrs. Ellis, having leased out the Lincoln Hotel, had men at work by the end of the year building a new house directly east of the court house.[18]

Some of this energy went into public buildings. John B. Wilson's saloon was purchased and turned into a church by February of 1885. Some time in June men began making adobes for the new school house, to be erected "directly east of the courthouse." That particular neighborhood must have been getting crowded. The school was still under construction in October but it may have been completed by the end of the year.[19] The court house came in for attention, too, with the construction of a vault for the safekeeping of county records in the northeastern corner of the first floor. More repairs and renovations continued there through 1886.[20]

Problems such as fires were bound to happen. On March 31 the court house fell a victim when the chimney in the sheriff's office "burnt out" and from appearances it looked like flames were enveloping the building. The reporter's concern about what could happen if a fire did break out was no doubt genuine, since the newspaper rented two rooms in the court house for its office.[21] Just behind the court house too things had been lively:

> A fire broke out about 8 o'clock this morning in the main room of the jail at this place, and if Jailor Lea had not have been close by it would have resulted in the cremation of two of the prisoners. It happened in this way. Mr. Lea had made a fire in the stove a few minutes before and a catridge happened to be among the chips. When the wood caught a fire, the catridge exploded, forcing a live coal from the front of the stove, which ignited in a pair of pants hanging on the wall. Two prisoners were in the cell opposite the main room and they immediately shouted for help, but it was not until they were nearly suffocated before the desired assistance arrived.

The side and top of the room was burnt to a crisp and had it been allowed to burn ten minutes longer nothing could have saved it.[22]

The jailor, J.C. Lea, had another tense moment in June. One of the prisoners sought to break out when it was time to go into his cell at night. The man threw an iron hearth which glanced off the jailor's head and then fled out the door as Lea cocked his .41 Colt. Mr. Lea pumped four bullets into the would-be escapee and he fell dead in the jail yard instead.[23] By July 2, three of the other prisoners were on their way to the penitentiary, smiling and seeming "to be perfectly contented with their lot," perhaps remembering the lot of their fellow jailbird just three weeks before. The only person still incarcerated in the Lincoln County calabozo was allowed to exercise his artistic talent:

> There is only one prisoner left in the county Jail, and he has decorated the cells and main corridor in a manner becoming one used to handling the brush. He letters very nicely and upon entering the jail, the words "Those who enter here leave all hopes behind," are in plain view. Over his cell the word "welcome" appears, while over the ones just vacated "to let" and "vacant."[24]

Gallows humor indeed.

Technological advances were coming. According to a news item in the summer of 1884 a telephone line was to connect Fort Stanton, which had not even had a telegraph connection until several years earlier, with the Mescalero Apache Agency. The line was working by the late fall of 1885.[25] Civilian communities had to wait much longer for telephone service; Roswell had a system in operation by 1900 and Lincoln had at least one telephone in 1905.

When the first term of a public school in Lincoln got under way in October 1885, forty scholars were in attendance, roughly twenty-five percent of the school-age children in the precinct. In those days students everywhere were examined publicly at the end of a term, when they gave recitations and poetry readings, put on skits and the like to display their new knowledge. At Lincoln this happened on Christmas Eve of 1885:

> The exercises at the school house Christmas eve were well attended, and the schol- ars did very well indeed. The room was decorated with evergreens, and the tree, as it hung full of presents, was a pretty sight. Everything passed off pleasantly, and the little folks were never happier.

The schoolteacher, Lee Rudisille, was happy, too, since he received a contract for the new three-month term.[26]

Lincoln also had a holiday tradition of a Christmas ball. It was held Christmas night at Sais' hall, which as the reporter noted was becoming too crowded for the occasion. The musicians came all the way from Albuquerque. Good order and feeling prevailed the entire evening, in contrast with what might have happened a few years before. The society editor described how Lincoln's citizens turned out in their best regalia for this occasion:

> The bon ton were all out wearing their best clothes. The ladies were well dressed, as usual, and looked too nice to hug, and where all appeared to the reporter like queens of some enchanted fairy land he has made no odious distinctions. As to the men—he has roped in a few specialties.
>
> Scripio Salazar wore tight pants and a dark colored roundabout with a long tail, and hair dressed down with a hat rack. Atanacio Martinez had on a red necktie import- ed from Fort Stanton, a black moustache dressed pompadour, and his best suit of mixed goods. Col. Brent wore blue pants, with overskirt of same ornamented with gold mounted brass buttons. Will Ellis had a frilled three-inch collar and gros-grained wedding garments, but sat a way back in one corner, his countenance ornamented with a second-hand grin, but did not dance—said he was not feeling well. Smith Lea

Lincoln's prosperity led to great merriment. The Curry-Thornton Saloon (earlier the Lincoln Saloon), ca. 1883. Courtesy Special Collections, University of Arizona Library.

The Lincoln Saloon, ca. 1906. Courtesy Special Collections, University of Arizona Library.

was gotten up regardless of expense, in a bombazine cashmere suit all of a kind and trimmed with leather belting cut bias. Jones Taliaferro wore flowing pants embroidered around the edges with worsted ruchings, and a Prince Albert coat polka-dotted with olemargarine. Charley Buford waltzed around the room wearing an undressed buckskin wamus ornamented with polished steel buttons as large as lamp reflectors, and also wore brown doeskin breeches and red leggins trimmed with bugles and rawhide tapaderos. Pat F. Garrett drove in with Mrs. Garrett, and appeared at the dance in a suit of the latest style of woolen clothes and tight boots, and looked tall enough for two. Clarence Warfield was in from the big government grocery at the post, and skipped through the sinuous measures of the Mexican quadrille in spike-tailed coat, satin drawers, and cotton socks. Murry Ellis did the same in cow-hide boots, and a suit of brown nuns' veiling cut gored and garnished with leather strings and gunny sack fringe around the bottom—hair pasted down with goat ile and a flat-iron. Charlie Bell was conspicuous in diagonal overalls trimmed with basket pleating, and coat too short to speak of—feet well developed.

Many other killing get-ups were present, but some one brushed the reporter off the door step just then and by the time he was able to prove his identity once more the dance was over and the key hole plugged up.[27]

Presumably the reporter had sobered up after sampling the first batch of local brew the evening before.

With this report on its 1885 yuletide festivities, Lincoln ended a year of impressive achievements.

⌒ 15 ⌒

THE LATER YEARS

1886–1913

Two Legal Hangings

Lincoln would soon see changes, but first the community witnessed an efficient law-and-order system at work. John Janes was tried, convicted, and sentenced to death in Lincoln County district court for murdering one Denham while they were out on the Llano Estacado the previous November.[1] Sheriff Jim Brent carried out Janes' execution "in a most perfect manner, the condemned dying without a tremor, and not a bungle occurring." The press went on to describe the event:

> The scaffold was erected in the jail yard, but a large crowd gathered to witness it, many of whom obtained admission to the grounds, while others occupied the windows of the court house. The prisoner remained comparatively easy during the morning, only complaining that the execution did not occur earlier. At half past one o'clock he was placed in position on the scaffold, the parish priest accompanying and administering the last sad rites to him.
>
> He was asked if he had anything to say, as is usually the custom but he did [not] make any remarks until after the rope was adjusted when he said "good-bye boys; God bless you all," and the black cap was drawn down and the trap sprung. So perfectly was everything arranged that his neck was broken instantly and there was not a struggle.[2]

This was quite in contrast with the spectacle that accompanied William Wilson's hanging at Lincoln almost eleven years before. Janes paid the penalty on June 18, 1886, Lincoln's second legal execution. His crime was described as having been heartless and cruel; shooting a companion in the back for his horse and a little money.

D.C. Johnson witnessed all of this from his jail cell where he was being held for the murder of a storekeeper in Tularosa cañon just eight days before. At the fall term of court he confessed and the jury took only ten minutes to find him guilty, setting the punishment at death by hanging. When he fell through the trap at Lincoln on November 19, 1886, the affair rated only one paragraph in the newspaper.[3]

Boom times for Lincoln continued at least through 1886. In March of that year the Santa Fe *Daily New Mexican* stated that

> Lincoln has been having a steady improvement during the past year. Since last April there have been completed nine new houses for dwelling and business places. Three more are nearly completed, and three new foundations have been laid within the last three weeks. . . . The foundation of Jack Weldon's and Vick's new saloon is now completed.[4]

Another paper confirmed the bustle in Lincoln but added a disturbing note:

> Lincoln has doubled its number of buildings in the past year. The cattle ranges are very dry and no grass the Angus "V" especially so.[5]

151

Lincoln and the Range Cattle Industry

While some newspaper accounts from 1886 told of a long, continued drought in Lincoln County, others claimed that cattle on the ranges owned by Riley and Rynerson on the Tularosa were in excellent condition, that the Agua Chiquita (vicinity of Weed, N.M.) had had good rain and every cow and cowman was happy, and that an overflow had ruined the corn crop for the year on the lower Peñasco![6] These conflicting reports suggest that the drought was localized and had little long-term effect on the range cattle industry. The more serious problem of overstocked ranges, especially in Lincoln County, was just gaining recognition.[7]

The prices for range beef dropped in 1887 and 1888, recovered somewhat, and slumped again in the early 1890s. Then, as now, livestock brought variable prices depending upon grade, condition, and market demands. One Carrizozo shipper received "the largest price New Mexico cattle have ever sold for" in May of 1887 while the El Capitan Land & Cattle Company sold their one-, two-, and three-year-old steers at $14., $18., and $23. per head in September 1889—"the best sale they have made for several years."[8] What was good for the range cattle business was good for Lincoln.

Through at least the spring of 1887 the cattle business was "looking up lively," as they said, and a group of local ranchers with familiar names—Wm. L. Rynerson, J.J. Dolan, J.A. LaRue, the Fritz brothers, Numa Reymond, and others—incorporated themselves as the Felix Cattle Co. With 5,000 head they still ranked as a small outfit. Dolan became the manager. They evidently met with all the calamities—rustlers, low prices, overstocked and depleted rangelands, droughts—that other cattle companies experienced during the early 1890s and sold off their herds in 1897 when range cattle prices improved.[9] The heyday of the large cattle ranches was a short one, only ten to twenty years, and even at the time some cattlemen were thinking that a cattle-feeding operation could produce a better profit than an open-range business.[10]

The Pecos Valley Develops

The New Mexico Legislature passed a law in 1887 that allowed companies to organize and sell stock for the purpose of constructing irrigation canals and reservoirs, with the object of promoting settlement and developing farm lands.[11] Cattlemen Pat Garrett and Charles B. Eddy quickly seized upon this to organize the Pecos Valley Irrigation and Investment Company, which built the Northern canal system. Others followed suit, until by 1890 eighteen of the thirty-two incorporated irrigation companies in New Mexico lay in Lincoln County. Even J.J. Dolan and Wm. L. Rynerson hedged their livestock interests by forming the Guadalupe Valley Reservoir Irrigating and Manufacturing Company to take waters from the lower Rio Peñasco by a canal twenty miles long. This proposal led immediately to litigation with the farmers at Hope, a recent settlement on the lower Peñasco.[12]

These new developments affected Lincoln in several ways. By 1889 small ditches taken from springs and surface streams in the Roswell area already watered more than 2,000 acres there. Roswell itself was booming and drawing a number of professional people away from Lincoln.[13] When the large irrigation companies failed, interest only shifted to the Roswell Artesian Basin that later assured a steady supply of water for irrigation. The 1889 Legislature voted to split off the eastern three-fifths of Lincoln County—the Pecos Valley and everything east to the Texas line, to form Chaves and Eddy counties. The developers undoubtedly inspired this law, which went into effect on January 1, 1891.

Economic opportunities in the Pecos Valley were drawing people from all over, including the older settled sections of Lincoln County. Farming itself changed to meet the needs of ranchers and stock-feeders:

> Range cattle can not compete in the eastern market with grain fed stock, and cattle-men are coming more and more to the conclusion that in order to make their business profitable they will be compelled to feed the stock intended for early spring market.[14]

Already one Roswell farmer had about 400 acres in alfalfa; as of 1889, over 24 percent of the tilled lands in still-undivided Lincoln County produced alfalfa. Along the tributaries to the west, the crops raised were largely for forage. While Lincoln's farmers kept pace with the changes in crops, the economic importance of the Bonito and Ruidoso valleys was dwindling by comparison with the new wealth from the Pecos Valley.

The "Old Town" of Lincoln

Lincoln in 1888 boasted five general mercantiles, three attorneys, two blacksmiths, one shoemaker, a photographer, and a druggist, plus a billiard hall and a livery stable.[15] Yet by the next summer it had no newspaper, this loss being a temporary one. Remarks in the Roswell paper about Lincoln coming to life for an upcoming term of court or the problem of getting a crowd in the town suggest that economic stagnation had already set in:

> The old town of Lincoln has again been aroused from its regular semi-annual sleep by the advent of the court and numerous contestants and witnesses, together with a goodly sprinkling of lawyers. The business men, all, have put their best foot forward ready for the rush of the coming week, the residents have cleaned up their yards and re-plastered the ancient adobes, hotels are busy, new restaurants have suddenly been started all along the single street, while the owners of private residences which have more rooms than is needed for their own use are rapidly filling them with lodgers, who are very glad indeed to pay a good round rent for them; the saloons have bands of music playing a merry accompaniment to the jingle of the glasses at the bar, while speculators in ivory abound on every side, ready and eager to build their stacks into towers of wealth; indeed the old town has taken on an air of business that is really encouraging.[16]

The revived *Lincoln Independent* replied with a touch of envy:

> Roswell is growing, slowly but surely. She now has sixty houses within her limits and it is safe to say by this time next year she will have 160. Roswell is all right.[17]

Unfortunately the published 1890 Census tells us little about Lincoln beyond the county's population total, which was 7,081. The decline in the number of school-age children at Lincoln, from 128 in December 1889 to 102 in January 1891, showed that the town was losing population. School enrollments were low too; Prof. B.J. Baca had about thirty pupils as of mid-March 1891.[18] Lincoln and Lincoln County already seem to have been genuinely depressed two years before the onset of a national depression in 1893:

> There is nothing Lincoln county needs so much as money to stimulate her industries. If this whole country had $50 per capita—instead of $5, as now estimated, our mines would boom, railroads would come in bringing immigration, create a demand for home products, stimulate the stock interests, everybody would prosper and this country blossom as the rose.[19]

Some Lincoln citizens had probably moved to White Oaks, which was booming then, thanks to development of the Old Abe mine.

Lincoln's main street, ca. 1910. Photo Archives, Museum of New Mexico.

Cocktail hour at the Penfield (Tunstall) Store, ca. 1920s. Courtesy Special Collections, University of Arizona Library.

The economy never revived. In 1894 the best offer at a probated property sale fell far short of expectations

> owning [*sic*] to the stringent time and scarcity of money, and [the] real estate [being] listed in a dull and non-progressive town.[20]

Through the last twenty years of the territorial period, Lincoln slumbered for about eleven months of the year, arousing itself for the semi-annual terms of the district court, then lapsing back.

Yet Lincoln did not live in the past. From 1889 on, a Lincoln baseball team scheduled games with Roswell, Fort Stanton, and White Oaks players. The high point for the Lincoln team came about 1891:

> We have seen the suits of the Lincoln "Red Socks." The caps are gray and white, the panties or knee-breeches gray, shirts cream colored with "Lincoln" in black across the breast, and red stockings. The belts are plain. Boys, when you don those new clothes may they inspire you to deeds that will smother you in glory.[21]

A few days later the team played a return game at Fort Stanton and lost it 28 to 14. This, the reporter noted, was not so bad as the score in the game played at Lincoln!

Visitors to Lincoln had a choice of two hotels—the Stanton House and the Lincoln Hotel. Mercantile companies came and went; J.J. Dolan sold his business in the old Tunstall store to a Las Cruces entrepreneur, Numa Reymond, who in turn disposed of his interest to Rosenthal & Co. William Rosenthal and Charles Beljean operated their firm for ten years, then sold out to the Lincoln Trading Company in 1900. From 1886 to 1896 Michael Cronin leased the mercantile and store rooms in the courthouse, just across the street from the Whelan & Co. general store.[22] George Barber reestablished his law office in Lincoln as of January 1891, in time to join the campaign for a $20,000. bond issue to build a new court house. Voters defeated this proposal, but the old county building did get a coat of plaster that fall.[23] Lincoln County used the original Murphy-Dolan store building as its court house for another twenty years.

A.J. Fountain and the Stock Growers Association

That court house saw plenty of use, thanks to the relentless work of Col. Albert Jennings Fountain, whom the southeastern New Mexico Stock Growers Association retained as a special investigator. This association was formed in March 1894 in response to wholesale losses to rustlers, mostly among the smaller cattlemen. Within three months Fountain had warrants issued in Lincoln County for the Slick Miller gang, who were rounded up and tried in Roswell on a change of venue. In the first year, Fountain's efforts sent no less than fifteen cattle thieves to the penitentiary for terms of up to ten years.[24]

Pushed by the association, Fountain went after another gang headquartered at Tularosa, where with the help of attorney Albert B. Fall they had been able to defy justice in Doña Ana County. Fountain hired a staff of special investigators to collect evidence of altered brands and other wrongdoing, including a hide with the former H changed to the pigpen brand used by Oliver Lee and Billy McNew. Court met in January 1896 and Fountain presented his case to the Lincoln County Grand Jury, complete with the steer hide spread on the floor of the old court house. The jury handed down thirty-two indictments against accused rustlers, including two against Lee and McNew for larceny in cattle and defacing brands. Fountain and his young son were on their way back to Las Cruces, when they disappeared at Chalk Hill in one of New Mexico's most famous unsolved murder mysteries.[25]

Old-Timers Pass, Old Ways Change

Sudden death at the wrong end of a six-gun was still common enough in Lincoln County, but no longer so in Lincoln itself. During the 1890s natural causes began to claim some of the old-timers prominent in the town's earlier years. Hugh M. Beckwith, an entrepreneur on the Rio Bonito before the Civil War and a Confederate sympathizer, later a participant in the Lincoln County War, had deep roots in New Mexico though he died in Texas around 1892. A.M. Clenny was truly a first settler, having come to the Bonito country in 1855 as a rancher and farmer. He passed away on May 19, 1898. His obituary said that he made the sixth old-timer who had crossed the great divide since the first of the year.

One of the others was James J. Dolan, who of all the people in the Lincoln County War probably came out of it the best. For the rest of his life Dolan seems to have worked for the interests of the Lincoln community. He became a successful merchant and rancher, held public offices, and was lauded in the newspapers as a solid citizen. For awhile in early 1892 he edited a paper himself, the *Lincoln Republican*. Three years later Dolan moved his family from their home in Lincoln to a new and comfortable dwelling at the Feliz ranch. After selling off his company's livestock holdings he died unexpectedly on February 20, 1898.[26]

Other large herd owners—the Block (El Capitan), VV, <u>CA</u>, and Carrizozo cattle companies—were selling their cattle about this same time. The open range and roundup were giving way to fenced pastures, windmills, and dipping vats.[27] Farmers along the Rio Bonito now grew alfalfa and fruit, with their fruit shipments in 1892 estimated at 250,000 pounds. Isaac Ellis had a show place, or model farm, just below Lincoln that produced apples, peaches, pears, and plums, as well as grapes.[28]

By 1900 more Lincoln family heads gave their occupation as farmer or farm laborer (84 of 203) than for any other employment. The census that year listed sixty-six farms in Precinct No. 1. A very detailed plat from the Territorial Engineer's Hondo Hydrographic Survey showed the Lincoln vicinity still heavily cultivated in 1908. Nearly all of the fields were small, between two and five acres in size, with at least ninety percent of the acreage planted to alfalfa and corn. The remainder was given over to orchard crops, wheat, and vegetables.[29] This emphasis on growing alfalfa, cereals, and orchard fruits in the small stream sections of Lincoln County persisted even as irrigation water along the Rio Bonito began to be diverted to other uses.[30]

Old Fort Stanton had only a small custodial force remaining when the army officially abandoned the place in 1896. Three years later President McKinley set aside the site as a tuberculosis sanatorium, administered by the U.S. Marine Hospital Service. By then the buildings were so dilapidated as to be uninhabitable, but they were rebuilt and the post became a principal employer in the area. The Fort Stanton Hospital had its own dairy and beef herds and raised the forage for these, producing part of the poultry and eggs consumed by the patients as well. Other commodities came mostly from merchants in nearby Capitan.[31]

Coal and Capitan

The gold mining town of White Oaks also had coal seams, with coal being mined there as early as 1880. Twenty miles to the south lay another coal field at what was called the Salado district. Sam Wortley had given up his hotel business in Lincoln and by 1889 he operated a small coal mine at the Salado fields. Developer Charles B. Eddy, a familiar figure from the Pecos valley, was looking for another venture and he recognized the need for a railroad

This scaffold was erected in 1907 for the execution of Rosario Emilio; the prisoner escaped. Photo Archives, Museum of New Mexico.

The House of Murphy as Lincoln County Courthouse in 1938. Hangings were conducted in the jail yard behind the building. Photo Archives, Museum of New Mexico.

to haul ore and coal from the mines at White Oaks, as well as other resources from a vast country lacking adequate transportation. He convinced eastern financiers to supply the capital for building an El Paso & Northeastern Railroad, primarily for hauling coal. Eddy, of course, had taken care to acquire the Salado coal mining properties. Construction began in December 1897.

The railroad was pushed vigorously and by August 1899 tracks had been laid to Carrizozo flat. Eddy sold the Salado coal properties to the New Mexico Fuel Company on the basis of advice that commercial quantities of high quality coal simply awaited the capital for development. From the railroad's temporary terminus at Carrizozo, Eddy built a twenty-one-mile branch to the Salado mines, completing this on September 29, 1899. Coal mining started that same year but the beds were soon found to be broken up by many intrusive dikes and faults. The field was a failure; coal could not be mined there in large quantities. Production reached a peak of 169,440 tons in 1901 and declined steadily until 1905, after which the mines were practically abandoned.[32]

The mining camp at the Salado fields was called Coalora, but Eddy had purchased a place about a mile beyond where he platted a townsite, named Capitan. The first building lot was sold there on March 4, 1900, and one year later the local paper optimistically estimated a current population of about 1,000. The El Paso & Northeastern Railway Co. extended its tracks and ran the first regular train into Capitan as of February 4, 1901. Meanwhile, on the flats fifteen miles to the west another townsite was booming at the rail junction called Carrizozo. Already it boasted two general merchandise stores and six saloons.[33]

With abandonment of the coal field, Capitan and Carrizozo became rail heads for shipping cattle, sheep, and wool out of Lincoln County as well as apples from the Rio Bonito valley. About this time, too, cattle raising in Lincoln County had stabilized at a new level:

> The country which was formerly practically controlled by a few large cattle companies is today furnishing homes for numberless small stockmen who have come here to engage in the live stock industry. Next to mining, stock raising is the leading industry of the county.[34]

The cattle business, then, was in better condition than it had been for several years. The territorial Bureau of Immigration estimated, perhaps optimistically, that Lincoln County had 150,000 sheep, 8,000 goats, and 75,000 head of cattle, many of the latter Herefords.[35]

Lincoln Enters the Twentieth Century

The Lincoln precinct had a population of 1,065 in the 1900 Census, with about 300 people in the town itself. It was the trading center for a fruit and grain producing and stock raising country, while awareness of its historical interest was growing.

> By reason of its being the county seat Lincoln is today and always has been an important trading point and a prosperous town. . . . Lincoln as seen today retains much suggestive of the early days of this part of New Mexico to the pioneers of this section. The houses that stood 25 or 30 years ago are today unchanged except for a few repairs that time has made necessary.

The reporter described Lincoln as composed of a single street with an abundance of shade trees, equally pleasant in winter and summer:

> The town of Lincoln has a population of between 500 and 600 while the population for the precinct is three or four times as great. Lincoln is the trading point for an immense territory the principal industries of which are agriculture and stock-raising.

Gov. John Miles presented the dedication address of the refurbished Lincoln Courthouse Museum in 1939. Photo Archives, Museum of New Mexico.

Lincoln girls' basketball team in the 1920s. Photo Archives, Museum of New Mexico.

The principal business houses of the town are the Aragon Bros. large mercantile establishment and J.J. Jaffa's extensive general merchandise store and bank. The town besides has one physician, a half dozen lawyers, two saloons, three hotels and a number of other business establishments.[36]

These mercantile businesses seem to have reorganized every few months, which may indicate instability or a squeeze on the prosperity. One firm, R. Michaelis & Co., had sold off its merchandise at cost when the principal partner retired.[37] Lincoln lost its last newspaper, the *Lincoln Weekly News*, about the time that J.J. Dolan died in 1898. Town boosters had hoped for twenty years that a railroad would come to Lincoln, but the nearest railhead remained at Capitan.

Lincoln's baseball team had a name now, the Lincoln Tigers, and 1900 promised to be a winning season. The Tigers beat a Fort Stanton team 36 to 9; came out 14 to 9 on top of a composite team made up of Capitan, Fort Stanton, and other players from Lincoln; then lost 24 to 9 to Capitan. Baseball also had some unusual hazards, as in a game played on July 31.

Astonishing was the game of base ball between the Lincoln Tigers, the regular nine of Lincoln, who in a few days expect to go to El Paso, and a nine organized by Manager D. Perea and captained by George Sena, called the Rough Riders. They played a matched game Tuesday for a chicken, and at the 9th inning the game stood 16 to 9 in favor of the Tigers. While the Riders complimented their opponents upon their victory, they still believe that with a week's practice the Riders can take all the spots off the Tigers, and several more games will be played this summer between the two nines. Captain Sena, while making a home run which was the best play in the game, fell through a prairie dog hole, and of course was put out. Had not this accident happened the Riders surely would have won the game.[38]

Sure they would. On San Juan Feast Day, June 24, 1906, Lincoln saw an unusual type of double-header when the home team lost to Fort Stanton 21 to 10 in baseball, followed that afternoon by a more traditional New Mexican sport, a *corrida de gallo* or "rooster pull."[39] This game, from an earlier description, was played as follows:

Yesterday was San Juan's Day. It is a day looked for by the Mexican people with great anxiety, for work is put to one side, and a general good time is had by all in horse racing, catching the rooster, etc. The last named is a very exciting and dangerous game, played in this manner: A hole is dug and a rooster is placed in it, so that nothing but the head of the fowl is above the ground. As many as wish to enter the game mount horses and get off some distance from the hole. When all are ready one of the riders starts out as fast as his horse can carry him towards the rooster, and as he passes it, endeavors to jerk it out of the ground. In turn the others do the same. When the lucky one succeeds in rescuing the fowl, then the real fun commences, for the rest of the number give him chase. Should his horse prove the fastest, the rooster is his, but if he is overtaken, the bird is again returned to the hole and the game is played over. The game is a dangerous one, but those that generally take part become quite proficient, grabbing the smallest article as they dash by.[40]

Capitan had more than a baseball team in 1900; it had seven telephones. For this Lincoln had to wait another six years until Dr. T.W. Watson became the sole owner of the telephone line between Capitan and Lincoln. Actually another medical doctor, J.W. Laws, had placed a professional card in the newspaper the previous December advertising a "Telefono en la casa," so the date when telephone service first came to Lincoln is not certain. In any case, Dr. Watson showed his progressiveness once more when he took delivery of a 1912 Ford Torpedo.[41]

The Lincoln (Wortley) Hotel, ca. 1905. Photo Archives, Museum of New Mexico.

Lincoln, looking northeast, ca. 1920s. (A) Courthouse; (B) 1889 jail; (C) 1921 school; (D) Watson house; (E) Tunstall store; (F) San Juan Church; (G) Convento. Courtesy Special Collections, University of Arizona Library.

One Lincoln resident in 1900 certainly harked back to an earlier era. This was Henry A. McCarty Jr., then residing in the county jail. It seems likely that something more than coincidence was involved in bringing a fifteen-year-old namesake of Billy the Kid to Lincoln. Yet the census taker recorded this lad as having been born in October 1884 in Texas, so he could not have been a rumored son of the Kid, said to have lived in Lincoln County.[42]

Lincoln at the turn of the century was no longer a violent town, but it remained a setting for controversies. The manager of the Lincoln Rough Riders baseball team, Demetrio Perea, was also the outgoing sheriff of Lincoln County. He received an appointment as the Lincoln postmaster. In less than a year, postal inspectors swarmed over his office when Perea took French leave after having failed to keep any records. One of the inspectors trailed him into Mexico and, after a standoff at a mining camp in Chihuahua, took Perea in charge and brought him back to face trial. He pleaded guilty and was sentenced to two years and two days in the penitentiary plus a fine. Another former postmaster at Lincoln pleaded guilty to embezzlement at the same court session and also received a fine and a jail sentence.[43]

Last Controversy: Lincoln Loses the County Seat

Judicial controversy of another kind followed the election for Lincoln County sheriff in 1902, when it took six months to decide the winner. Robert D. Armstrong contested his opponent's election and finally, at the end of August 1903, John W. Owen relinquished the office. In the meantime the district judge who decided this contest was publicly removed from office by President Roosevelt on charges of general immorality. The judge protested in vain.[44] At that same 1902 election, two Lincoln County War veterans sought election as probate judge. Francisco Gomez won the office over Saturnino Baca.

Lincoln's decline after 1906 can be traced in the school enrollment figures. By February 1906 the two mining towns of White Oaks and Capitan had lost population to an extent where neither had more than about half the number of people as lived in Precinct No. 1 (Lincoln). Lincoln still held to its claim of being the paramount community in Lincoln County. Carrizozo technically did not yet exist, since the townsite was platted and the sale of lots began only in 1907. Yet there was already agitation for what would be the most serious blow to Lincoln since the violence of the late 1870s. Carrizozo became a railroad division terminal with repair shops and a roundhouse, and it was said that the next session of the legislature would see an effort to move the county seat there or to create a new county. During 1908 the population at Carrizozo had boomed while that at Lincoln had declined, until by mid-October school enrollment at the new town was up by more than 100 just since May and stood almost sixty percent higher than the figure for Lincoln.[45]

The trend was clear. In July 1909 the Lincoln County Commission received a petition requesting that an election be held on the proposition to remove the county seat to Carrizozo. The election was held on August 17, 1909; out of 1,513 votes cast, Lincoln received 614 and Carrizozo, 899. Lincoln responded immediately with an injunction to prevent the commissioners from removing the county seat.[46]

The people at Lincoln soon filed a suit attacking the regularity of the election and the validity of the law under which the election was held. The one thing in their favor was that they had a good lawyer—Thomas B. Catron. Through an endless series of hearings, rehearings, decisions, appeals, and other legal entanglements, Carrizozo won at every turn. In the meantime, bonds were issued for the construction of a new court house in Carrizozo. The Lincoln adherents managed to get an injunction that stopped further work after the shell of the building had already been put up. At the request of the county officers, the Lincoln County District Attorney delivered his opinion concerning the removal of county

San Juan Church, ca. 1920s. Courtesy Special Collections, University of Arizona Library.

J.J. Dolan house, restored. Courtesy Special Collections, University of Arizona Library.

offices and records. He found no valid excuse for not removing at once to Carrizozo.

The treasurer and county clerk agreed to move (the district court was already being held in Carrizozo). They asked for teams and wagons to move their records, but

> when the conveyances reached Lincoln a mob of over forty people were at the Court house and when an attempt was made to get the records, both Clerk Riggle and Treasurer Watson claimed that the people of Lincoln had control of the records and refused to allow them to be taken to Carrizozo.

The sheriff wrung his hands; he was unable to control the mob.

> Treasurer Watson stated that he had started for Carrizozo in an automobile Tuesday morning with his records and was stopped at the court house by a committee of Lincoln citizens who seized his records and placed them in a vault in the court house of which he did not know the combination. Mr. Riggle stated that he attempted to open the vault door in his office and two men setting against the same refused to allow it to be opened.[47]

This last Lincoln County war was fought with arguments, opinions, and appeals, rather than bullets, with the legal battle eventually reaching the U.S. Supreme Court. There on January 20, 1913, Mr. Justice Oliver Wendell Holmes delivered the opinion that finally settled the Lincoln County seat cases. The decree of the Supreme Court of the Territory was affirmed; Carrizozo was the county seat. Attorney T.B. Catron immediately sought to lift the injunction so that work on the buildings at Carrizozo could go ahead and the contractor could be paid. The feeling in the county was relief, mixed with exhaustion. The last chapter was written in August of 1913 with shipment of the Lincoln County Clerk's records to Carrizozo.[48]

With loss of the county seat, Lincoln was left with little more than memories. The population numbers drifted downward, from about 250 as of 1912, to slightly more than 100 in the 1930s, down to some 50 full-time residents today. A rich history remained in the town itself and with those who continued to live there. A visitor back in 1911 seemed to have sensed this in the word portrait that he titled "Lincoln: Quaintest Town in the World":

> Lying high above the banks of the Rio Bonita (Beautiful River), between ranges of stately foothills, is one of the quaintest settlements in the New World. Lincoln is not a city, it is not a town, not even a village; it is simply Lincoln. There is one street, which might be called Bonita boulevard, or Broadway, or Lincoln road, but no resident ever calls it by any name. The courthouse is on "this" side of the main thoroughfare, the postoffice on "that" side, and the leading mercantile establishment "down that way a little". Private residences and business houses join hands, or walls, rather, and aside from the new sanitarium, which is built along the most advanced lines of modern thought, there is hardly a structure in the place that is not suggestive of days long since past and gone. The two-story courthouse has an outside wooden stairway leading from the street to the upper floor. An adobe wall, reinforced by some tall posts and a variegated assortment of boards, makes a fairly satisfactory livery stable. The population is almost solidly Mexican, as that term is generally understood in New Mexico.
>
> There is not, so far as I know, a Protestant meeting house anywhere in the region. Little Catholic churches are quite common, usually having a burying ground in connection. Isolated graveyards are frequent, and solitary graves, protected by a wooden fence, dot the landscape here and there. . . .
>
> Lincoln has no daily or weekly publication. My impression is that a live quarterly would prove attractive. Nobody ever hurries; brain fag and nervous prostration, according to one of the oldest citizens, are unknown. These remarks apply to the

Lincoln public school in 1887. Lincoln's school opened its doors in October 1885, with forty scholars attending. Photo Archives, Museum of New Mexico.

Lincoln public school, ca. 1909. Photo Archives, Museum of New Mexico.

Railroad lines to southwestern New Mexico, 1899–1900.

The men of Lincoln, ca. 1900. Courtesy Rio Grande Historical Collections, New Mexico State University.

George W. Peppin, one of Lincoln's first citizens. Courtesy Special Collections, University of Arizona Library.

citizen as he walks the street of the settlement. Now, when he mounts a horse, he is all energy and excitement. One young man sat under a shady retreat for two hours, lazily masticating tobacco and whittling a stick. At last he arose, gave a tremendous yawn and sauntered off to a hitching post, where his saddled quadruped was dozing between efforts at nibbling some loose hay. Once in the saddle our young man appeared to have been stung by a regiment of yellow jackets. He applied spurs and left behind him a cloud of dust that would have done credit to a squadron of cavalry in action. . . .

It is said that more melons are devoured in Lincoln than any place of its size on the planet. Watermelon is looked upon as a prime necessity, something on a par with bread and meat. As melons do not thrive in that region, thousands of them are hauled in from Roswell and other towns in the valley of the Pecos.

One who visits this place cannot fail to be impressed with the uniform courtesy and general spirit of neighborly helpfulness that may almost be said to be universal. The Mexicans are hospitable and generous entertainers. Their ways and methods are not what many of us are accustomed to, but it is only the narrow-minded fanatic who does not respect the inborn custom of an old and chivalrous people.[49]

⌒ 16 ⌒

THE COMMUNITY AS
A HISTORICAL MONUMENT

B y 1900 popular interest in such aspects of Lincoln County history as Billy the Kid and the Lincoln County War had pretty well died out. The first revival came between 1901 and 1907 when author Emerson Hough resurrected the Kid's legend and gave it heroic dimensions. Then in 1926 Walter Noble Burns' *The Saga of Billy the Kid* burst onto the scene, ensuring both the Kid and the Lincoln County War a permanent place in western American history.[1]

Many Lincoln residents met early deaths as a result of the War and its aftermath, but others lived to see the renewed interest in events of the 1870s and 1880s. Two adherents of the House, J.B. "Billy" Mathews and George W. Peppin, both died in 1904. John H. Riley lived until 1916 and rustler John Kinney to August of 1919. Jessie Evans escaped from custody in Texas in 1882 and disappeared, but if a story told to historian Eve Ball is true, then Evans might have outlived all of his contemporaries.[2]

Martin Chavez of Picacho, the principal leader of McSween's Hispanic allies, survived until 1931, as did Frank Coe and Sue McSween Barber. Doc Scurlock had passed away two years earlier; Robert Widenmann only one year before. Yginio Salazar, the pal of Billy the Kid, survived his wounds from the Five-Days Battle and lived at Lincoln until 1936. George Coe, the last of the Regulators, returned to Lincoln County and lived on the Ruidoso for many years. He died at Roswell on November 12, 1941. Frank and George Coe, Sue Barber, and Yginio Salazar all gave interviews during the 1920s and 1930s when interest in the Lincoln County War had revived. For Mrs. Barber this left a bitter aftertaste; she felt that Walter Noble Burns ignored or misused the information that she gave him.[3]

Governor Lew. Wallace's autobiography, published the year after his death in 1905, made mention of his Lincoln County experiences. Capt. Henry Carroll died from blood poisoning in 1908, the same year that ex-sheriff Pat Garrett suffered a fatal case of lead poisoning. Lt. Col. N.A.M. Dudley, his last years cushioned by a promotion to brigadier general on the retired list, outlived many of his enemies and survived until 1910. Another veteran, Capt. Saturnino Baca, remained a prominent citizen of Lincoln until his death in 1924. Francisco Gomez, who had an interesting life during his two years with the McSweens, apparently outlived everyone else of the Lincoln County War generation. He lived on in Lincoln until July 1946.[4]

By this time the town itself was being recognized as a historical resource. In April 1934 the Southern Pacific Railroad transferred the torreon lot to the State of New Mexico. The Chaves County Historical Society, with support from the Federal Economic Recovery Act, sponsored reconstruction of this stone-walled tower from the few feet that remained, completing work in February 1935.[5]

Meanwhile the Murphy-Dolan store, the later Lincoln County court house, was standing vacant and abandoned. Early in 1937 a group of county residents interested in the preservation of Lincoln organized the Lincoln County Society of Art, History, and Archaeology. Through this group's efforts the court house was deeded to the State of New Mexico. Ren-

169

TOWN OF LINCOLN

1. Courthouse Museum, 1874 (formerly Murphy-Dolan Store). Owned by the State of New Mexico.

2. Schoolhouse.

3. Gibson house.

4. Sheriff Brent house. Owned by the State of New Mexico.

5. Community Church (formerly the first schoolhouse, 1885).

6. R. Pryor house.

7. Garcia house (former Lesnett house).

8. Salas house.

9. James Ramsey home (Aragon house).

10. Ramsey Store.

11. Shreecengost home (originally the Dolan house, later Bonito Inn).

12. C. Zamora home.

13. San Juan Church, 1887.

14. Convento (formerly first courthouse & Wilson's Saloon). Owned by the State of New Mexico.

15. Maes (Rufina) home.

16. Hall home (Sandoval house).

17. Anderson house (formerly Montaño house & store). Owned by the Lincoln County Heritage Trust.

18. Booky home (originally the Juan Patron house and store).

19. M. Perry home.

20. Tode's Store.

21. Román Maes home.

22. Maes Museum and La Paloma Bar.

23. Bank Exchange Saloon (formerly Curry-Thornton Saloon).

24. Wortley Hotel. Owned by the State of New Mexico.

25. J. Zamora home and Aragon Store.

26. Wright house (formerly Dr. Wood's). Owned by the Lincoln County Heritage Trust.

27. Wright Annex (also a drug store, winery, movie house at various times).

28. Watson house. Owned by the State of New Mexico.

29. Fresquez house. Owned by the State of New Mexico.

30. Site of McSween house, 1877–78. Owned by the State of New Mexico.

31. Tunstall Store, 1877. Owned by the State of New Mexico.

32. Penfield shop and home.

33. Racher home.

34. Dunlap La Placita shop.

35. Torreon, built by early Hispanic settlers, 1850s. Owned by the State of New Mexico.

36. Locke shop (on site of Saturnino Baca home).

37. Deel house (former Gallegos house). Owned by the Lincoln County Heritage Trust.

38. Ramon Luna home. Owned by Lincoln County Heritage Trust.

39. Zamora (Rita) home.

40. Ray Taylor home.

41. Dockery Red Geranium shop and house (formerly Perea house).

42. Ramey house (formerly Isaac Ellis & Sons Store, also Dr. Laws' T.B. sanatorium).

43. Nurses' quarters (formerly Ellis' mill house).

44. Evans house.

Town of Lincoln (from 1974 New Mexico State Planning Office report).

RIO BONITO

TOWN OF LINCOLN · 1974 ·

ovation of the old building began the following year under the direction of J.W. Hendron from the Museum of New Mexico, with funds provided by the Works Progress Administration. This was a substantial project, not completed until 1939, the aim being to restore the building as nearly as possible to its appearance at the time Billy the Kid made his escape in 1881. Governor John E. Miles dedicated the court house as the Lincoln County Museum on July 30, 1939.[6]

These two projects were the genesis of Lincoln State Monument. Through the years the State acquired other properties, all of which are now administered under the Museum of New Mexico as units of Lincoln State Monument. At present the buildings in the monument system are:

North side of the street: Wortley Hotel
Watson site
McSween site & Fresquez House
Tunstall Store
Torreon
South side of the street: Convento (first court house)
Wilson property
San Juan Church
Sheriff Brent House
Court House

The Lincoln County Heritage Trust, formed in 1976, has refurbished several of Lincoln's historical structures and opens these to visitors between Memorial Day and Labor Day each year. In 1980 the Trust also built their Historical Center on what is known as the Luna property, linked to the old Luna House by a courtyard. The Trust properties are:

Dr. Wood's House and Annex
Montaño's Store
Luna House
Gallegos House
Aragon Store site
Whelan & Co. Store site

Other historical buildings in Lincoln are owned by individuals and used as residences, shops, a museum, and a saloon. The architectural integrity of the village is assured by a Lincoln County Historical Ordinance approved in 1972.[7]

During August the pageant grounds just west of the court house are the setting for the outdoor folk-pageant *The Last Escape of Billy the Kid*. This began in 1949 and is sponsored by Lincoln Pageants & Festivals, Inc., a local organization that currently operates the Wortley Hotel as well. In this annual event, some of Lincoln's most exciting moments are relived by visitors and residents alike.

Lincoln looking northwest, 1980. Photograph by Thomas Caperton.

APPENDIX

DOCUMENT 1

A disinterested party (Charles Scase?) explains the Lincoln County War, May 31, 1878

Printed in the Grant County Herald,
June 8, 1878.

TROUBLES IN LINCOLN.

A Statement.

What an honest and disinterested Man Says.

We publish the following communication because we are convinced that the writer tells the *truth*:

Silver City, N.M.
May 31, 1878.

Mr. Editor of The Herald:

I have been going through your town from Lincoln county and in talking to your people, I find that you would not be afraid to tell the truth about the Lincoln county row, if you had a fair show. I think the thing ought to be showed up and I believe you will publish my letter. I use poor grammar but you can fix it up so as to look right in the paper.

I was in Lincoln county through the whole fight and this is just how it was. I had a ranche down on the Panasco. I came in there last summer, and went through the whole trouble and am pretty well posted. The difficulty was because McSween won't pay over the life insurance of $10,000 to Fritz's sister who ought to have it. Tunstall came in the county and tried to run out Murphy and Dolan. McSween thought Murphy was throwing off on him, and then for spite went in with Tunstall. In the fight afterwards, Widerman the marshal, crowded down everybody who was not in favor of Tunstall and McSween. If it hadn't been for Brady he would have had everything in his own hands.

Where I lived on my ranche I tried to be a fair man to both sides. Men on both sides were going by nearly every day, and I tried to treat both the same. I wouldn't hold up one side or the other. I went in, on business to Lincoln and Widerman says to me that he killed a lot of my friends the other day. I told him they were no friends of mine nor no particular enemies. Then Widerman says why don't you come in with us if you are no friend of theirs you ought to be with us. And I said it was no fight of mine, and I didn't intend to put myself up to be shot at as long as I could make a living by work.

I went back to my ranche and a day after, a friend of mine come out to the ranche from Lincoln and said, you better leave because Widerman and his party think you are no friend and say they intend to put you out of the way if you stay here. The next day I thought the matter over and then traded my ranche for a horse, to travel on. I left nearly fifteen acres of grain and it was the 7th of May and before long I could have had a good crop, but I considered my life worth more. I had no quarrel with either party but was afraid Widerman might send some one to kill me in the dark.

Then I left my ranche and started for Tularosa and at daylight I came to the ranche south of Fort Stanton. One of Widerman's men met me. He says Widerman wants to see you at the plaza in Lincoln. I went back to the plaza because I was afraid I would be killed on the road if I refused. Widerman told me he wanted to know what Murphy and Dolan's party intended to do. I said I knew nothing about it and they let me go. Then I started for Mesilla and on the road met two other men who were afraid of their lives from Widerman and his party. After I met these men a party met us and spread out on both sides of the road. We jumped off the horses and showed fight. Then they said they were looking for cattle, but I knew three of them to belong to Widerman's party.

Roberts was killed only because Dolan had him to work for him taking charge of his herd. The whole business was because McSween and Tunstall wanted to run Murphy and Dolan out, and then when I didn't want to do anything on either side, they drove me out too, because they thought I was a friend of Dolans, when I was just as much a friend of Widerman before he commenced to try to make me fight for him.

I wouldn't have left even by the threats of my life, only I found out that John Chisum, who before hated Widerman, was making a job with him and McSween to go together and clean out the whole county. I knew that Chisum would be glad to see me killed and so I just left my crops and sailed out. Lots of men are leaving the county in the same way, because they say that McSween and Widerman and Chisum are paying four dollars a day for a man and his rifle and intend to drive everybody else out. It was no fight of mine, but they drove me away from a good ranche where I thought I could make a first class farm, and I think the thing ought to be showed up. If you will publish this you will do justice to many men who have been crowded almost to the death, only because they wouldn't take up Widerman and McSween's fight, and although they were not the friends of the other side, because that party had the power they drove them out of the county or left them no show for their lives. It ought to be published and I think you will do it. I have left there, and now I ain't afraid to tell just how the thing was. Every word I write is true and the people ought to know it.

S.

DOCUMENT 2

Lt. Col. Dudley reports on the Five-Days Battle, July 20, 1878

National Archives Microcopy M-666. Letters Received by the Office of the Adjutant General (Main Series) 1871–1880. Roll 397 (1878), file No. 1405-AGO-1878.

★★★

(*Jacket*) Lieut. Col. N.A.M. Dudley makes report of affairs in Lincoln County, N.M. (13 Enc.).

(*4th Endors't*) Adjutant General's Office, Washington, Aug. 13, 1878.
Respectfully submitted to the *Secretary of War* in Connection with papers submitted by the General of the Army on the 8th instant.

(*Letter*)   Headquarters
Fort Stanton, N.M.
Midnight. July 20" 1878

Act. Asst. Adjutant General
District of New Mexico
Santa Fe, N.M.

Sir

As I anticipated as will be seen by my last communication on the subject of affairs in Lincoln County, which was dated the 18" inst. I having received reliable information that the firing between the two belligerent parties in Lincoln, the County seat, actually or nearly so interrupted the traveling of non combattants through the town since the 15th inst., and being almost hourly approached by parties asking for protection of lives of women and children, and for private property, they having been threatened by the lawless foreigners of the county, whom I verily and honestly believe are attached to the late A.A. McSweens party, who has openly and defiently resisted the sheriff of the county of Lincoln and Special Deputy U.S. Marshal Geo. W. Peppin, I deemed it my imperative duty as commanding Officer, after consulting the opinion of every officer of my Command, as will be seen by paper marked "A" to take all the available force at my command, to proceed to Lincoln, and go in temporary camp near the seat of War, for the sole purpose of giving protection to women and children, and such non combattants as might be disposed to avail themselves of the protection of my small Command.

On the morning of the 19" inst. I took every officer of the post including the post surgeon, leaving the Post under the Command of 2 Lieut. S.S. Pogue A.A.Q.M. I in person proceeded to Lincoln taking with me the Gatling Gun with 2000 rounds of ammunition, also the Howitzer with ample supply of ammunition for any emergency that might arise, with three days rations.

The Command left the post promptly at the hour designated, reaching a point near Wortley's Hotel without resistence, where I met Special Deputy U.S. Marshal and Sheriff of Lincoln County, G.W. Peppin and told him in the presence of the officers that I had not come down for the purpose of assisting him in making arrests, but simply for the purpose of protecting the lives of women and children, "the men could take care of themselves", that I proposed to go in camp within half a mile of the town, and if my camp was attacked, or an officer or man was killed or wounded from a shot fired by either party from any house, I should demand the parties who did the firing to be turned over to me, and in case of failure, I should request women and children to leave the house, and I should open fire on it with my Howitzer, and arrest the parties in the house. I further stated I did not know what houses his party or McSween's occupied, I should treat both parties exactly alike. I ordered the command to advance. I personally headed the column, taking the precaution to give my soldiers orders to pay no attention to slurs or jeers that they might receive from either party in passing through the town.

While passing through the town I did not see after leaving Wortley's Hotel a single human being, until I arrived at the lower end of the town, and placed my command in Camp with the intention of remaining overnight, my intention at the time being to proceed down the Rio Bonito, and making a reconnaissance of a day's march below Lincoln. Before unsaddling or unpacking my wagons I was informed by a Mexican that the house of Mr. Montana was occupied as a Fortification by a detachment of men under control of A.A. McSween. The house was located within 20 yards of where I proposed to pitch my own tent, and when a man made his appearance from a side door of Montana's house, I told him that I understood there was a party of McSween's men in that house, that I had no interest in this quarrel, I was going in camp there. I came there simply to protect women and children if a shot was fired from that house into my command, wounding or killing any of my officers or men, I should open fire with my Howitzer on it at once, and in that case I would earnestly request that if women or children were in the house they would retire from it, and stating the fact that I had come there to protect women and children alone, and would take no action on either side.

In less than three minutes there was a large number of women and children assembled around me, and welcomed the advent of my command. I went into Camp, posting the necessary Sentinels, and sending a mounted patrol of three men under a reliable non-commissioned Officer to examine the front and rear, to ascertain whether or not my position was a safe one. In ten minutes I withdrew this patrol which had not approached within 200 yards of Mr. McSween's residence in the mean time I received through a little girl about 7 years of age a communication (copy marked "B") signed A.A. McSween, probably the last letter he ever wrote, to which I returned the following reply in lead pencil, through my Adjutant Lieutenant Goodwin, by the same messenger—viz—I am directed by the Commanding Officer to inform you that no soldiers have surrounded your house, and that he desires to hold no correspondence with you; if you desire to blow up your house, the Commanding Officer does not object—providing it does not injure any U.S. soldiers.

From this time the firing was almost constant, except occasionally a lull of ten or fifteen minutes; during this time Mrs. McSween, wife of the deceased made her appearance in my camp in a very excited condition, trying to lead me into a discussion of the position of the two parties, demanding that I would give an order prohibiting the Sheriff from firing her house, to which demand I replied by saying that I had no control over the Sheriff, or his *posse*, that I understood he had warrants for the arrests of various parties, among them her husband; and he must be the Judge of the means to be used in carrying out his instructions; that I was there but to prevent wanton destruction of property and protect women, and children, she then returned in much anger, as before stated the firing was not only kept up—but was increasing between the Sheriffs *posse* and McSween's party, so severe was the fire, that I required my Officers and men, even taking the sentinel off of his Post to seek cover behind an unfinished "adobe" building, in the mean time a fire was reported by some of the men of my command in the direction of Worthlys Hotel, which for some three hours was observed, the firing from McSweens house,. and their positions, that his men occupied made it imprudent for me (being a non-combattants) to expose the lives of my command.

About 5.30 P.M. I received copies of communications, marked "C" and "D". Notwithstanding it was a hazardous duty, Capt. Blair and Lieut. Goodwin were requested by me, to visit the building occupied by Rev. Mr. Ealy and family. These Gentleman reported to me that they were convinced that some of the McSween party were in the building occupied by Mr. Ealy the (Tunstal Building), and as I had been informed that the Sheriff's party were determined to attempt to carry out the edicts of the Court, in attempting to make arrests, of parties which they supposed were in this Building and fearing that they might attack the building—I ordered a wagon hitched up, on the additional application of Miss Yates, member of Dr. Ealy's family, and as the duty was a hazardous one, I called for volunteers from my command. Capt. Blair, Dr. Appel, Corpl. Bergold and 4 Privates of the 15' Infantry volunteered to go down and get the household property of said Dr. Ealy—which was safely conveyed at the risk of the lives of the party to a house under the protection of my command.

The fire at the time that this duty was done, was a fusillade, fortunately no one was injured. I personally witnessed the Conduct of this party, which I take occasion here to officially commend. I might here add that Mrs. McSween—wife of deceased came to Cap't Blair, and (asked if she could have protection also) Cap't Blair told her certainly she could have the same protection as every-one else, and all that our command could afford, and asked her to come to camp immediately, which she did, and occupied a building within 30 paces of the command.

Shortly after this it became so dark, and the firing became so general, I directed that every Officer and man should get under cover, which order was carried out for the next two hours. Shots frequently passed over my camp, at one time over 20 passed within a few feet of the heads of the men, 2 or 3 more striking the buildings which sheltered both Officers and men. The estimate made by my Officers was that over two thousand shots were exchanged during the evening.

On my arrival at the point where I camped the party occupying the Montana house to the number of some 16 to 20 men thoroughly armed, left by the back door and went to the residence of Mr. Ellis some 400 yards east of my camp, where they remained for at least half an hour, when they left with their horses which were in his corral and took to the bluffs north of my camp, taking position opposite my camp in a body, when a posse headed by Sheriff Peppin on foot (the latters horses being secured in a canon some miles distant) demanded their surrender, which was not heeded, and fire was opened upon them, when they deployed as skirmishers and advanced over the bluffs, at least six hundred yards, under partial cover of the buildings occupied by the sheriff's posse when they were received by a galling fire from Peppin's men. Sheriff Peppin alone with a Winchester Gun from the tower in the centre of the town, where he had retreated dispersed them, and I believe their detachment did not again appear. The next fire from this direction came from a party of six or seven men from a point directly opposite my camp about 500 yards distant, and fired promiscuously into the western portion of the town. At this period the fire was promiscuous, general, and incessant for several minutes, by what parties fired I am unable to say.

During most of the time referred to in this communication, my officers and soldiers were inactive spectators and more or less exposed to the fire referred to, and I am proud to say that they never returned a single shot. The result of this conflict between the Sheriff's posse in the execution of their duty, and the party resisting them headed by McSween I regret to report as follows. A.A. McSween, Jose Chavis, Vencinta Romero, Harvey Morris were killed. Thomas Culliens, and another man name unknown were wounded or killed and reported as buried in the burned house of McSween, and since the commencement of the firing between the two belligerent parties, it is reported that one man was killed on the 18" inst, and buried in the cellar of McSween's house. Hinio Salacar was dangerously wounded, and Benjamine Ellis seriously wounded, and a detachment that I sent out this afternoon to visit the late Sheriff Brady's widow reported that blood was tracked over a mile and a half on the trail of McSween's men retreating from the Town.

Jim French "and Kid Antrim" are reported missing and it is generally supposed they are in the ruins of the building, as during the burning of the building a large number of cartridges were heard exploding. In regard to the two latter parties I can not vouch for. On the part of the Sheriff's party, I have to announce the killing of Mr. Robert Beckwith of the P-cos near seven rivers, a gentleman well known in the country, and recognized as one of the most upright, energetic, and industrious men of the community, who I believe lost his life in the conscientious discharge of loyal duty. He belonged to one of the best families in his section of the County, and his loss will be deplored by every good citizen, who had the good fortune to know him. I personally know that this slight tribute to his memory is equally appreciated by the Officers of my command, and the citizens of this county.

There has been I believe only one casualty besides the one referred to in the Sheriff's *posse* of one man (Crawford) being dangerously wounded, he is now in the Post Hospital, and a slight wound on the neck of William Johnson, and two other men slightly wounded.

In regard to the destruction of the building occupied by A.A. McSween, I would say, my camp was so far from it, and the firing from it, and its vicinity, my command remained in camp, and myself, and I am unable to make any report in regard to it.

The Command did not reach the Post till near sun-down. I trust that the report made out as it is by different Clerks will account for its form. I respectfully enclose copy of proceedings of "Coroners Inquest" marked "E" also Affidavit marked "F".

I am Sir, Very Respectfully,
Your Obedient Servant
N.A.M. Dudley
Lieutenant Colonel 9' Cavalry Commanding

DOCUMENTS 3 AND 4

Lt. Col. Dudley reports on affairs in Lincoln County, September 7 and 29, 1878

National Archives Microcopy M-666. Letters Received by the Office of the Adjutant General (Main Series), 1871–1880. Roll 397 (1878), file No. 1405-AGO-1878.

(*Jacket*) Lieut. Col. N.A.M. Dudley. Weekly Report of affairs in Lincoln County, N.M. 2 Encls.

(*Letter*)   Headquarters
Fort Stanton N.M.
September 7" 1878

Act'g Asst Adjutant General
District of New Mexico
Santa Fe N.M.

Sir.

I have little to report of interest to the District Commander this week.

Jim French, Kidd, Scroggins, Waite, and three others of the McSween ring hold the town of Lincoln. Stock stealing is being reported as occurring daily, the animals taken being driven towards the Pecos and Seven Rivers.

The Sheriff has no posse now and is making no attempt to arrest anyone. French's Party by threats and acts has forced County Commissioner Baca to leave the town, and seek protection for himself and family within the limits of the post.

French makes his Headquarters with Mrs. McSween. Easton the present business manager of the affairs of J.B. Catron Esq, who only about a week ago reported to me that he was sleeping in the hills, being afraid to sleep in the Murphy building, is now reported on intimate terms with, and a daily visitor of Mrs. McSween has stated that he has no fears now from that party. There is some thirty armed men between old Fort Sumner and Roswell. Scurlock and Middleton is reported to be with this party.

Kinney and his party I am unable to locate just now positively.

Another party of some fifteen men are in the mountains near Tulerosa, the two Coe Brothers are in this Band.

I have one non-com-officer and three men at the Agency. Their instructions are strictly within the authority given in Par. II and III G.O. #28 c.s. of 1870 Dept. of Mo. furnished me for my guidance from District Headquarters. The N.C.O. reports by each mail any information that is of importance.

I enclose copy of his report received last night marked No. 1.

Very Respectfully
Your Obdt Servant

N.A.M. Dudley
Lieut Col 9" Cavalry
Comd'g Post

Indiana Historical Society Library microfilm of Lew Wallace Papers 1878–1881.

Head Quarters, Fort Stanton, N.M.
Sept. 29" 1878
3 o'clock P.M.

To the Asst. Adj't General
District of New Mexico.

Sir:

I avail myself of the opportunity to send this in advance of the next mail, by Mr. Dolan, who leaves here tonight for Santa Fe, N.M.

The party of men styling themselves the "Wrestlers" made up of renegades from Texas principally, some of whom have been partizans with both of the leading factions here, since I assumed command, have renewed their raiding with almost unparalleled vigor. Yesterday they attacked a party of laborers cutting hay near the Ranch of Jose Chaves, five miles below Fritz's Farm, and without the least provocation killed three of the party, two of the sons of Chaves. None of these men have in any possible way been partizans, or given their sympathy to either of the partys. They stole what horses they could find on the Ranch, and proceeded to another Ranch further south some fifteen miles, where they attacked another party of citizens, putting three balls into one man, mortally wounding him, and wounding another. An express came in for surgical aid, and I have allowed Dr. Lyon, who volunteered to go down. Mr. Kline, the mail driver, says the man who drives below him, stated to him, he would not make another trip with the mail without a military guard. Kline stated the same. I shall send an officer with twenty men to meet the broken link in the transit of the mail early in the morning, with instructions to give necessary protection to the mail, and in case it has been molested in any way, to follow the trail of the robbers, and either arrest or kill them if possible.

I have reliable information that the gang of which these men are a part, are from sixty to eighty strong, and are en route here now from Seven Rivers, and south of there.

I respectfully and earnestly ask in the name of God and humanity, that I may be allowed to use the Forces at my command, to drive these murderers, horse-thieves, and escaped convicts out of the county. The wives and daughter of quiet and good citizens are being daily insulted by these desperadoes, driven into the mountains, hiding to save their lives. This, too, almost in sight of the Garrison.

I am, sir, very respectfully,
Your obedient servant,
(signed)   N.A.M. Dudley
Lieut. Col. 9" Cav.
Commanding Post

DOCUMENT 5

Las Vegas Gazette account of the Five-Days Battle

Printed in the Albuquerque Review, *August 31, 1878, from the* Las Vegas Gazette

THE FIGHT IN LINCOLN

Knowing the interest felt by the public in the late desperate fight in Lincoln, a Gazette reporter availed himself of the opportunity to interview a reliable gentleman who recently arrived from that place, upon the circumstances of the contest. He stated in brief that McSween and party had arrived in Lincoln on the evening of the 14th of July. He had about 40 men who took up quarters at his own house and in different points in the town. The sheriff and posse arrived in the town on Monday the 15th ult. and the fighting began at once and continued until Friday evening, when it terminated in the death of McSween and the destruction of his house. The sheriff's posse numbered also about 40 men. They took possession of the Indian tower, a three story building constructed for the purpose of fighting Indians and which commanded McSween's house, as likewise the hotel corral on the opposite side. On Friday the final fight took place. McSween's forces were divided, a part of them being in the mountains. Those in the mountains were prevented from joining by General Dudley pointing a cannon towards them, which intimidated them. The cannon was first pointed in the direction of the house of Ellis & Sons. For fear that the house would be burned, Mrs. Shield asked permission to go into her part (it was a double house) and take out her household goods. This was granted, but some of the sheriff's posse went in with her, and poured coal oil on the floor and set fire to it. She begged them not to do so, as she wanted to save her goods, but they said it was necessary to get those men out of there. This was about 2 o'clock.

The posse approached the house from every point they could. They took possession of some of the windows. McSween's men fought desperately, contending against the fire within and the posse without. They expected to wait until night and take their chances of getting out under cover of darkness. No quarter was given and no quarter was asked from the sheriff's posse. McSween offered to surrender to Col. Dudley; but he was not authorized to take them. Bob Beckwith attempted to reach one of the windows from the back yard about 4 o'clock in the afternoon. He was shot in the head and died instantly. When night approached and it was seen that the house was no longer tenable, Mrs. McSween kissed her husband and bid him goodbye. The men one by one made their escape across the river, by the backyard. They all got out of the house; McSween was killed in the backyard. He appeared to have given up all hope of escape and sat down on the woodpile, where he was discovered and killed. His clothes were badly scorched from the fire. Thus ended the five day's fight. The remaining forces of McSween did not come to the rescue. Had they done so the result would undoubtedly have been different. Four men of McSween's party were killed and two of the sheriff's posse.

NOTES

Chapter 1   *The First Settlement, 1855–1860*

1. Map of the Territory of New Mexico Compiled by Bvt. Second Lt. Jno. G. Parke, U.S.T.E. Santa Fe, 1851.
2. Frank D. Reeve, 1961: *History of New Mexico, Vol. II*, pp. 170–72; Averam B. Bender, 1974: *A Study of Mescalero Apache Indians, 1846–1880*, pp. 91–118
3. William G. B. Carson, 1964: *William Carr Lane Diary*, p. 277.
4. Steck to Lane, February 7, 1853, National Archives (NA), Record Group 75, OIA, LR, N Mex., W-224. Published in the *Santa Fe Weekly Gazette*, February 19, 1853, p. 2.
5. C. L. Sonnichsen, 1958: *The Mescalero Apaches*, pp. 74–81; Robert M. Utley, 1967: *Frontiersmen in Blue*, pp. 149–52; Carole Gorney, 1969: *Roots in Lincoln*, pp. 1–6; Bender 1974: 121–128.
6. Extracts from two private letters dated April 11, 1855, published in the *Santa Fe Weekly Gazette*, April 28, 1855, p. 2.
7. *Santa Fe Weekly Gazette*, November 3, 1855, p. 2; *Roswell Record*, May 27, 1898, p. 3.
8. Wm. Pelham, Santa Fe, to Commissioner, General Land Office, August 31, 1855; Microfilm of Papers Relating to New Mexico Land Grants, Reel 56, U.S. Surveyor General, Letters Sent, Vol. I.
9. *Lincoln County Leader*, December 23, 1882, p. 1.
10. Maj. Thos. H. Holmes, Fort Stanton, to A.A.G. Santa Fe, February 15, 1857; University of New Mexico Library, Special Collections, Michael Steck Papers, Box 2 Folder 4 (collection hereafter cited as "Steck Papers"). Ibid. to Ibid., April 12, 1857; NA, Microcopy M1120 Roll 6, Department of New Mexico, Letters Received, File No. H-9.
11. D.S. Garland, Albuquerque, to Surveyor General of New Mexico, May 3, 1856; Microfilm of Papers Relating to New Mexico Land Grants, Reel 60, U.S. Surveyor General, Letters Received, 1854–1876, No. 379.
12. Charles N. Beach, Fort Stanton, to Michael Steck, December 19, 1857; Steck Papers, Box 2 Folder 5. Maj. Thos. H. Holmes, Fort Stanton, to A.A.G. Santa Fe, September 27, 1857; NA, Microcopy M1120 Roll 6, File No. H-33.
13. Capt. Thos. Claiborne, Fort Stanton, to Col. Collins, Supt. Ind. Affairs, November 6, 1859; Steck Papers, Box 3 Folder 1.
14. Capt. Thos. Claiborne, Fort Stanton, to A.A.A.G. Santa Fe, November 9, 1859; NA, Microcopy M1120 Roll 9, File No. C-31.
15. Capt. Thos. Claiborne, Fort Stanton, to A.A.A.G. Santa Fe, November 16, 1859; NA, Microcopy M1120 Roll 9, File No. C-33.
16. See Notes 8 and 15; also Capt. Thos. Claiborne, Fort Stanton, to A.A.A.G. Santa Fe, November 3, 1859; NA, Microcopy M1120 Roll 9, File No. C-30.
17. Timothy McGowan et al., Fort Stanton, to Col. B.L.E. Bonneville, February 2, 1859; NA, M1120 Roll 10, File No. R-8. See Notes 15 and 16; also Capt. Thos. Claiborne, Fort Stanton, to A.A.G. Santa Fe, July 13, 1860; NA, M1120 Roll 11, File No. C-15.
18. 35th Cong. 2d Sess. Sen. Ex. Doc. 1 (Serial 975), p. 308.
19. Robert W. Frazer, 1983: *Forts and Supplies*, pp. 154–55. NMSRCA, U.S. Census Records, 1860. Socorro County, Schedule 4 (Productions in Agriculture), Rio Bonito.
20. Frazer 1983: 101. Voucher abstract to Moore & Rees, February 2, 1857; Steck Papers, Box 2 Folder 4. Chas. N. Beach, Fort Stanton, to Michael Steck, November 23, 1857, and voucher to Chas. N. Beach, December 30, 1857; both in Steck Papers, Box 2 Folder 5.
21. Voucher to Chas. N. Beach, December 30, 1857; Steck Papers, Box 2 Folder 5. Voucher to Moore and Rees, March 25, 1858; Steck Papers, Box 2 Folder 6.
22. Frazer 1983: 119. Voucher to Chas. N. Beach, December 30, 1858; Steck Papers, Box 2 Folder 7. Voucher to B.L. Rees, March 30, 1859; Steck Papers, Box 2 Folder 8. NMSRCA, U.S. Census Records, 1860. Socorro County, Schedule 4 (Productions in Agriculture), Rio Bonito.
23. NA, Microcopy T-7 Roll 158; Population Schedules, 8th Census (1860), Rio Bonito,

Socorro County, N.M.

24. Carson 1964: 277. NMSRCA, Socorro County Deed Records, Book A, pp. 262–63, 290–91, 324–25, 344. Michael Steck to J.L. Collins, Supt. Ind. Affairs, March 5, 1860; Steck Papers, Box 3 Folder 2.

25. Philip J. Rasch and Lee Myers, 1963: *Tragedy of the Beckwiths*; Lily Klasner, 1972: *My Girlhood Among Outlaws*, p. 67.

26. See Note 23.

27. Frazer 1983: 103–5. Chas. N. Beach to M. Steck, November 23, 1857; Steck Papers, Box 2 Folder 5. For additional information on the population of Rio Bonito in 1860, see Darlis A. Miller, 1986: *Women of Lincoln County*, pp. 170–72.

28. Lt. Col. J.V.D. Reeve, Fort Stanton, to A.A.A.G. Santa Fe, November 24, 1858; NA, Microcopy M1120 Roll 8, File No. R-35.

29. Reeve to A.A.A.G. Santa Fe, December 14, 1858; NA, Microcopy M1120 Roll 8, File No. R-37. NMSRCA, Territorial Archives of New Mexico, Roll 21 frames 143, 147.

30. Gorney 1969: 8.

31. Capt. Thos. Claiborne, Fort Stanton, to A.A.A.G. Santa Fe, November 3, 9, 16, 1859; all in NA Microcopy M1120 Roll 9, File Nos. C-30, C-31, C-32. Also Capt. Thos. Claiborne, Fort Stanton, to J.L. Collins, Supt. Ind. Affairs, November 6, 1859; Steck Papers, Box 3 Folder 1.

32. See Note 22; also NMSRCA, Territorial Archives of New Mexico, Roll 21 frame 166.

33. Letter from "C" dated Mesilla, January 1, 1860; in *Tri-Weekly Missouri Republican* (St. Louis), January 18, 1860, p. 2.

Chapter 2   *Civil War on the Rio Bonito, 1861–1862*

1. *Daily Alta California*, December 21, 1860, p. 1; The *San Francisco Herald*, December 27, 1860, p. 3; January 1, 1861, p. 3; January 28, 1861, p. 3 (reprinting from various issues of the *Mesilla Times*). Utley 1961; Benjamin H. Sacks, 1962: *New Evidence*.

2. The *Semi-Weekly Southern News* (Los Angeles), February 27, 1861, p. 3; The *Daily Picayune*, March 9, 1861, p. 5; The *San Francisco Herald*, February 25, 1861, p. 1 (reprinting from the *Mesilla Times*). Bender 1974: 165.

3. Bender 1974: 165–66.

4. NA, Microcopy 617 Roll 1216; Post Returns, Fort Stanton, New Mexico, February 1861.

5. Bender 1974: 167; *War of the Rebellion: Official Records* (hereafter cited as WR, OR), Ser. I Vol. 1, p. 604. NA, Microcopy 617 Roll 1216; Post Returns, Fort Stanton, New Mexico, March and April 1861.

6. *Santa Fe Weekly Gazette*, June 8, 1861, p. 2. Bender 1974: 167–68.

7. *Santa Fe Weekly Gazette*, July 13, 1861, p. 2. Fayette Jones, 1968: *Old Mines and Ghost Camps*, pp. 176–77; Bender 1974: 168–69.

8. "Report of the Commissioner of Indian Affairs, . . . for the year 1861," p. 122.

9. WR, OR, Ser. I Vol. 4, pp. 36–7, 51–2. "Report of the Joint Committee on the Conduct of the War," Part III, pp. 364–72. Lt. Col. B.S. Roberts, Fort Stanton, to Col. E.S. Canby, Santa Fe, July 7, 1861;

NA, Microcopy M1120 Roll 28 (July 1861).

10. WR, OR, Ser. I Vol. 1, p. 604.

11. Lt. Col. B.S. Roberts, Fort Stanton, to Col. E.S. Canby, Santa Fe, July 7, 1861; NA, Microcopy M1120 Roll 28 (July 1861).

12. WR, OR, Ser. I Vol. 4, p. 22.

13. WR, OR, Ser. I Vol. 4, p. 19.

14. *Daily Picayune*, September 5, 1861, p. 1 (reprinting from the *Mesilla Times* of August 10, 1861).

15. WR, OR, Ser. 1 Vol. 4, p. 23.

16. *Daily Picayune*, September 27, 1861, p. 1 (reprinting from the *Mesilla Times* of August 29, 1861).

17. Capt. Saturnino Barrientos, Sierra de la Gallina, to Senor Commandante Gral. de Santa Fe, August 24, 1861; NA, Microcopy M1120 Roll 13, File No. B-16.

18. Capt. W.B. Rossell, Albuquerque, to A.A.A.G. Santa Fe, August 19, 1861; NA, Microcopy M1120 Roll 28 (August 1861).

19. Anonymous to Amigo mio (Lorenzo Labadie?), Rio B., August 15, 1861; NA, Microcopy M1120 Roll 13, File No. B-17 (encl.).

20. WR, OR, Ser. I Vol. 4, pp. 24–5.

21. *Tri-Weekly Telegraph* (Houston,Texas), November 1, 1861, p. 3(?) (reprinting from *Mesilla Times* of October 10, 1861).

22. See Note 20.

23. Capt. I. Moore, Camp near Manzana, N.M., to A.A.A.G. Santa Fe, September 20, 1861; NA, Microcopy M1120 Roll 14, File No. M-75.

24. Col. B.S. Roberts, Fort Craig, to Col.

E.R.S. Canby, Santa Fe, January 6, 1862; NA, Microcopy M1120 Roll 29 (January 1862). *Santa Fe Gazette*, November 15, 1862, p. 2.

25. Capt. I. Moore, Camp near Manzana, to A.A.A.G. Santa Fe, September 29, 1861; NA, Microcopy M1120 Roll 14, File No. M-83.

26. *The Texas Republican* (Marshall, Texas), January 11, 1862, p. 2. A similar article appeared in the Denver *Rocky Mountain News* on January 4, 1862, p. 4. Both articles may have been reprinted from the *Santa Fe Gazette*, for which there are no extant issues between mid-October 1861 and mid-January 1862.

27. See Note 19. Capt. I. Moore, Camp near Manzana, N.M., to A.A.A.G. Santa Fe, September 20, 29, 1861; NA, Microcopy M1120 Roll 14, File No. M-75, M-83.

28. WR, OR, Ser. I Vol. 4, pp. 85–9. H.M. Beckwith, Fort Stanton, to Major J. Francisco Chaves, Manzano, August 18, 1861; NA, Microcopy M1120 Roll 13, File No. B-17 (encl.).

29. Edward D. Tittmann, 1929: "Exploitation of Treason," p.138. *Rio Abajo Weekly Press* (Albuquerque), April 21, 1863, p. 3. Brig. Gen. James H. Carleton, Santa Fe, to Col. Christopher Carson, Fort Stanton, November 26, 1862; also to Col. Joseph R. West, Mesilla, September 23, October 8, 1862; all in NA Microcopy M1072 Roll 3, Vol. 9, File Nos. 781, 862, 1064 (for 1862). 1st Lt. Cyrus H. DeForrest, ADC, Santa Fe, to C.O. Fort Stanton, February 27, 1863; NA, Microcopy M1072 Roll 3, Vol. 9, File No. 161 (for 1863).

30. Brig. Gen. James H. Carleton, Santa Fe, to Col. C. Carson, November 26, 1862; NA, Microcopy M1072 Roll 3, Vol. 9, File No. 1064 (for 1862). Published in J.R. Doolittle, 1867: "Condition of Indian Tribes," pp. 102–3.

31. F. Stanley, 1964: *Fort Stanton*, pp. 43, 60.

32. Bender 1974: 176–78.

33. *Santa Fe Gazette*, December 27, 1862, p. 2.

34. *El Paso Daily Herald*, February 13, 1899, p. 2.

35. Ibid. January 30, 1899, p. 3. See also William A. Keleher, 1962: *Fabulous Frontier*, pp.102–3, and R. Jack Sandoval, 1983: *History of St. Francis*.

Chapter 3 *Resettlement, 1862–1869*

1. WR, OR, Ser. I Vol. 15, pp. 576–77, 579.

2. Bender 1974: 183; *Santa Fe Gazette*, December 27, 1862. p. 2.

3. Bender 1974: 179–88; Sonnichsen 1958: 98–101. WR, OR, Ser. I Vol. 15, p. 670.

4. Bender 1974: 192–97.

5. WR, OR, Ser. I Vol. 15, pp. 669–70. Doolittle 1867: 102, 106; Bender 1974: 183–88.

6. *Santa Fe Gazette*, December 27, 1862, p. 2.

7. Col. C. Carson, Fort Stanton, to A.A.G. Santa Fe, January 4, 1863; NA, Microcopy M1120 Roll 18, File No. C-24.

8. Major Joseph Smith, Fort Stanton, to A.A.G. Santa Fe, May 20, 1863; Capt. Fran^co Abreu to Post Adjt., Fort Stanton, July 23, 1863; both in NA Microcopy M1120 Roll 20, File Nos. S-97, S-142.

9. Capt. Geo. Hollister to Post Adjt., Fort Stanton, September 15, 1863; NA, Microcopy M1120 Roll 19, File No. H-90.

10. Major Joseph Smith, Fort Stanton, to A.A.G., Santa Fe, July 30, 1863; NA, Microcopy M1120 Roll 20, File No. S-150.

11. Klasner 1972: 51–2; Nora Henn, 1979: *Historical Survey*, pp.12–13.

12. Journal of John A. Clark, entry for December 15, 1863. Museum of New Mexico History Library, Manuscript collection (extract courtesy of Dr. Robert W. Frazer).

13. John A. Clark, Santa Fe, to Hon. Joseph S. Wilson, August 15, 1866; Microfilm of Papers Relating to New Mexico Land Grants, Reel 56, U.S. Surveyor General, Letters Sent, Vol. I, pp. 538–42.

14. Capt. Wm. Brady, Fort Stanton, to A.A.G. Santa Fe, September 8, 1865; NA, Microcopy M1088 Roll 1, District of New Mexico, Letters Received, File No. B-417.

15. Bvt. Lt. Col. Emil Fritz, Fort Stanton, to Maj. Cyrus H. DeForrest, Santa Fe, March 12, 1866; Ibid. to Ibid., January 6, 1866; both in NA Microcopy M1088 Roll 3, File Nos. F-17, F-5.

16. Maj. Emil Fritz, Fort Stanton, to A.A.G. Santa Fe, October 16, 1865; NA, Microcopy M1088 Roll 1, File No. F-79. See also letter of April 27, 1865, from Brig. Gen. James H. Carleton to Capt. Wm. Brady, Fort Stanton, asking the people to put in all the crops they can that spring (NA, RG 393; Letters Received, Fort Stanton, N.M.).

17. Bvt. Maj. L.G. Murphy, Fort Stanton, to Maj. C.H. DeForrest, ADC Santa Fe, June 10, 1866; NA, Microcopy 1088 Roll 3, File No. M-95.

18. Bureau of Land Management (BLM), New Mexico State Office: Field Notes, Subdivisional Lines in T10S R16E, Vol. S1010 (October 1867), p. 65.

19. BLM, New Mexico State Office; Field Notes, Subdivisional Lines of T9S R16E, Vol. S976 (October 1867), p. 66.

20. BLM, New Mexico State Office; Field Notes, Exterior Boundaries, Vol. R57 (April 1867), pp. 167–68.

21. Klasner 1972: 53–55.

22. Journal of march by detach. of Co. I 37th U.S. Inf. by Lt. Geo. W. Baird, August 17–21, 1868; Fort Stanton, August 26, 1868. NA, Microcopy M1088 Roll 10, File No. S-250.

23. Stanley 1964: 62.

24. Stanley 1964: 70.

25. Bender 1974: 256–58.

26. NMSRCA, Territorial Archives of New Mexico, Roll 3; 18th Legislative Assembly, House of Representatives Journal, pp. 269–70, 321. Charles R. Coan, 1922: *County Boundaries of New Mexico*, pp. 258–60.

27. Richard W. Helbock, 1981: *Post Offices of New Mexico*, p. 27.

28. NMSRCA, Territorial Archives of New Mexico, Roll 21 frames 335, 338–339, 345.

29. Klasner 1972: 54. NA, Microcopy 617 Roll 1216: Post Returns, Fort Stanton, New Mexico, May 1855–December 1867. Special Orders No. 27, Headquarters, Fort Stanton, March 8, 1867; NA, M1088 Roll 7, File No. D-15 (filed with Q-72).

Chapter 4   *The Rise and Decline of the House of Murphy, 1867–1873*

1. Robert N. Mullin, 1968: *Fulton's History of Lincoln County War*, p. 8.

2. Deposition of A.A. McSween, June 6, 1878; in Report on the Death of John H. Tunstall by Frank W. Angel (hereafter cited as Angel Report), pp. 5–6. NA, Record Group 60 (General Records of the Department of Justice), File No. 44-4-8-3.

3. Capt. James F. Randlett, Fort Stanton, to Hon. Sec. of War, July 18, 1873, and Randlett to Adjutant General U.S.A., July 22, 1873; both in NA Microcopy M666 Roll 120, Letters Received by the Office of the Adjutant General 1871–1880, File No. 3211 AGO 1873.

4. Klasner 1972: 95, 98.

5. L.G. Murphy & Co. ledger, May 1871–December 1872; L.G. Murphy & Co. journal, May 1873–January 1874 (hereafter cited as Murphy ledger and Murphy daybook), both at University of Arizona Special Collection Library. First National Bank of Santa Fe General ledger Vol. I, 1871–1873, and Individual ledger No. 2, 1873–1878 (hereafter cited as FNB Gen. ledg. and FNB Indiv. ledg.); University of New Mexico Library, Special Collections, First National Bank of Santa Fe Collection. NA, Record Group 192 (Records of the Office of the Commissary General of Subsistence), Entry 74, Vols. 2,3,4; also Record Group 92 (Records of the Office of the Quartermaster General),

Entry 1238 Vols. 16, 17, Entry 1239 Nos. 1, 2 (extracted from notes of Dr. Darlis Miller). NA, Microcopy M782 Roll 1. Internal Revenue Assessment Lists for Territory of New Mexico, 1862–1870, 1872–1874. Lawrence Lindsay Mehren, 1969: *History of Mescalero Apache Reservation*.

6. NA, Microcopy M427 Roll 15, Compiled Service Records of Volunteer Union Soldiers Who Served . . . from the Territory of New Mexico, Lawrence G. Murphy service record, 1st Cav. N. Mex. Vols. Doolittle 1867: 346.

7. Klasner 1972: 94.

8. Ibid.; also Mullin 1968: 46–47. Deposition of A.A. McSween, Exhibit 5, in Angel Report.

9. "One of the First" (brief biographical sketch of J.H. [*sic*] LaRue) in The *Roswell Daily Record*, September 4, 1905, p. 2. NA, Microcopy M782 Roll 1, Record of Personal Taxes 1865–1870.

10. Murphy ledger, distribution of liabilities, May 1, 1871. Deposition of A.A. McSween, Exhibit 6, in Angel Report.

11. NA, Microcopy M782 Roll 1, Record of Licenses assessed and issued, N. Mex., 1863–1868, and Record of Personal Taxes 1865–1870.

12. NA, Microcopy M1097, Registers of Letters Received, District of New Mexico 1865–1890, Roll 1 Vol. 3 (1867), File No.

S-127, and Roll 2 Vol. 4 (1868), File No. M-253.

13. Wm. D. Whipple A.A.G. Washington, D.C., to Lawrence G. Murphy, Washington, D.C., February 15, 1871; NA, Microcopy M1088 Roll 13, File No. M-64.
14. R. H. McKay, 1918: *Little Pills*, p. 108.
15. NA, Microcopy M782 Roll 1, Record of Personal Taxes 1865–1870.
16. NA, RG192, Entry 74 Vol. 2, pp. 91, 130.
17. NA, RG92, Entry 1238 Vol. 17, pp. 34, 109.
18. Affidavits of Agapito Lucero and Juan Jose Martinez, February 16, 1869; NA, Microcopy M1088 Roll 11, File No. H-3.
19. Endorsement on Commissioner of Indian Affairs E.S. Parker to Brig. Gen. E.D. Townsend, Adjt. Gen. U.S.A., July 21, 1871; NA, Record Group 94, Letters Received by the Appointment, Commission and Personal Branch, 1871–1894, File 3172 ACP 1871. Mehren 1969: 27.
20. A summary of the laws and regulations covering sutlers and post traders from 1776 through 1876 is in 46th Cong. 3d Sess. Senate Report 829 (1881).
21. See Note 19.
22. See NA Microcopy M1097 Roll 2 Vol. 6, File Nos. S-115, S-160, S-167. Proposal and report, Post Traders Store at Fort Stanton for use as a hospital, August 18–September 24, 1870; NA, Microcopy M1088 Roll 11, File No. S-143.
23. Printed endorsements of L.G. Murphy & Co., December 19, 1870, through May 4, 1874; also Wm. W. Belknap, Sec. of War, to C.O. Fort Stanton, August 20, 1873; both in NA Microcopy M666 Roll 120, File No. 3211 AGO 1873. Murphy ledger, pp. 388, 518.
24. Rasch, 1957a: *Rise of House of Murphy*, pp. 62–70; Andrew Wallace, 1975: *Duty in the District*, p. 262; Mehren 1969: 28. Lt. Col. August V. Kautz, Fort Stanton, to Adjt. Gen. U.S.A., January 10, 1872; NA, Record Group 393, Letters Sent, Headquarters, Fort Stanton, N.M.
25. NA, Microcopy 593 Roll 894; Population Schedules, 9th Census (1870), Lincoln County, N.M.
26. See Note 24 (Kautz letter).
27. William J. Parish, 1961: *Charles Ilfeld Company*, pp. 44–60.
28. See Murphy ledger and Murphy daybook (Note 5).
29. Klasner 1972: 95–96.
30. *Golden Era* (Lincoln, N.M.), January 1, 1885, p. 1.

31. Murphy ledger.
32. *The Daily New Mexican*, August 29, 1872, p. 1.
33. See Note 28.
34. NMSRCA, U.S. Census Records, 1870. Lincoln County, Schedule 3 (Productions in Agriculture), Precincts Nos. 1–4.
35. See Note 28.
36. See Note 28; also Klasner 1972: 96.
37. NA, RG92, Entry 1238 Vol. 17, p. 136; also published in Serial No. 1440, 41st Cong. 3d Sess. Sen. Ex. Doc. 21 (1871).
38. NA, RG92, Entry 1242 No. 1, pp. 24–44 (from notes of Dr. Darlis Miller).
39. When an awardee could not fill his contract, the balance owing might be filled by another contractor or by purchases on the open market, the original contractor being held liable for the difference in cost. For examples see C.W. Conrad to Post Adjutant, Fort Stanton, December 30, 1869; NA, RG 393, Letters Sent, Fort Stanton, N.M.; also file concerning Peter Ott hay contract (& others) in University of New Mexico Library, Special Collections, Catron Collection, Sect. 803 Box 2, Miscellany (Folder 1); also S.B. Bushnell, Fort Stanton, to L.E. Dudley, Supt. Ind. Affairs, May 8, 1873, concerning Van Smith beef contract, in NA Microcopy T21 Roll 18, Letters Received from the Mescalero Apache Agency, 1873.
40. "Report of the Commissioner of Indian Affairs, . . . for the Year 1871," p. 371. See also Note 24 (Kautz letter).
41. Mehren 1969: 28, 67–68.
42. "Report of the Commissioner of Indian Affairs, . . . for the Year 1871," pp. 371, 401.
43. Ibid., p. 402.
44. Mehren 1969: 25–27.
45. Ibid., p. 30. Also Wm. Vandever, U.S. Ind. Inspector, Fort Stanton, to Sec. of the Interior, September 3, 1873; NA, Microcopy M1070 Roll 29, Reports of Inspections of the Field Jurisdictions of the Office of Indian Affairs 1873–1900.
46. Mehren 1969: 25–26, 30–32.
47. Ibid., pp. 34–35.
48. Vouchers dated March 31, 1873, to Emil Fritz with cover letter of May 17, 1873; vouchers dated May 31, 1873, to Emil Fritz with cover letters of November 8 and 24, 1873; voucher of June 30, 1873, to J.J. Dolan with cover letter of June 14, 1873; voucher dated July 25, 1873, to L. G. Murphy & Co. with cover letter of Aug. 8, 1873; NA, Microcopy 234 Roll 561, frames

0678–0683, 0576–0579, 0691–0693, 0532–0537.

49. Mehren 1969: 35.

50. See Note 48: also contract with L.G. Murphy and Emil Fritz for delivery of 364,000 lbs. of corn dated June 26, 1873. NA, Microcopy 234 Roll 561, frames 0098–0100. "Report of the Commissioner of Indian Affairs, . . . for the Year 1873," p. 263.

51. Mehren 1969: 52; Hana Samek, 1982: "No Bed of Roses," pp. 143–44.

52. Ibid. 1969: 52; Ibid. 1982: 144.

53. FNB Gen. ledg., FNB Indiv. ledg. (see Note 5). Financial and business records, Second National Bank of Santa Fe, Deposit ledger January 1, 1873–March 31, 1876, and Individual ledger No. 2 (hereafter cited as 2NB Gen. ledg. and 2NB Indiv. ledg.); Museum of New Mexico History Library, Manuscript Collection.

54. See Note 48 and similar vouchers on the same microfilm; also Geo. H.B. White, National Metropolitan Bank, Washington, to Hon. Commissioner of Indian Affairs, May 18, 1874, with attached (?) assignment by L.G. Murphy & Co. to First National Bank of Santa Fe, dated Aug. 28, 1874. NA, Microcopy 234 Roll 563, frame 0802.

55. FNB Indiv. ledg., L.G. Murphy & Co. account.

56. Printed endorsements of L.G. Murphy & Co., December 19, 1870 through May 4, 1874; NA, Microcopy M666 Roll 120, File No. 3211 AGO 1873. See also Note 24 (Kautz letter).

57. Rasch 1957a: 65–69; Mehren 1969: 61–63. "Annual Report of the Commissioner of Indian Affairs . . . for the Year 1872," pp. 263–264.

58. Lincoln County Clerk's Office, Carrizozo, N.M., Book E - M1sc., pp. 78–80. Quitclaim deed of Emil Fritz and L.G. Murphy to the U.S.A., June 13, 1873. Notes on voucher in University of Arizona Special Collections Library, Maurice Fulton Papers, Box 11 Folder 1: Lincoln County History (collection hereafter cited as "Fulton Papers"). S.B. Bushnell, Fort Stanton, to Supt. L.E. Dudley, Santa Fe, May 24, 1873, recommending purchase of L.G. Murphy & Co. building; NA, Microcopy T21 Roll 18.

59. Endorsement of Capt. Ch. McKibbin on letter of Capt. James F. Randlett, Fort Stanton, to Hon. Sec. of War, July 18, 1873; NA, Microcopy M666 Roll 120, File

No. 3211 AGO 1873. See also Murphy daybook.

60. Rasch 1957a: 66–68. S.B. Bushnell, Fort Stanton, to L.E. Dudley, Supt. Ind. Affairs, Santa Fe, May 8, 1873; NA, Microcopy T21 Roll 18. The army compiled a substantial file on the Randlett-Murphy affair; see File No. 3211 AGO 1873 in NA Microcopy M666 Roll 120.

61. Voucher dated May 31, 1873, to Emil Fritz, with endorsements, enclosed with cover letter of November 8, 1874; NA, Microcopy 234 Roll 561, frames 0576–0579.

62. L. Edwin Dudley, New York City, to Commissioner of Indian Affairs, August 31, 1874; C.B. French, Second Auditor's Office, to Hon. Commissioner of Indian Affairs, Sept. 18, 1874; NA, Microcopy M234 Roll 562, frames 0099 and 0632. Z. Staab & Co., New York, to Commissioner of Indian Affairs, October 6, 1874; NA, Microcopy M234 Roll 563, frame 0507.

63. L. Edwin Dudley, Wing's Station, Dutchess Co., New York, to Messrs. Z. Staab & Co., October 3, 1874; NA, Microcopy M234 Roll 563, frame 0508.

64. See Note 61.

65. Maj. Wm. Redwood Price, Santa Fe, to Lt. J.P. Willard, A.A.A.G., December 13, 1873; NA, Microcopy M234 Roll 563, frame 0780.

66. See Note 3.

67. Meaning the Military Reservation; emphasis in original. See endorsement by Wm. H. Belknap, Sec. of War, September 25, 1873, on letter from Randlett to Adj. Gen. U.S.A., July 22, 1873 (see Note 3). The actual order was in a letter from the Adj. Gen. U.S.A. to Capt. Ch. McKibbin, Fort Stanton, September 30, 1873; NA, Microcopy M666 Roll 120, File No. 3211 AGO 1873.

68. Maj. Wm. Redwood Price, Fort Stanton, to A.A.A.G. Santa Fe, November 25, 1873; NA, Microcopy M666 Roll 120, File No. 3211 AGO 1873. Printed reply to statements of Capt. James F. Randlett, May 25, 1874, and printed endorsements of L.G. Murphy & Co., December 19, 1870 through May 6, 1874; NA, Record Group 94, Letters Received by the Appointment, Commission and Personal Branch, 1871–1894, file 2461 ACP 1874.

69. See Note 3, also endorsement of Capt. Ch. McKibbin on Randlett letter of July 22, 1873. See also Note 68 and Comm. of Ind. Affairs to Hon. Sec. of War, Washington, D.C., August 21, 1873; all in NA

Microcopy M666 Roll 120, File No. 3211 AGO 1873.

70. See Note 68.

71. "Annual Report of the Commissioner of Indian Affairs . . . . for the Year 1873," p. 264.

72. Samek 1982: 157.

73. Mullin 1957: 72; Rasch 1957a: 70.

74. Murphy daybook. *The Daily New Mexican*, August 29, 1874, p. 3, announcing dissolution of the Murphy-Fritz partnership due to death; Ibid., August 31, 1874, p. 2, giving notice that the firm of L.G. Murphy & Co. will consist of L.G. Murphy and J.J. Dolan after this date.

75. J.W. Hendron, 1939: *Old Lincoln Courthouse*; Thomas J. Caperton, 1983: *Historic Structure Report*, pp. 134–37; Murphy daybook, p. 318.

76. Murphy daybook, pp. 137, 206, 220, 257, 288, 290, 320, 335, 351. Deposition of A.A. McSween, Exhibit 6 p. 14, in Angel Report.

77. Murphy ledger, pp. 250, 258, 523.

78. Lincoln County Clerk's Office, Carrizozo, N.M., Record Book A.

79. See Keleher, 1957: *Violence in Lincoln County*, pp. 16–20, for examples.

Chapter 5   *The Horrell War, 1873–1874*

1. Klasner 1972.

2. Rasch, 1968: "Tularosa Ditch War"; Miller, 1982: *California Column in New Mexico*, pp. 107–9.

3. General Orders No. 3, AGO, Fort Leavenworth, Ks., February 14, 1874; NA, Microcopy M666 Roll 142, File No. 554 AGO 1874.

4. Rasch, 1956c: 223–26; Fulton 1957.

5. Rasch, 1956c: "Horrell War," pp. 226–27; *Mining Life* (Silver City, N.M.), December 20, 1873, p. 2; *The Daily New Mexican*, December 9, 1873, p. 1. Also Jacinto Gonzales and Manuel Guiterra, Lincoln, N.M., to Gov. Marsh Giddings, Santa Fe, December 26, 1873, and Major Jno. S. Mason, Fort Stanton, to A.A.G. Dept. of the Missouri, December 25, 1873; both in NA Microcopy M666 Roll 142, File No. 554 AGO 1874.

6. Major Jno. S. Mason, Fort Stanton, to A.A.G. Dept. of the Missouri, December 25, 1873; NA, Microcopy M666 Roll 142, File No. 554 AGO 1874.

7. Jacinto Gonzales and Manuel Guiterra, Lincoln, N.M., to Gov. Marsh Giddings, Santa Fe, December 26, 1873; NA, Microcopy M666 Roll 142, File No. 554 AGO 1874.

8. See Note 6, also Gov. Marsh Giddings, Santa Fe, to Sec. of the Interior, January 12, 1874; Warren Bristol, Santa Fe, to the Governor, January 10, 1874; L.G. Murphy, Lincoln, N.M., to Gov. Giddings, December 26, 1873; all in NA Microcopy M666 Roll 142, File No. 554 AGO 1874.

9. See Note 6.

10. See Note 6.

11. See Notes 6 and 7, also *The Borderer* (Las Cruces, N.M.), December 27, 1873, and *Mining Life*, January 10, 1874, p. 2.

12. See Notes 6 and 7, also Rasch 1956c: 228–29; Caperton 1983: 89–91; *Daily New Mexican*, January 2, 1874, p. 1. A.A.G. Dept. of the Missouri, Fort Leavenworth, Ks., to C.O. Dist. of New Mexico, Santa Fe, December 30, 1873; NA, Microcopy M666 Roll 142, File No. 554 AGO 1874.

13. *Daily New Mexican*, January 9, 1874, p. 1. Judge Warren Bristol, Santa Fe, to Sheriff of Lincoln County, January 17, 1874; Maj. Wm. Redwood Price, Santa Fe, to A.A.A.G. Santa Fe, January 18, 1874; both in NA Microcopy M1088 Roll 23, File No. P-2 N.M. 1874 (Enclosures).

14. Klasner 1972: 104. Maj. Wm. Redwood Price, Fort Stanton, to A.A.G. Santa Fe, January 23, 1874; entered in NA Microcopy M1097 Roll 3 Vol. 8 as File No. P-3 N.M. 1874.

15. Maj. Wm. Redwood Price, Fort Stanton, to A.A.G. Santa Fe, January 25, 1874; NA, Microcopy M1088 Roll 23, File No. P-4 N.M. 1874.

16. Maj. Wm. Redwood Price, Fort Stanton, to A.A.G. Santa Fe, January 28, 1874; NA, Microcopy M1088 Roll 23, File No. P-5 N.M. 1874.

17. Enclosures with C. Delano, Sec. of the Interior, Washington, D.C., to Hon. W.H. Belknap, January 28, 1874; NA, Microcopy M666 Roll 142, File No. 554 AGO 1874.

18. W.H. Belknap, Washington, D.C., to Hon. Sec. of the Interior, February 3, 1874; NA, Microcopy M666 Roll 142, File No. 554 AGO 1874.

19. Maj. Wm. Redwood Price, Fort Stanton, to A.A.G. Santa Fe, February 5, 1874; NA, Microcopy M1088 Roll 23, File No. P-6 N.M. 1874.
20. *Mesilla News*, March 7, 1874, p. 2.
21. Maj. D.R. Clendenin, Fort Stanton, to A.A.A.G. Santa Fe, February 18, 1874; NA, Microcopy M1088 Roll 23, File No. S-17 N.M. 1874.
22. *The Daily New Mexican*, March 13, 1874, p. 1.
23. *The Daily New Mexican*, January 20, 1874, p. 1.
24. NMSRCA, Territorial Archives of New Mexico, Roll 21 frame 398.
25. Capt. James F. Randlett, Fort Stanton, to Hon. Sec. of War, October 17, 1874; NA, Microcopy M666 Roll 120, File No. 3211 AGO 1873.
26. Lincoln County Clerk Records, Carrizozo, N.M., Causes 73, 79, 80; Socorro County District Court Journal, October 31, 1874, Causes No. 22–26; both from, notes in Philip C. Rasch file No. 28—"The Horrell

War." *The Mesilla News*, November 14, 1874, p. 2.
27. Deposition of Juan B. Patron, June 6, 1878, in Angel Report, p. 275.
28. Murphy daybook, p. 348.
29. The original notes are in the Fulton Papers, Box 11 Folder 9. One other note for $900. was payable March 1, 1874. See also Lincoln County Clerk's Office, Carrizozo, N.M., Record Book A, Articles of Agreement, J.J. Dolan and Charles Miller, February 3, 1874.
30. George G. Anderson, 1907: *History of New Mexico, Vol. I*, pp. 232–33.
31. Maj. John L. Mason, Fort Stanton, to Capt. Chambers McKibbin, December 5, 1873; Lt. A.G. Hennisee, Post Adjt. Fort Stanton, to Capt. E.G. Fechit, December 24, 1873; both enclosed with C. Delano, Sec. of the Interior, Washington, D.C., to Hon. W.H. Belknap, January 28, 1874; NA, Microcopy M666 Roll 142, File No. 554 AGO 1874.

Chapter 6   *A Tradition of Violence, 1874–1877*

1. Maj. Wm. Redwood Price, Fort Wingate, to ???, March 14, 1874; NA, Microcopy M1088 Roll 23, File No. P-13 N.M. 1874 (copy).
2. *Mesilla News*, December 5, 1874, p. 2.
3. J. Evetts Haley, 1930: *Horse Thieves*; Harwood P. Hinton, 1956: "John Simpson Chisum," pp. 177–90; Sonnichsen 1958: 150–54. Robert A. Casey interview with J. Evetts Haley, June 25, 1937, in Haley History Center, Midland, Texas (collection hereafter cited as HHC).
4. E.C. Watkins, U.S. Indian Inspector, Santa Fe, to Commissioner of Indian Affairs, June 27, 1878 (hereafter cited as Watkins Report), pp. 16, 41–42. NA, Microcopy M1070 Roll 29.
5. *Daily New Mexican*, November 6, 1874, p. 1; Miller 1982: 214.
6. *Mesilla News*, December 26, 1874, p. 2.
7. *Mesilla News*, January 16, 1875, p. 2.
8. *Daily New Mexican*, March 22, 1875, p. 1.
9. *Daily New Mexican*, April 26, 1875, p. 1.
10. *Daily New Mexican*, May 20, 1875, p. 1.
11. Mullin 1968: 26–27; *Mesilla News*, May 1, 1875, p. 2. Lincoln County Legal Records, 1875, Cause No. 157; from notes in Philip C. Rasch file No. 30—"They Fought for the House II."
12. NMSRCA, Territorial Archives of New

Mexico, Roll 21 frames 425, 463, 509.
13. *Daily New Mexican*, October 28, 1875, p. 1.
14. Klasner 1972: 124–136.
15. *Daily New Mexican*, August 9, 1875, p. 1; *Weekly New Mexican*, August 31, 1875, p. 2; *Mesilla News*, August 14, 1875, p. 2.
16. Rasch, 1957b: "The Gun and the Rope"; Robert A. Casey interview with J. Evetts Haley, June 25, 1937. HHC. *Daily New Mexican*, November 3, 1875, p. 1; *Weekly New Mexican*, November 9, 1875, p. 1; *Mesilla News*, December 25, 1875, p. 2; *The Herald* (Silver City, N.M.), February 20, 1876, p. 2; *Lincoln County Leader* (White Oaks, N.M.), June 26, 1886.
17. Klasner 1972: 134–35.
18. Ibid., pp. 135–36. *Weekly New Mexican*, December 28, 1875, p. 1.
19. The *Mesilla News*, December 18, 1875, p. 2.
20. Ibid.
21. Victor Westphall, 1965: *Public Domain in New Mexico*, pp. 45, 67–68.
22. Klasner 1972: 6–7. Frank Coe interview with J. Evetts Haley, August 14, 1927, HHC.
23. *Mesilla News*, December 18, 1875, p. 2. "Sundry memorials," pp. 118–19, 23d

Legislative Assembly, Territory of New Mexico (1878); in NA, Microcopy M364 Roll 8, Interior Department Territorial Papers, New Mexico, 1851–1914. Frank Coe interview with J. Evetts Haley, August 14, 1927, HHC.

24. Caperton 1983: 49–51, 137–38, 279, 326–29, 420, 470.
25. Murphy daybook, pp. 258, 266, 312.
26. Frank Coe interview with J. Evetts Haley, March 20, 1927, HHC.
27. Mullin 1968: 64; Klasner 1972: 96. Deposition of A.A. McSween, June 6, 1878, in Angel Report, pp. 6–7.
28. Lincoln County Clerk's Office, Carrizozo, N.M., Record Book A.
29. Deposition of A.A. McSween, June 6, 1878, in Angel Report, p. 5. Letter from M. Turner in the *Las Vegas Gazette* (Las Vegas, N.M.), May 4, 1878. Susan E. Barber interview with J. Evetts Haley, August 16, 1927, HHC.
30. Susan (McSween) Barber, "Notes of Correction on The Saga of Billy the Kid," p. 38; Fulton Papers, Box 1 Folder 4. W.L. Patterson, "The Lincoln County War," p. 4; Fulton Papers, Box 11 Folder 1.
31. Klasner 1972: 142.
32. Hinton 1956: 190; FNB Indiv. ledg. (see Chapter 4 Note 5).
33. Utley, 1985: *Four Fighters of Lincoln County*, p. 1.
34. Mehren 1969: 34, 62–3, 66.
35. Ibid. 1969: 84, 108–9.
36. Mehren 1969: 126–27, 158–59.
37. Ibid. 1969: 144.
38. Mullin 1968: 8; Klasner 1972: 97.
39. Klasner 1972: 290–91.
40. Ibid. 1972: 97.
41. Mehren 1969: 144, 163–65.
42. FNB Indiv. ledg.
43. NA, RG192, Entry 74 Vol. 4.
44. A two-company post with a garrison of 140 officers and men at the regulation ration of 1¼ pounds of fresh beef per day required 5,250 pounds of beef each month. Converted to live weights this would be about twelve steers.
45. Mullin 1968: 95.
46. Hinton 1956: 310–14; Keleher 1957: 42–51. McSween replied to these accusations in *Eco Del Rio Grande*, January 24, 1878. Although a grand jury later refused to indict him on the embezzlement charge, McSween never produced the insurance money.
47. Hinton 1956: 312; Keleher 1957: 44–9; Klasner 1972: 261–71.

48. Don Rickey Jr., 1963: *Forty Miles a Day on Beans and Hay*, p. 128.
49. Keleher 1957: 49–51; Mullin 1968: 34.
50. Mehren 1969: 163–64.
51. Keleher 1957: 272.
52. FNB Gen. ledg., FNB Indiv. ledg. (see Chapter 4, Note 5); 2NB Gen. ledg., 2NB Indiv. ledg. (see Chapter 4, Note 53).
53. NA, RG192, Entry 69, Vol. for years 1863–1871, p. 140; Entry 74 Vol. 4NA, RG92, Entry 1242 No. 1 and No. 2 (from notes of Dr. Darlis Miller). Mehren 1969: 127, 144, 163–164.
54. Westphall, 1973: *Thomas Benton Catron and His Era*, p. 77.
55. *Mesilla Valley Independent*, April 27, 1878, p. 2; Hinton 1956: 191–92, 196; Mullin 1968: 51, 166; Klasner 1972: 97, 255. Deposition of James H. Farmer, June 4, 1878, in Watkins Report; NA, Microcopy M1070, Roll 29. W.L. Patterson, "The Lincoln County War," p. 4; Fulton Papers, Box 11 Folder 1. Robt. A. Widenmann to Hon. C. Schurz, March 11, 1878; typescript in Fulton Papers, Box 11 Folder 7. George Coe interview with J. Evetts Haley, March 20, 1927, HHC. Gov. Lew. Wallace, Santa Fe, to Hon. C. Schurz, April 25, 1879; in Indiana Historical Society Library, Lew.Wallace Papers (collection hereafter cited as Lew. Wallace Papers).
56. Mullin 1968: 166. George Coe interview with J. Evetts Haley, March 20, 1927, HHC.
57. Mehren 1969: 84, 109–10.
58. See Mullin 1968: 213 for a roster; "Billie's" letter names other rustlers (see Note 59).
59. Letter/testimony signed "Billie," ca. 1880; Lew. Wallace Papers.
60. Hinton 1956: 191–192; Rasch, 1956d, "Pecos War," p. 103; Mullin 1968: 35–6.
61. *Mesilla Valley Independent*, June 23, 1877, p. 5. Rasch 1956d; Mullin 1968; 35–43.
62. *Grant County Herald* (Silver City, N.M.), August 24, 1878, p. 1.
63. Mullin 1968: 89.
64. *Mesilla Valley Independent*, August 18, 1877, pp. 2, 3; August 25, 1877, pp. 1–2; September 8, 1877, p. 1; September 22, 1877, p. 3. Rasch, 1960: "Story of Jesse J. Evans"; Mullin 1968: 66–7, 75–87; Klasner 1972: 156–57; Grady E. McCright & James H. Powell, 1983: *Jessie Evans: Lincoln County Badman*, pp. 41–53.
65. *Grant County Herald*, September 1, 1877; Rasch, 1955: "Twenty-One Men He Put Bullets Through," p. 9.
66. *Mesilla Valley Independent*, October 6,

1877, p. 2; October 13, 1877, p. 1.
67. Robert A. Casey interview with J. Evetts Haley, June 25, 1937, HHC.
68. Susan Barber, "Notes of Correction on The Saga of Billy the Kid," no page number;

Fulton Papers, Box 1 Folder 4.
69. *Grant County Herald*, October 6, 1877, p. 3.
70. See Note 67; also Klasner 1972: 174.

Chapter 7   *John H. Tunstall Comes to Lincoln, 1876–1878*

1. FNB Indiv. ledg. (see Chapter 4 Note 5).
2. Keleher 1957: 38–9; Frederick W. Nolan, 1965: *Life and Death of J.H. Tunstall*, pp. 152–80.
3. J.H. Tunstall to "My Much Beloved Father," April 27, 1877; photocopy in Fulton Papers, Box 14 Folder 3. See also Nolan 1965: 213.
4. J.H. Tunstall to "My Much Beloved Governor," March 23, 1877; photocopy in Fulton Papers, Box 14 Folder 3.
5. Nolan 1965: 205–206.
6. J.H. Tunstall to Father, addition to letter of June 8 (1877); photocopy in Fulton Papers, Box 14 Folder 3. See also Nolan 1965: 220, 224.
7. Nolan 1965: 206.
8. Ibid., p. 207.
9. Deposition of A.A. McSween, June 6, 1878, in Angel Report, pp. 9–10.
10. For a similar opinion see Cecil Bonney, 1971: *Looking Over My Shoulder*, p. 61.
11. NA, RG92, Entry 1242 No. 1 and No. 2. Mehren 1969: 127–28, 159–60, 191–92.
12. NA, RG92, Entry 1242 No. 2. pp. 245–46, 249. *Rio Grande Republican* (Las Cruces, N.M.), November 10, 1883, p. 2.
13. *Lincoln County Leader*, May 3, 1890, p. 1; May 24, 1890, p. 4; May 9, 1891, p. 1. *Liberty Banner* (Lincoln, N.M.), June 25, 1891, p. 3.
14. Deposition of Juan B. Patron, June 6, 1878, in Angel Report, p. 273. *Grant County Herald*, August 18, 1877, p. 1. Mullin 1968: 168, 186; Caperton 1983: 70.
15. U.S. Department of the Interior, General Land Office, 1924: 31–32.
16. A.A. McSween to "My Dear Mr. Tunstall," April 17, 1878; photocopy in Fulton Papers, Box 14 Folder 4.
17. Nolan 1965: 397.
18. J.P. Tunstall to J.H. Tunstall, March 10, 1877; Fulton Papers, Box 14 Folder 2.
19. J.H. Tunstall to Father, addition to letter of June 8 (1877); photocopy in Fulton Papers, Box 14 Folder 3. See also Nolan 1965: 204, 208.
20. J.P. Tunstall to J.H. Tunstall, March 21,

1877; Fulton Papers, Box 14 Folder 2.
21. J.P. Tunstall to J.H. Tunstall, undated (probably February 1878); Fulton Papers, Box 14 Folder 2.
22. On March 19, 1878, Rev. Taylor Ealy wrote to Sheldon Jackson that Tunstall "Had just drawn on a bank of London for several thousand pounds, which had not reached here at the time of his death" (Norman J. Bender, 1984: *Missionaries, Outlaws, and Indians*, p. 27).
23. Nolan 1965: 420.   23a. FNB Indiv. ledger (see Chapter 4 Note 5).   23b. Warranty deed, Lawrence G. Murphy to A.A. McSween, February 9, 1877; Fulton Papers, Box 12 Folder 4.
24. Keleher 1957: 34–38, 149; Rasch, 1964a: "War in Lincoln County," p. 2; 1970: 4. Deposition of A.A. McSween, Exhibit 7 pp. 121–22, Exhibit 8 pp. 127–28, in Angel Report.
25. *Grant County Herald*, August 18, 1877, p. 1.
26. Daniel T. Kelly, 1972: *The Buffalo Head*, pp. 21–22. J.P. Tunstall to J.H. Tunstall, March 21, 1877; Fulton Papers, Box 14 Folder 2.
27. The *Mesilla Valley Independent*, August 25, 1877, p. 3.
28. *Mesilla Valley Independent*, October 13, 1877, p. 2.
29. Pat. F. Garrett, 1954: *Authentic Life of Billy the Kid*, p. 85.
30. Keleher 1957: 88–90; Mullin 1968: 87–92. *Weekly New Mexican*, December 4, 1877, p. 2; *Mesilla Valley Independent*, December 15, 1877, p. 2. Message of the Governor to the 23d Legislative Assembly, Territory of New Mexico, delivered January 8, 1878; in NMSRCA, Territorial Archives of New Mexico, Roll 21.
31. Depositions of Jessie Evans, June 14, 1878, and Andrew Boyle, June 17, 1878, in Watkins Report; NA, Microcopy M1070 Roll 29 (see Chapter 6 Note 4).
32. Nolan 1965: 255–56.
33. Attachment and sale of 64 head of Casey

cattle; same for 145 head of Casey cattle; both by Sheriff Wm. Brady, April 4–June 6, 1877; photocopies in Fulton Papers, Box 12 Folder 2.

34. Nolan 1965: 239, 247–50; Mullin 1968: 83–4; Klasner 1972: 147–49.

35. Keleher 1957: 105–6; Nolan 1965: 257–60, 263.

36. Nolan 1965: 245, 275.

37. Abneth McCabe to Mrs. E.E. Casey, December 23, 1877; typescript copy in Fulton Papers, Box 11 Folder 7.

38. Inventory of Property Belonging to Estate of John H. Tunstall, January 16, 1879, by Isaac Ellis. Notice of Administrative Sale and List of Property to be Sold, Tunstall Estate, May 28, 1881, by Sue E. Barber. Photocopies of both in Fulton Papers, Box 14 Folder 7.

39. Mehren 1969: 59. *Mesilla Valley Independent*, October 13, 1877, p. 2. NA, RG92, Entry 1242 No. 2.

40. Thirty-day note for $4.00 or 175 pounds of clean wheat in sacks, Jose Madril to J.H. Tunstall, February 2, 1878; Fulton Papers, Box 11 Folder 9.

41. First endorsement dated May 2, 1878 to letter of Maj. Gen. Jno. Pope, Fort Leavenworth, Ks., to A.A.G. Division of the Missouri, Chicago, April 24, 1878; NA, Microcopy M666 Roll 397, File No. 1405 AGO 1878.

42. See Note 3.

43. Mullin 1968: 47–49; Klasner 1972: 94–95.

44. Deposition of James J. Dolan, June 17, 1878, in Watkins Report; NA, Microcopy M1070, Roll 29.

45. A.A. McSween to Hon. Carl Schurz, February 11, 1878, and A.A. McSween to Dr. Lowry, February 25, 1878; both in NA, RG75, LR, Office of Indian Affairs, File Nos. M319/1879 and L147/1879 (Encl. 1). An undated, unsigned letter to Hon. Carl Schurz stamped received October 27, 1877 made similar charges and appeared to be in Tunstall's handwriting. Photocopies of all in Fulton Papers, Box 11 Folder 7. See also Keleher 1957: 66–68.

46. Deposition of Morris J. Bernstein, June 14, 1878, in Watkins Report; NA, Microcopy M1070, Roll 29.

47. Deposition of A.A. McSween, June 18, 1878, in Watkins Report; NA, Microcopy M1070, Roll 29.

48. E.C. Watkins to Commissioner of Indian Affairs, June 27, 1878, in Watkins Report, p. 39; NA, Microcopy M1070, Roll 29 (see Chapter 6 Note 4).

49. Deposition of Juan B. Patron, June 6,

1878, in Angel Report, pp. 275–76.

50. Deposition of Florencio Gonzales, June 8, 1878, in Angel Report, pp. 324–25.

51. Deposition of James J. Dolan, June 25, 1878, in Angel Report, pp. 235–37.

52. Deposition of A.A. McSween, June 6, 1878, in Angel Report, p. 13.

53. FNB Indiv. ledg. (see Chapter 4 Note 5).

54. Keleher 1957: 63–65; Nolan 1965: 279, Fig. 29 (illustration of McSween check); *Mesilla Valley Independent*, January 26, 1878, p. 5; February 2, 1878, p. 3. Undated 4 pp. statement (in Robert Widenmann's handwriting) in Fulton Papers, Box 14 Folder 8. See also depositions by A.A. McSween, June 6, 1878, and Juan B. Patron, June 6, 1878, in Angel Report, pp. 13–14, 278. Montague Leverson, Lincoln, N.M., to "Dear Sir" (U.S. Marshal John Sherman Jr.?), March 20, 1878, in Angel Report (unpaginated addenda).

55. Keleher 1957, 78–9, 103; Mullin 1968: 203–4; *Mesilla News*, July 13, 1878, p. 2. Robt. A. Widenmann, Lincoln, N.M., to Hon. C. Schurz, March 11, 1878; typescript copy in Fulton Papers, Box 11 Folder 7. Mortgage deed, John H. Riley and J.J. Dolan to Thomas B. Catron, January 19, 1878; photocopy in Fulton Papers, Box 12 Folder 4.

56. Keleher 1957: 60–3, 76–80; Nolan 1965: 258–59, 263, 267–68, 280; Mullin 1968: 97, 101–2, 111, 201, 223–24.

57. Mullin 1968: 103–8. Depositions of A.A. McSween, June 6, 1878, and A.P. Barrier, June 11, 1878, in Angel Report, pp. 26–30, 289–95.

58. Keleher 1957: 81, 85–7, 104–5; Nolan 1965: 268–70; Mullin 1968: 109–111. Depositions of A.A. McSween, June 6, 1878, Robert A. Widenmann, June 6, 1878, and James J. Longwill, May 14, 1878, all in Angel Report, pp. 32–4, 193–94, 248–49.

59. Rasch, 1962: "How the Lincoln County War Started"; James D. Shinkle, 1966: *Reminiscences of Roswell Pioneers*, pp. 38–9; *Las Vegas Gazette*, May 4, 1878, p. 2; *Grant County Herald*, June 8, 1878, p. 1. (Reprinted in the *Weekly New Mexican*, June 22, 1878, p. 1). George Taylor to President Hayes, April 4 and June 3, 1879; copies in Fulton Papers, Box 11 Folder 8. See also Note 48.

60. *Mesilla Valley Independent*, April 27, 1878, p. 2; April 19, 1879, p. 2; May 24, 1879, p. 2.

61. Keleher 1957: 364–66; *Thirty-four* (Las Cruces, N.M.), December 31, 1879, p. 2.

Chapter 8 *The Lincoln County War I, February–March 1878*

1. Keleher 1957: 85–88; Mullin 1968: 111–112.
2. Deposition of William H. Bonney, June 8, 1878, in Angel Report, pp. 314–16.
3. Deposition of Robert A. Widenmann, June 6, 1878, in Angel Report, p. 197.
4. See Note 2.
5. Report of Frank W. Angel, Special Agent (November 27, 1878), "In the Matter of the cause and circumstances of the death of John A. Tunstall, a British Subject," in Angel Report (4 pp.; unpaginated section). Mullin 1968: 239–40.
6. Keleher 1957: 82–4; Nolan 1965: 272–74; Mullin 1968: 115–20.
7. Maurice G. Fulton, ed., "Mrs. Ealy's Own Account" in undated issue of *New Mexico Writers*, ed. Haniel Long; Fulton Papers, Box 12 Folder 8. Nolan 1965: 285–87.
8. Mullin 1968: 126–27. Deposition of A.A. McSween, Exhibits 12, 13, 14, pp. 139–51, in Angel Report. Sir Edward Thornton to Hon. Wm. M. Evarts, March 9, 1878, in Angel Report (unpaginated addenda).
9. Depositions of Robert A. Widenmann, June 6, 1878, pp. 332–336; Atencio Martinez, April —, 1878, pp. 340–41; Capt. Geo. A. Purington, March 14, 1878, pp. 344–46; 2d Lt. M.F. Goodwin, June 24, 1878, pp. 370–72; Jas. J. Longwill, May 14, 1878, pp. 248–55, all in Angel Report. See also *Mesilla Valley Independent*, March 30, 1878, p. 2; Nolan 1965: 287–88; Mullin 1968: 130–31. The chronology of events is badly confused and the depositions by McSween, June 6, 1878, and Widenmann, June 6, 1878, pp. 41–43 and 205–7 in Angel Report make conflicting claims. Bonney and Waite may never have been arrested; Capt. Purington said later that most of McSween's statements were false (pp. 348–50 in Angel Report).
10. Capt. Geo. A. Purington, Fort Stanton, to A.A.A.G. Santa Fe, February 21, 1878; NA, Microcopy M666 Roll 397, File No. 1405 AGO 1878. Orders No. 18, Fort Stanton, February 22, 1878, in Angel Report, pp. 374–75.
11. Nolan 1965: 288–304; Mullin 1968: 131–32; Bruce T. Ellis, 1975: "Lincoln County Postscript." See transcripts of numerous letters by Widenmann, McSween, Leverson and Thornton in Angel Report (unpaginated addenda) and Fulton Papers, Box 14 Folder 4.
12. Keleher 1957: 80–81; Nolan 1965: 283–84, 304; Mullin 1968: 121–23. Although dated February 14, 1878, McSween may have written it when he heard of Tunstall's death. See also documents accompanying Sir Edward Thornton to Hon. Wm. M. Evarts, March 27, 1878, in Angel Report (unpaginated addenda).
13. Keleher 1957: 159; Nolan 1965: 288–89, 383; Mullin 1968: 134–36.
14. Capt. Geo. A. Purington to F.W. Angel, June 25, 1878, in Angel Report, pp. 348–50. Wm. Morton, a Murphyite, and George Coe, a Regulator, both claimed that their pay was $60. per month: see Keleher 1957: 99 and Shinkle 1966: 39. It seems doubtful that either Dolan or McSween had the cash to pay such wages. McSween's account at the First National Bank of Santa Fe was virtually inactive after January 1878 but never overdrawn; the final entry on June 27, 1878, showed a balance of 21¢; see FNB Indiv. ledg. By this time McSween may have been carrying his accounts with a St. Louis bank; see Nolan 1965: 316.
15. Deposition of A.A. McSween, June 6, 1878, and Exhibit 13, in Angel Report, pp. 52, 143–47. Keleher 1957: 96–100; Mullin 1968: 137–41; Rasch, 1980: "These Were the Regulators."
16. J.P. Meadows, "Kid's Explanation of the Killing of Morton and Baker" in his manuscript "Billy the Kid As I Knew Him"; Philip C. Rasch files. *Mesilla Valley Independent*, March 16, 1878, p. 3; Keleher 1957: 96–100; Mullin 1968: 138–41.
17. *Mesilla Valley Independent*, March 23, 1878, p. 3; Mullin 1968: 147–48; McCright and Powell 1983: 109–12, 118.
18. J.P. Meadows, "Billy the Kid As I Knew Him"; Philip C. Rasch files.
19. Keleher 1957: 90–5; Mullin 1968: 143–47, 150–57; deposition of A.A. McSween, June 6, 1878, in Angel Report, pp. 50–1.
20. A.A.A.G. Santa Fe to Comdg. Officer, Fort Stanton, N.M., March 24, 1878; NA, Microcopy M666 Roll 397, File No. 1405 AGO 1878; copy also in Angel Report.
21. Mullin 1968: 147; Bender 1984: 28–29. Capt. Geo. A. Purington, Fort Stanton, to A.A.A.G. Santa Fe, March 29, 1878; NA, Microcopy M666 Roll 397, File No. 1405 AGO 1878.

22. Keleher 1957: 95–6, 107; Rasch, 1964b: "Loquacious Mr. Leverson"; Nolan 1965: 292–314, 339–43; Mullin 1968: 163, 169–71; Lee Scott Theisen, 1976: "Frank Warner Angel's Notes," p. 356; see also Leverson letters in Angel Report (unpaginated addenda).

23. *Weekly New Mexican*, March 23, 1878; transcript in Fulton Papers. Box 11 Folder

7. On the microfilm of the *New Mexican* half of the first sheet of this issue is shown as torn away and the inside pages were not filmed at all. Maurice Fulton found another copy somewhere. The newspaper reprinted this article in Spanish on March 30, 1878, p. 4. See also Nolan 1965: 289–92, 299–300; Mullin 1968: 150–52.

24. Mullin 1968: 152–57.

Chapter 9 *The Lincoln County War II, April–July 1878*

1. Deposition of A.A. McSween, June 6, 1878, and Montague Leverson to President Hayes, April 2, 1878, both in Angel Report, pp. 55–56 and unpaginated addenda.

2. Francisco Trujillo, "Billy the Kid," May 10, 1937; NMSRCA, WPA files.

3. There are a number of unresolved questions such as whether Brady and his deputies were on their way to or were returning from the courthouse; whether French was wounded; and whether it was French or the Kid concealed under the floor. With bullets flying, confusion later about what happened is understandable. This reconstruction is based upon Garrett 1954: 61–62; *Mesilla Valley Independent*, April 13, 1878, p. 3; April 27, 1878, p. 2; Gorgonio Wilson, "Billy the Kid Story" (1937?), WPA transcript in Philip C. Rasch files; Rasch 1964a; Mullin 1968: 158–62; Bender 1984: 30–31, 181.

4. Rasch 1964a: 11.

5. John P. Meadows, "Billy the Kid As I Knew Him"; Philip C. Rasch files. For another anecdotal version attributed to the Kid, see Keleher 1957: 329.

6. Deposition of A.A. McSween, June 6, 1878, pp. 55–60; Montague Leverson letters of April 1, 1, 2, 1878, unpaginated addenda; Capt. Geo. A. Purington to F.W. Angel, June 25, 1878, pp. 348–50, all in Angel Report. See also Rasch 1964a: 6; Keleher 1957: 110; Mullin 1968: 161–68.

7. Bender 1984: 33.

8. Lt. Col. N.A.M. Dudley, Fort Stanton, to A.A.A.G. Santa Fe, May 4, 1878; NA, Microcopy M666 Roll 397, File No. 1405-AGO 1878.

9. Colin Rickards, 1974: *Gunfight at Blazer's Mill*.

10. *Mesilla Valley Independent*, April 13, 1878, p. 3; Keleher 1957: 124–26; Mullin 1968: 195, 201, 227–29. Arrest warrant

(original) for murderers of Wm. Brady and appointment of John Copeland, April 8, 1878; in Fulton Papers, Box 12 Folder 2.

11. Supplement to *Mesilla Valley Independent*, April 20, 1878. See also Mullin 1968: 196–99.

12. Keleher 1957: 118–23; Mullin 1968: 195–203; Rickards 1974.

13. Keleher 1957: 129–30; Mullin 1968: 189–92, 206–22.

14. Mullin 1968: 203, 210–26; Klasner 1972: 95; Rickards 1974; Bender 1984: 42–46; Utley 1985: 28. Also various from May 1878 in NA, Microcopy M666 Roll 397, File No. 1405 AGO 1878.

15. Dwight Greenly, "Military Career of N.A.M. Dudley," 1986.

16. H.I. Chapman, Lincoln, N.M., to Gov. Lew. Wallace, November 25, 1878; NA, Record Group 153, Records Relating to the Dudley Court of Inquiry (QQ1284) (hereafter cited as Dudley Court Record), Exhibit 24. See also Mullin 1968: 208–209; Utley 1986: 77.

17. Col. E. Hatch, Santa Fe, to Gov. Lew. Wallace, April 9, 1879, in Lew. Wallace Papers.

18. *Mesilla News*, July 13, 1878, p. 2; Mullin 1968: 203; Mehren 1969: 163–65, 191; Westphall 1973: 87–8. NA, RG192, Entry 74 Vol. 4. Various from May 17–31, 1878 in NA, Microcopy M666 Roll 397, File No. 1405 AGO 1878.

19. *Grant County Herald*, June 8, 1878, p. 1; Keleher 1957: 124–27; Mullin 1968: 225–29; Westphall 1973: 87–90.

20. Westphall 1973: 90, 124–27; McCright and Powell 1981.

21. Angel Report (see Chapter 4 Note 2); also Cleaveland 1975; McCright and Powell 1981.

22. Watkins Report (see Chapter 6 Note 4).

23. Lt. Col. N.A.M. Dudley, Fort Stanton, to A.A.A.G. Santa Fe, May 4, 11, 1878; NA,

Microcopy M666 Roll 397, File No. 1405
AGO 1878. Col. Edward Hatch, Santa Fe,
to A.A.G. Fort Leavenworth, Ks., June 1,
1878; in LS, HQ District of New Mexico,
pp. 191–192 (transcript in Philip C. Rasch
File No. 70). See also Chapter 7 Note 48.
24. E.C. Watkins to Commissioner of Indian
Affairs, June 27, 1878, in Watkins Report,
p. 14; NA, Microcopy M1070 Roll 29.
25. Mullin 1968: 232–33. Lt. Col. N.A.M.
Dudley, Fort Stanton, to Hon. S.B.
Axtell, Santa Fe, June 20, 1878, in Dudley
Court Record, Exhibit 77 (Fort Stanton
correspondence), Vol. I No. 28. Lt. Col.
N.A.M. Dudley, Fort Stanton, to
A.A.A.G. Santa Fe with enclosures, June
22, 1878; NA, Microcopy M666 Roll 397,
File No. 1405 AGO 1878.
26. Bender 1984: 47.
27. *Mesilla News*, June 29, 1878, p. 2; Keleher
1957: 125–27, 155–58; Mullin 1968: 129,
204, 233–34; 1973; Westphall 1973: 90–2,
127–28. Lt. Col. N.A.M. Dudley, Fort
Stanton, to A.A.A.G. Santa Fe, June 22,
1878; NA, Microcopy M666 Roll 397, File
No. 1405 AGO 1878. Angel submitted
thirty-one questions or "interrogatories"
as he called them, to Governor Axtell on
August 11, 1878. These with the
governor's reply and some other
correspondence between them were
published in a newspaper, probably an
August issue or issues of the Santa Fe
Rocky Mountain Sentinel; editorial
comment on this exchange between the
two appeared in *Mesilla Valley
Independent*, August 31, 1878, p. 2.
Clippings of the published interrogatories
and related correspondence may be seen in
the NMSRCA copy of the Angel Report,

in their Westphall Collection (personal
communication, Dr. Robert M. Utley,
January 31, 1986).
28. *Mesilla News*, July 6, 1878, p. 1; *Weekly
New Mexican*, July 6, 1878, p. 2; *Grant
County Herald*, August 24, 1878, p. 1;
Mullin 1968: 234–35. Lt. Col. N.A.M.
Dudley, Fort Stanton, to Capt. H. Carroll,
midnight June 27–28, 1878; Dudley to
A.A.A.G. Santa Fe with enclosures, June
29, 1878; Capt. H. Carroll to Post
Adjutant, Fort Stanton, July 1, 1878; all in
NA Microcopy M666 Roll 397, File No.
1405 AGO 1878.
29. 57th Cong. 2d Sess. Senate Doc. 209
(Serial No. 4430), pp. 206–7, 336–37 (1903).
Mullin 1968: 235. Lt. Col. N.A.M. Dudley,
Fort Stanton, to A.A.A.G. Santa Fe, June
29, 1878, also Special Orders No. 49, HQ
Fort Stanton, June 28, 1878, both in NA
Microcopy M666 Roll 397, File No. 1405
AGO 1878.
30. Mullin 1968: 243–45; Lt. Col. N.A.M.
Dudley, Fort Stanton, to A.A.A.G. Santa
Fe with enclosures, July 6, 1878; NA,
Microcopy M666 Roll 397, File No. 1405
AGO 1878. *Mesilla News*, July 13, 1878, p.
2.
31. Mullin 1968: 244–46; 1973: 229; Lt. Col.
N.A.M. Dudley, Fort Stanton, to
A.A.A.G. Santa Fe with enclosures, July
13, 1878; NA, Microcopy M666 Roll 397,
File No. 1405 AGO 1878.
32. Keleher 1957: 139–41; Nolan 1965: 374;
Mullin 1968: 242–43; *Mesilla News*, July
20, 1878, p. 2. R.W. Beckwith to Josie
Beckwith, Lincoln, July 11, 1878;
transcript in Fulton Papers, Box 11 Folder
7.
33. Bender 1984: 49.

Chapter 10   *The Lincoln County War III,
July–September 1878*

1. Rasch, 1956a: "Five Days of Battle," pp.
299–300; Mullin 1968: 249–52. *Mesilla
News*, July 27, 1878, p. 1; *Weekly New
Mexican*, August 10, 1878, p. 2;
Albuquerque Review, August 31, 1878, p.
1. Lt. Col. N.A.M. Dudley, Fort Stanton,
to A.A.A.G. Santa Fe, July 18, 1878; NA,
Microcopy M666 Roll 397, File No. 1405
AGO 1878.
2. Lt. Col. N.A.M. Dudley, Fort Stanton, to
A.A.A.G. Santa Fe, July 16, 1878; NA,
Microcopy M666 Roll 397, File No. 1405
AGO 1878.

3. Rasch 1956a: 299; Mullin 1968: 249; N.
Mex. State Planning Office 1974: 52–53;
Caperton 1983: Fig. 3. Asst. Surg. D.M.
Appel to Post Adjt., Fort Stanton, July
15, 1878; NA, Microcopy M666 Roll 397,
File No. 1405 AGO 1878.
4. Rasch 1956a: 320–21.
5. Rasch 1956a: 300–1; Mullin 1968: 250–52;
Dr. Taylor Ealy, Anton Chico, N.M., to
Sheldon Jackson, August 13, 1878;
typescript copy in Fulton Papers, Box 11
Folder 7. Asst. Surg. D.M. Appel to Post.
Adjt., Fort Stanton, July 15, 1878; NA,

Microcopy M666 Roll 397, File No. 1405
AGO 1878.

6. Rasch 1956a: 300; Mullin 1968: 251–52;
Ealy to Jackson, August 13, 1878; Fulton
Papers, Box 11 Folder 7 (see Note 5).

7. Mullin 1968: 252–53; Bender 1984: 50.

8. Sheriff Geo. W. Peppin, Lincoln, N.M., to
Gen'l N.A.M. Dudley, July 16, 1878, and
Lt. Col. N.A.M. Dudley, Fort Stanton, to
G.W. Peppin Esq., July 16, 1878; both in
NA Microcopy M666 Roll 397, File No.
1405 AGO 1878. See also Mullin 1968: 253.

9. Mullin 1968: 253–54. Proceedings of a
Board of Officers Convened at Fort
Stanton, New Mexico . . . July 17, 1878
. . . To investigate and report upon the
firing at a U.S. Soldier near Lincoln, New
Mex.; NA, Microcopy M666 Roll 397, File
No. 1405 AGO 1878.

10. Bender 1984: 51.

11. Rasch 1956a: 302–3; Mullin 1968: 254–55;
Bender 1984: 50–51.

12. Mullin 1968: 257; Bender 1984: 51–52.

13. Lt. Col. N.A.M. Dudley, Fort Stanton, to
A.A.A.G. Santa Fe, July 18, 1878; NA,
Microcopy M666 Roll 397, File No. 1405
AGO 1878.

14. Rasch 1956a: 303–4; Mullin 1968: 255–56;
Statement of Asst. Surgeon D.M. Appel,
November 9, 1878, from notes made July
20, 1878; in Dudley Court Record, Exhibit
B6. Lt. Col. N.A.M. Dudley, Fort
Stanton, to A.A.A.G. Santa Fe, Midnight,
July 20, 1878; NA, Microcopy M666 Roll
397, File No. 1405 AGO 1878.

15. Bender 1984: 55.

16. *Mesilla News*, August 10, 1878, p. 2;
Rasch 1956a: 303; Mullin 1968: 258–59.

17. Statement of Asst. Surg. D.M. Appel,
November 9, 1878, in Dudley Court
Record, Exhibit B6 (see Note 14); Dudley
to A.A.A.G., July 20, 1878, in NA
Microcopy M666 Roll 397, File No. 1405
AGO 1878 (see Note 14); Affidavit of
deputy John Long, July 21(?), 1878; NA,
Microcopy M1088 Roll 34, File No. LR,
1718, DNM 1878 Encl.

18. Mullin 1968: 260–61; Statement of Asst.
Surg. D.M. Appel, November 9, 1878, in
Dudley Court Record, Exhibit B6; also
Dudley to A.A.A.G., July 20, 1878, in NA
Microcopy M666 Roll 397, File No. 1405
AGO 1878 (see Note 14).

19. Mullin 1968: 262; Dudley to A.A.A.G.,
July 20, 1878, in NA Microcopy M666 Roll
397, File No. 1405 AGO 1878 (see Note
14).

20. Testimony of William Bonney, in Dudley
Court Record, pp. 320–27; published in

part in Keleher 1957: 233–34.

21. Dudley to A.A.A.G., July 20, 1878, in NA
Microcopy M666 Roll 397, File No. 1405
AGO 1878 (see Note 14); see also Utley
1986: 49.

22. See Note 18; also Rasch 1956a: 307–10;
Mullin 1968: 265–67; undated affidavit of
John B. Wilson in Lew. Wallace Papers.

23. See Note 17; also *Mesilla News*, July 27,
1878, p. 1; Rasch 1956a: 310–13; Mullin
1968: 263–69; Bender 1984: 52–54.

24. Rasch 1956a: 313–18; Mullin 1968: 270–73.

25. Lt. Col. N.A.M. Dudley, Fort Stanton, to
A.A.A.G. Santa Fe, July 23, 1878; original
in NA, Microcopy M666 Roll 397, File No.
1405 AGO 1878, copy in NA, M1088 Roll
34, File No. LR, 1719, Dist. N.M. 1878.

26. See Note 25; also Rasch 1956a: 317–20;
Keleher 1957: 146–49; Mullin 1968: 273–82.

27. Lt. Col. N.A.M. Dudley, Fort Stanton, to
A.A.A.G. Santa Fe, July 27, August 3,
1878; NA, Microcopy M666 Roll 397, File
No. 1405 AGO 1878.

28. Keleher 1957: 131–33; Mullin 1968: 282–85.
Lt. Col. N.A.M. Dudley, Fort Stanton, to
A.A.A.G. Santa Fe, August 8, 10, 1878;
Capt. Thos. Blair, Fort Stanton, to Post
Adjutant, August 9, 1878; all in NA,
Microcopy M666 Roll 397, File No. 1405
AGO 1878.

29. Nolan 1965: 379–88.

30. See Frank Warner Angel to Governor
S.B. Axtell and Axtell to Angel, August
11–13, 1878, in NMSRCA copy of Angel
Report (see Chapter 9 Note 27); also
Westphall 1973: 127–29; *Mesilla Valley
Independent*, August 31, 1878, p. 2; C.
Schurz to "Dear Mr. President," August
31, 1878; partial typescript copy in Fulton
Papers, Box 11 Folder 7, original in Hayes'
Memorial Library, Fremont, Ohio.

31. Hinton 1956: 325–28; Keleher 1957: 148;
Mullin 1968: 288–89; Mary Watley Clarke,
1984: *John Simpson Chisum*, pp. 97–103.

32. Nolan 1965: 380; Mullin 1968: 278.

33. S.R. Corbet, Lincoln, N.M., to Mr. Lee
Keyser, August 22, 1878; NA, Microcopy
M666 Roll 397, File No. 1405 AGO 1878.

34. G. Gauss, Lincoln, N.M., to J.P. Tunstall,
August 22, 1878; photocopy in Fulton
Papers, Box 14 Folder 4. Published in part
in Nolan 1965: 385–86.

35. Lt. Col. N.A.M. Dudley, Fort Stanton, to
A.A.A.G. Santa Fe, August 24, 1878; NA,
Microcopy M666 Roll 397, File No. 1405
AGO 1878.

36. McCright and Powell 1983: 180.

37. Thomas Gardner, Seven Rivers, N.M., to
Gen'l N.A.M. Dudley; August 18, 1878;

NA, Microcopy M666 Roll 397, File No. 1405 AGO 1878.

38. Lt. Col. N.A.M. Dudley, Fort Stanton, to A.A.A.G. Santa Fe, September 7 and 3 p.m. September 7, 1878; NA, Microcopy M666 Roll 397, File No. 1405 AGO 1878. Fritz recognized the horse thieves when they returned in December; see Chas. Fritz, Fort Stanton, to General N.A.M. Dudley, December 16, 1878, in Dudley Court Record, Exhibit 79 (Fort Stanton correspondence), Vol. III No. 12.

39. Keleher 1957: 131–33. Deposition of Geo. W. Peppin, August 15, 1878; NA, Microcopy M666 Roll 398, File No. 1405 AGO 1878. Another copy of Peppin's deposition is in the Angel Report, unpaginated section. Both are original, signed copies in the same hand, but only the one in File 1405 AGO 1878 bears a date.

40. See Note 35.

41. Report of Frank W. Angel, Special Agent, October 7, 1878, "In the Matter of the Troubles in Lincoln County, New Mexico" (4 pp.); also Lt. Col. N.A.M. Dudley, Fort Stanton, to Hon. Charles Devens, August 15, 1878; both in Angel Report, unpaginated section.

42. Mullin 1973: 230; Henry F. Hoyt, 1980: "A Frontier Doctor," p. 56; McCright and Powell 1983: 154–55.

43. Asst. Surg. Wm. B. Lyon to Post Adjutant, Fort Stanton, October 1, 1878; NA, Microcopy M666 Roll 398, File No. 1405 AGO 1878.

44. See Note 39 (Peppin deposition).

45. Petition of Florencio Gonzales, Saturnino Baca, George Kimbrell, and Jose Montano, Lincoln, N.M., to His Excellency the Governor, n.d. (ca. August 15, 1878); NA, Microcopy M666 Roll 398, File No. 1405 AGO 1878.

46. Governor S.B. Axtell, Santa Fe, to His Excellency the President, August 20, 1878; NA, Microcopy M666 Roll 398, File No. 1405 AGO 1878.

47. Nolan 1965: 413.

48. Lt. Col. N.A.M. Dudley, Fort Stanton, to A.A.A.G. Santa Fe, September 28, 29 (2), October 3, 1878; Asst. Surg. Wm. B. Lyon to Post Adjutant, Fort Stanton, October 1, 1878; all in NA Microcopy M666 Roll 398, File No. 1405 AGO 1878. The *Mesilla Valley Independent*, October 5, 1878, p. 2. See also Nolan 1965: 388; Mullin 1968: 290–96; McCright and Powell 1983: 148–150.

49. Nolan 1965: 388–389; Mullin 1968: 293–295; McCright and Powell 1983: 151. Lt. Col. N.A.M. Dudley, Fort Stanton, to A.A.A.G. Santa Fe, October 4, 10, 1878; both in NA Microcopy M666 roll 398 File No. 1495 AGO 1878.

50. Lt. Col. N.A.M. Dudley, Fort Stanton, to A.A.G. Santa Fe, September 29, 1878; NA, Microcopy M666 roll 398, File No. 1405 AGO 1878. See also Mullin 1968: 295 and A.A.A.G. Santa Fe to Comd'g Officer, Fort Stanton, October 1, 1878 (telegram), in Dudley Court Record, Exhibit 78 (Fort Stanton correspondence), Vol. II No. 50.

Chapter 11 *Governor Lew. Wallace: New Hope for New Mexico, October–December 1878*

1. Keleher 1957: 164, 176–78, 357, 367; Calvin Horn, 1963: *New Mexico's Troubled Years*, p. 213; Oakah L. Jones, 1985: "Lew Wallace-Hoosier Governor," p. 147. Lew. Wallace Papers.

2. Keleher 1957: 178–79, 183; Theisen 1976; McCright and Powell 1981: 20.

3. Governor Lew. Wallace, Santa Fe, to Hon. C. Schurz, Sec. of the Interior, October 5, 1878, enclosing Lt. Col. N.A.M. Dudley, Fort Stanton, to A.A.G. Santa Fe, September 29, 1878, also U.S. Marshal John Sherman Jr., Santa Fe, to Wallace, October 4, 1878, and Judge Bristol, Mesilla, N.M., to U.S. Marshal Sherman, October 4, 1878, all in Lew. Wallace Papers. Lt. Col. N.A.M. Dudley,

Fort Stanton, to Governor Lew. Wallace, October 10, 1878; Dudley Court Record, Exhibit 61. See also Mullin 1968: 299. The Southwestern Stockmen's Association organized January 17, 1881 in Silver City, N.M., may have been the earliest one in New Mexico (*Newman's Thirty-Four*, January 26, 1881, p. 3). Other livestock associations were in existence by 1884.

4. Keleher 1957: 183–89.

5. Keleher 1957: 189–90; Rasch, 1957c: "Exit Axtell: Enter Wallace," pp. 236–37. Endorsement by Judge Advocate General S.M. Dunn, August 21, 1878, on telegram of Brig. Gen. Ord, San Antonio, to Adjt. Gen. Washington, D.C., August 19, 1878; in NA, M666 Roll 397, File No. 1405 AGO

1878. The problem at this time was in the Dept. of Texas.

6. Keleher 1957: 191. A.A.A.G. John S. Loud, Santa Fe, to Comdg. Officer, Fort Stanton, October 27, 1878, in Dudley Court Record, Exhibit 79 (Fort Stanton correspondence), Vol. III No. 1; copy also in Lew. Wallace Papers.

7. Capt. Henry Carroll to Post Adjt., Fort Stanton, March 10, 1879; NA, RG 393, U.S. Army Commands, Fort Stanton, LR, Box 3.

8. Eve Ball, 1969: *Ma'am Jones of the Pecos*, pp. 125–29, 149. Gov. Lew. Wallace, Lincoln, N.M., to Hon. C. Schurz, March 21, 1879, and Ira E. Leonard, Lincoln, N.M., to Gov. Lew. Wallace, May 20, 1879; both in Lew. Wallace Papers.

9. Lt. Col. N.A.M. Dudley, Fort Stanton, to A.A.A.G. Santa Fe, November 2, 1878, and Dudley to A.A.A.G. Santa Fe with enclosures, November 6, 1878; Dudley Court Record, Exhibits 18, 19A–E. *Mesilla Valley Independent*, October 26, 1878, p. 3; November 9, 1878, p. 3. NMSRCA, Territorial Archives of New Mexico, Roll 21 frame 509.

10. Lt. Col. N.A.M. Dudley, Fort Stanton, to A.A.A.G. Santa Fe, November 16, 1878; Dudley Court Record, Exhibit 22.

11. *Mesilla News*, November 23, 1878, p. 2.

12. Keleher 1957: 192; Mullin 1968: 287–88, 303–4.

13. H.I. Chapman, Las Vegas, N.M., to Gov. Lew. Wallace, October 24, 1878; original in Lew. Wallace Papers, copy in Dudley Court Record, Exhibit 4. See also Keleher 1957: 192.

14. Gov. Lew. Wallace, Santa Fe, to Gen. Edward Hatch, October 28, 1878, in Dudley Court Record, Exhibit 14; another copy in Lew. Wallace Papers.

15. Rasch, 1965, "Trials of Lt. Col. Dudley"; Leckie 1967: 112, 181–83.

16. Lt. Col. N.A.M. Dudley, Fort Stanton, to His Excellency Lew. Wallace, November 9, 1878, in Dudley Court Record, Exhibit 13.

17. Lt. Col. N.A.M. Dudley, Fort Stanton, to A.A.A.G. Santa Fe with enclosures, November 7, 9, 1878, in Dudley Court Record, Exhibit 6.

18. Deposition of George W. Peppin, November 6, 1878, in Dudley Court Record, Exhibit 8. The other seven affidavits are Exhibits 6B, 6C, 7, and 9–12 in the Dudley Court Record.

19. Francisco Gomez, "Pioneer Story," August 15, 1938; Museum of New Mexico History Library, WPA City Files, Manzano.

20. Mullin 1968: 319.

21. Lew. Wallace, Santa Fe, to Col. N.A.M. Dudley, November 16, 1878; Dudley Court Record, Exhibit 3.

22. Printed copy of the proclamation in Lew. Wallace Papers, also in Dudley Court Record, Exhibit 3'; published in the Santa Fe *Rocky Mountain Sentinel*, November 14, 1878 (clipping in Lew. Wallace Papers). See also Keleher 1957: 193–95; Rasch 1957c: 239–40; Mullin 1968: 301.

23. Rasch 1957c: 239; Utley 1986: 65; *Mesilla Valley Independent*, December 21, 1878, p. 2.

24. Keleher 1957: 193, 197–98; *Mesilla News*, November 23, 1878, p. 2; November 30, 1878, p. 2; December 14, 1878, p. 2; *Mesilla Valley Independent*, November 23, 1878, p. 2. Lt. Col. N.A.M. Dudley, Fort Stanton, to A.A.A.G. Santa Fe, November 30, 1878; in Dudley Court Record, Exhibit 23; also Dudley to A.A.A.G. Santa Fe, December 9, 1878, in NA, Microcopy M666 Roll 398, File No. 1405 AGO 1878.

25. Mullin 1968: 308–9, Lew. Wallace, Santa Fe, to Lt. Col. N.A.M. Dudley with enclosure, November 30, 1878, in Dudley Court Record, Exhibit 26. Dudley also regarded this as a strange affair; see Lt. Col. N.A.M. Dudley, Fort Stanton, to A.A.A.G. Santa Fe, December 8, 1878, in Dudley Court Record, Exhibit 79 (Fort Stanton correspondence), Vol. III No. 6.

26. Rasch 1957c: 233, 237–38; see also Note 21.

27. *Mesilla News*, November 23, 1878, p. 2; *Mesilla Valley Independent*, December 7, 1878, p. 2; Dudley "Open Letter" in *Weekly New Mexican*, December 14, 1878. See also Keleher 1957: 198; Mullin 1968:312.

28. Gov. Lew. Wallace, Santa Fe, to Hon. C. Schurz, December 21, 1878, in Lew. Wallace Papers.

29. Gov. Lew. Wallace, Santa Fe, to Hon. C. Schurz, November 13, 1878; NA, Microcopy M364 Roll 8, Interior Department Territorial Papers, New Mexico, 1851–1914.

30. Lt. Col. N.A.M. Dudley, Fort Stanton, to A.A.A.G. Santa Fe, December 17, 1878, in Dudley Court Record, Exhibit 79 (Fort Stanton correspondence), Vol. III No. 13.

31. H.I. Chapman, Lincoln, N.M., to Gov. Lew. Wallace, November 25, 25, 29, 1878; in Dudley Court Record, Exhibits 24, 25. See Keleher 1957: 198–200; Mullin 1968: 310–13.

32. Gov. Lew. Wallace, Santa Fe, to Col. Edward Hatch, December 7, 1878, with endorsements; NA, Microcopy M666 Roll 398, File No. 1405 AGO 1878. Keleher 1957: 200–202.
33. See Note 32 (endorsements).
34. Proceedings of a Board of Officers convened at Fort Stanton, N.M. . . . under Special Orders No. 157, Headquarters, Fort Stanton, December 14, 1878; in Dudley Court Record, Exhibit 28. Lt. Col. N.A.M. Dudley, Fort Stanton, to A.A.A.G. Santa Fe, December 15, 1878; in Dudley Court Record, Exhibit 79 (Fort Stanton correspondence), Vol. III No. 9. See also Rasch, 1959, "Murder of Huston I. Chapman": pp. 69–72.
35. See Note 30.
36. Sheriff George Kimbrell made this point at the time of Chapman's murder. See

Kimball [sic], Lincoln, N.M., to Lt. Col. N.A.M. Dudley, February 19, 1879, in Dudley Court Record, Exhibit 79 (Fort Stanton correspondence), Vol. III No. 40.
37. See Note 27; also Mullin 1968: 317 and *Mesilla News*, December 14, 1878, p. 2.
38. General Orders No. 62, HQ Fort Stanton, December 20, 1878, in Dudley Court Record, Exhibit 45. *Mesilla Valley Independent*, January 11, 1879, p. 3.
39. Special Orders No. 167, HQ Fort Stanton, December 27, 1878, in Dudley Court Record, Exhibit 79 (Fort Stanton correspondence), Vol. III No. 18.
40. NMSRCA, Territorial Archives of New Mexico, Roll 21 Frame 509. Garrett 1954: 85.
41. Jas. J. Dolan, Lincoln, N.M., to Governor Lew. Wallace, December 31, 1878, in Lew. Wallace Papers.

Chapter 12   *The Lincoln County War IV, January–July 1879*

1. *Mesilla Valley Independent*, January 25, 1879, p. 5. Lew. Wallace, Santa Fe, to John B. Wilson Esq., January 18, 1879, in Lew. Wallace Papers.
2. *Mesilla News*, January 18, 1879, p. 2.
3. *Mesilla News*, February 1, 1879, p. 1.
4. Mullin 1968: 319–21. *Las Vegas Gazette*, March 1, 1879.
5. Mrs. Sue E. McSween, Lincoln, N.M., to Col. N.A.M. Dudley, February 11, 1879, in Dudley Court Record, Exhibit 79 (Fort Stanton correspondence), Vol. III No. 32.
6. Lt. Col. N.A.M. Dudley, Fort Stanton, to Mrs. Sue E. McSween, February 13, 1879, in Dudley Court Record, Exhibit 79 (Fort Stanton correspondence), Vol. III No. 33.
7. Lt. Col. N.A.M. Dudley, Fort Stanton, to A.A.A.G. Santa Fe, February 15, 1879, in Dudley Court Record, Exhibit 79 (Fort Stanton correspondence), Vol. III No. 35.
8. Special Constable Emil Powers, Roswell, N.M., to Capt. Henry Carroll, February 1, 1879, with endorsement by Carroll; Lt. Col. N.A.M. Dudley, Fort Stanton, to Carroll, February 4, 1879; Dudley to A.A.A.G. Santa Fe, February 5, 1879; all in NA, Microcopy M666 Roll 398, File No. 1405 AGO 1878.
9. Capt. Henry Carroll, Camp at Roswell, N.M., to Post Adjutant, Fort Stanton, February 25, 1879, in Lew. Wallace Papers. For Capt. Carroll's report on this trip see Chapter 11 Note 7. The following

are all in the Dudley Court Record, Exhibit 79 (Fort Stanton correspondence): Sheriff George Kimball [sic], Fort Stanton, to Comdg. Officer, Fort Stanton, February 18, 1879, Vol. III No. 37; Special Orders No. 25, HQ Fort Stanton, February 18, 1879, Vol. III No. 38; Lt. Col. N.A.M. Dudley, Fort Stanton, to A.A.A.G. Santa Fe, February 19, 1879, Vol. III No. 42; Dudley to A.A.A.G. Santa Fe, February 21, 1879, Vol. III No. 43; 2d Lt. M.F. Goodwin, Fort Stanton, to Capt. Henry Carroll, February 25, 1879, Vol. 3 No. 49; Dudley to J.B. Wilson Esq., February 27, 1879, Vol. III No. 50; Dudley to A.A.A.G. Santa Fe, March 1, 1879, Vol. III No. 51; 2d Lt. M.F. Goodwin, Fort Stanton, to Capt. Carroll, March 3, 1879, Vol. III No. 53. Marion Turner, whose cattle were taken up by Capt. Carroll and who himself was made a prisoner until the troops returned to the Rio Peñasco, wrote a long, biased account of this affair published in *Mesilla News*, August 16, 1879, p. 1.
10. *Mesilla Valley Independent*, July 5, 1879, p. 4.
11. Lt. Col. N.A.M. Dudley, Fort Stanton, to A.A.A.G. Santa Fe, February 21, 1879, in Dudley Court Record, Exhibit 79 (Fort Stanton correspondence), Vol. III No. 43. Contrary to the claim by Fulton (Mullin 1968: 324), *Mesilla Valley Independent*

never published these "terms."

12. Lt. Col. N.A.M. Dudley, Fort Stanton, to A.A.A.G. Santa Fe, February 19, 1879, in Dudley Court Record, Exhibit 79 (Fort Stanton correspondence), Vol. III No. 42.
13. 1st Lt. Byron Dawson to Post Adjutant, Fort Stanton, February 19, 1879, in Dudley Court Record, Exhibit 79 (Fort Stanton correspondence), Vol. III No. 41.
14. *Las Vegas Gazette*, March 1, 1879. See also Ira E. Leonard, Las Vegas, N.M., to Gov. Wallace, February 24, 1879, in Lew. Wallace Papers.
15. See Note 10.
16. *Thirty-Four* (Las Cruces, N.M.), March 5, 1879, p. 2.
17. *Mesilla Valley Independent*, March 22, 1879, p. 3; July 5, 1879, p. 4.
18. See Chapter 11 Note 41.
19. 2d Lt. M.F. Goodwin, Fort Stanton, to Post Adjutant, February 23, 1879, in Lew. Wallace Papers. The following are all in the Dudley Court Record, Exhibit 79 (Fort Stanton correspondence): Sheriff George Kimball [sic], Lincoln, N.M., to Lt. Col. N.A.M. Dudley, February 19, 1879, Vol. III No. 40; Special Orders No. 26, HQ Fort Stanton, February 19, 1879, Vol. III No. 39; Lt. Col. N.A.M. Dudley, Fort Stanton, to A.A.A.G. Santa Fe, February 21, 1879, Vol. III No. 43.
20. Gov. Lew. Wallace, Santa Fe, to Hon. C. Schurz, February 27, 1879, in Lew. Wallace Papers. Wallace to Col. Edward Hatch, February 27, 1879; NA, Microcopy M666 Roll 398, File No. 1405 AGO 1878.
21. Keleher 1957: 199, 204–205; Ira E. Leonard, Las Vegas, N.M., to Gov. Wallace, February 24, 1879, in Lew. Wallace Papers.
22. Ira E. Leonard, Las Vegas, N.M., to Hon. Secretary of War, March 4, 1879; NA, Microcopy M666 Roll 398, File No. 1405 AGO 1878. Edward Hatch, Santa Fe, to Gov. Lew. Wallace, April 6, 1879, in Lew. Wallace Papers.
23. Rasch, 1966: "Governor meets the Kid," pp. 8–9; Mullin 1968: 331–32. Gov. Lew. Wallace, Lincoln, N.M., to Gen. Edward Hatch, March 6, 1879; Wallace to Hon. C. Schurz, March 21, 1879; both in Lew. Wallace Papers.
24. Gov. Lew. Wallace, Lincoln, N.M., to General Edward Hatch, March 7, 1879; Special Field Orders No. 2, HQ Dist. of N. Mex., Fort Stanton, March 8, 1879; Wallace to Hon. C. Schurz, March 21, 1879; B. Maj. Genl. Edward Hatch, Santa Fe, to the Governor of New Mexico,

March 11, 1879; all in Lew. Wallace Papers. Lt. Col. N.A.M. Dudley, Fort Stanton, to Adj. Gen. Army, telegram (with endorsements), March 10 (13), 1879; Dudley to Gen. Sherman, March 18, 1879; both in NA Microcopy M666 Roll 398, File No. 1405 AGO 1878.
25. Gov. Lew. Wallace, Lincoln, N.M., to General Edward Hatch, March 9, 1879; Capt. Henry Carroll, Fort Stanton, to His Excellency the Governor, March 11, 1879; Gov. Lew Wallace, Lincoln, N.M., to Capt. Henry Carroll, March 11, 12, 1879; Wallace to Hon. C. Schurz, March 21, 1879; all in Lew. Wallace Papers. Mullin 1968: 332–33.
26. Various dated March 13–14, 1879, in Lew. Wallace Papers; Keleher 1957: 209–11; Mullin 1968: 335–37.
27. Keleher 1957: 210–14; Rasch 1966; Mullin 1968: 335–38.
28. *Mesilla Valley Independent*, March 29, 1879, p. 2.
29. W.H. Bonney, San Patricio, N.M., to Friend Wilson, March 20, 1879, in Lew. Wallace Papers. Keleher 1957: 213–14.
30. Lew. Wallace, Fort Stanton, to W.H. Bonney, March 20, 1879, in Lew. Wallace Papers. Keleher 1957: 214.
31. W.H. Bonney, San Patricio, N.M., to Gen. Lew. Wallace, March 20, 1879, in Lew. Wallace Papers. Keleher 1957: 214–15; Mullin 1968: 338.
32. Mullin 1968: 339.
33. Gov. Lew. Wallace, Lincoln, N.M., to Hon. Carl Schurz, March 31, 1879, in Lew. Wallace Papers.
34. Statements by Kid, Sunday night March 23, 1879 (in Lew. Wallace's handwriting), in Lew. Wallace Papers.
35. Gov. Lew. Wallace, Santa Fe, to Hon. C. Schurz, October 4, 22, 1878; Brig. Gen. S.V. Benét to Gov. of N.M., October 12, 1878; Sec. of War to Gov. of N. Mex., November 13, 1878; all in Lew. Wallace Papers. Larry D. Ball, 1981: "People as Law Enforcers," p. 3; *Thirty-Four*, December 3, 1879, p. 2.
36. NMSRCA, Territorial Archives of New Mexico, Roll 87, Campaign records, Lincoln County outbreak, 1879, frame 188. Also Juan Patron to Gov. Wallace, January 10, 1880, in Territorial Archives of New Mexico, Roll 99, Records of the Territorial Governors, Lew. Wallace, frames 20–21. *Mesilla Valley Independent*, April 5, 1879, p. 2.
37. Gov. Lew. Wallace, Lincoln, N.M., to Dn. Juan Patron, March 19, 1879; Wallace to

Capt. Com'g Fort Stanton, March 21, 1879; Capt. Geo. A. Purington, Fort Stanton, to His Excellency the Governor, March 21, 1879; Juan B. Patron, Lincoln, N.M., to His Exc. Lew. Wallace, March 29, 1879; Wallace to Sheriff George Kimbrell, April 2, 1879; Wallace to Ben. Ellis Esq., April 9, 1879; B.H. Ellis, Lincoln, N.M., to Gov. Lew. Wallace, April 9, 1879; Juan B. Patron, Fort Sumner, N.M., to Dear Gov., April 12, 1879; John B. Wilson, Lincoln, N.M., to Hon. Lew. Wallace, May 18, 1879; all in Lew. Wallace Papers. See also Keleher 1957: 213, 216, 218–19; Jones 1985: 135–36.

38. Lew. Wallace, Fort Stanton, to Hon. C. Schurz, April 18, 1879, in Lew. Wallace Papers.

39. *Mesilla News*, April 26, 1879, p. 1; May 10, 1879, p. 2; *Mesilla Valley Independent*, May 10, 1879, p. 2; May 24, 1879, p. 2; *News and Press*, May 22, 1879.

40. *Rocky Mountain Sentinel*, undated clipping late April or early May 1879 in Lew. Wallace Papers.

41. *Mesilla Valley Independent*, April 26, 1879, p. 4; Keleher 1957: 221–22.

42. Ira E. Leonard, Lincoln Plaza, to Dear Gov., April 20, 1879, in Lew. Wallace Papers.

43. John B. Wilson, Lincoln, N.M., to Governor Wallace, April 21, 1879; in Lew. Wallace Papers.

44. *Mesilla News*, April 26, 1879, p. 1; *Thirty-Four*, May 7, 1879, p. 3; May 14, 1879, p. 3; *Mesilla Valley Independent*,

May 10, 1879, p. 4; *News and Press*, May 22, 1879. Keleher 1957: 222; Mullin 1968: 347–48.

45. *Thirty-Four*, May 7, 1879, p. 3. The assault case tried was that of Dan Dedrick.

46. Keleher 1957: 222–24; Mullin 1968: 346–49.

47. *Mesilla News*, June 21, 1879, p. 2; Mullin 1968: 349.

48. Dudley Court Record. Ira E. Leonard, Lincoln and Fort Stanton, N.M., to Gov. Lew. Wallace, May 20, 23; June 6, 13, 1879; Gov. Lew. Wallace, Santa Fe, to Hon. C. Schurz, July 30, 1879, all in Lew. Wallace Papers. Keleher 1957: 226–44; Rasch 1965; Mullin 1968: 356–65; Utley 1986: 57.

49. Maj. Gen. Jno. Pope, Fort Leavenworth, Ks., to Adj. Gen. U.S.A. with enclosure, October 15, 1878; opinion of Judge Advocate General, October 22, 1879 with endorsements of Sec. of War, December 27, 1879, and Gen. W.T. Sherman, December 30, 1879; NA, Microcopy M666 Roll 398, File No. 1405 AGO 1878.

50. Keleher 1957: 283–88; Mullin 1968: 380–81.

51. *Mesilla Valley Independent*, April 19, 1879, p. 2. See also Rasch, "Who Killed Who in Lincoln," 1969b. In the July 12, 1879 issue of the Santa Fe *Weekly New Mexican* a Lincoln County correspondent who signed himself "Quago" said that lead fever became an epidemic last season "and forty two died out of a voting population of one hundred and sixty."

Chapter 13 *Lincoln in Transition, 1879–1884*

1. Caperton 1983: 140–41.
2. S.R. Corbet, Lincoln, N.M., to John Middleton, February 3, 1880; original in Fulton Papers, Box 11 Folder 8.
3. Keleher 1957: 159; Nolan 1965: 383.
4. Caperton 1983: 345, 347, 353; see also Note 2.
5. Mullin 1968: 83, 413; Marc Simmons, 1985: "History of Flying H Ranch." Note by Maurice Fulton concerning W.L. Rynerson & Co., in Fulton Papers, Box 10 Folder 6. Susan Barber to Maurice Fulton, March 21, 1928; Fulton Papers, Box 1 Folder 4. S.R. Corbet, Lincoln, N.M., to My Dear Mr. Tunstall, October 31, 1879; Fulton Papers, Box 14 Folder 4.
6. Keleher 1957: 52–3, 347.
7. *Thirty-Four*, September 3, 1879, p. 4.

8. Lt. Col. N.A.M. Dudley, Fort Union, to Atty. Gen. Charles Devens, September 16, 1879; NA, Microcopy M666 Roll 398, File No. 1405 AGO 1878.
9. *Thirty-Four*, July 9, 1879, Supplement, p. 1.
10. Capt. Geo. A. Purington, Fort Stanton, to A.A.A.G. Santa Fe, August 17, 1879; NA, Microcopy M666 Roll 398, File No. 1405 AGO 1878.
11. Garrett 1954: 86–92.
12. Jones 1968: 168–75; David F. Myrick, 1970: *New Mexico's Railroads*, 18; *Thirty-Four*, December 31, 1879, p. 2; March 24, 1880, Supplement, p. 1; June 23, 1880, p. 1; *Rio Grande Republican* (Las Cruces, N.M.), May 19, 1883, p. 2.
13. *Thirty-Four*, December 3, 1879, p. 2.

14. *Weekly New Mexican*, July 19, 1880, p. 1.
15. Gov. Lew. Wallace, Santa Fe, to Hon. C. Schurz, July 23, 1880, in Lew. Wallace Papers.
16. NA, Microcopy T9 Roll 802; Population Schedules, 10th Census (1880), Lincoln County, N.M.; Microcopy 593 Roll 894; Population Schedules, 9th Census (1870), Lincoln County, N.M.
17. See Note 16.
18. NMSRCA, U.S. Census Records, 1870. Lincoln County, Schedule 3 (Productions in Agriculture), Precinct No. 1; also U.S. Census Records, 1880, Lincoln County, Schedule 2, Town of Lincoln. Miller (1986: 181) suggested that this decline in the number of farms and farmers was due to the census taker's failure to record many small farms.
19. NMSRCA, U.S. Census Records, 1880. Lincoln County, Schedule 2, Town of Lincoln.
20. See Note 19.
21. See Note 18; also NA, RG92, Entry 1242 No. 2 (from notes of Dr. Darlis Miller); *Rio Grande Republican*, November 10, 1883, p. 2. NMSRCA, Territorial Archives of New Mexico, Roll 41 (1885 Territorial Census, Lincoln County).
22. NA, Microcopy T9 Roll 802; Population Schedules, 10th Census (1880), Lincoln County, N.M. NMSRCA, Territorial Archives of New Mexico, Roll 41.
23. Keleher 1957: 159–60; Miller 1986: 188–90; Mullin 1968: 419–21; *Lincoln County Leader* (White Oaks, N.M.), March 26, 1892, p. 1. Sonnichsen, *Tularosa*, 1980: 249, 260.
24. Keleher 1962: 68–73; Metz 1974: 36–41; NMSRCA, Territorial Archives of New Mexico, Roll 21 frame 557.
25. Keleher 1957: 287.
26. Keleher 1957: 312–15; *Santa Fe Daily New Mexican*, April 3, 1881, p. 4.
27. Garrett 1954: 122–32; Keleher 1957: 286–93, 314–31; Rasch, "Hunting of Billy," 1969a; Leon C. Metz, *Pat Garrett*, 1974: 60–77.
28. G. Gauss, "Reminiscences of Lincoln County," 1890; Garrett 1954: 132–40; Keleher 1957: 332–34; Mullin 1968: 392–96; Metz 1974: 77–9.
29. Garrett 1954: 142–49; Wilson 1983.
30. Rasch, "Would-Be Judge," 1964c; Ira E. Leonard, Lincoln, N.M., to Commissioner of Indian Affairs, August 23, 1881; typescript copy in Philip J. Rasch File No. 38.
31. *Daily Optic* (Las Vegas, N.M.), February 13, 1882.
32. J.C. Lea, *New Mexico*, 1881.
33. *Rio Grande Republican*, August 20, 1881, p. 3.
34. NMSRCA, Territorial Archives of New Mexico, Roll 41.
35. *Golden Era* (Lincoln, N.M.), July 23, 1885, p. 1.
36. *Thirty-Four*, September 15, 1880; *Rio Grande Republican*, April 29, 1882, p. 1; May 19, 1883, p. 2.
37. *White Oaks Golden Era*, March 20, 1884, p. 1.
38. Sonnichsen 1971: 41–46, 63, 94, 117; *Thirty-Four*, May 5, 1880, p. 3; *Lincoln County Leader*, October 27, 1888, p. 3.
39. NMSRCA, Territorial Archives of New Mexico, Roll 21 frame 517; Roll 99 frames 20–21; *Thirty-Four*, September 3, 1879, p. 2; November 12, 1879, p. 3; December 3, 1879, p. 2; March 12, 1880, p. 3.
40. *Rio Grande Republican*, September 17, 1881, p. 3; February 25, 1882, p. 1. General Orders No. 4, 8, 13, 14, Executive Dept., Santa Fe, N.M., September 1881–June 1882, in NA Microcopy M364 Roll 8. Gibson 1965: 103–37; Ball 1980.
41. *Newman's Thirty-Four*, January 26, 1881, p. 3.
42. *Lincoln County Leader*, December 9, 1882, p. 3 (from notes in Fulton Papers, Box 12 Folder 7); Miller 1973: 117; Metz 1974: 112; *Rio Grande Republican*, April 26, 1884, pp. 1, 4.
43. Miller, "Wm. L. Rynerson in New Mexico," 1973: 117–18.
44. Gov. Lew. Wallace, Santa Fe, to Hon. C. Schurz, September 23, 1879; NA, Microcopy M364 Roll 8.
45. Murphy ledger; Klasner 1972: 118–23; Church 1982: 20–21; *Daily New Mexican*, May 20, 1875, p. 1; *Las Vegas Daily Optic*, February 13, 1882; *Rio Grande Republican*, April 22, 1882, p. 1.
46. *Compiled Laws of New Mexico, 1884*, pp. 544–56; *Golden Era*, May 28, 1885, p. 3; June 18, 1885, p. 1; October 15, 1885, p. 1; *Lincoln County Leader*, October 27, 1888, p. 3.
47. *Sadlier's Catholic Directory, 1869*, p. 266.
48. Bender 1984.
49. *White Oaks Golden Era*, February 7, 1884, p. 4; Caperton 1983: 94–95.
50. *Golden Era*, February 19, 1885, p. 1.
51. Caperton 1983: 95–6; Sandoval 1983; *Golden Era*, April 2, 1885, p. 1.
52. *Golden Era*, June 25, 1885, p. 1.
53. Caperton 1983: 471–72.
54. Metz 1974: 256.

55. Henn 1979: 124, 129–30, 134.
56. Metz 1974: 103–106; *Rio Grande Republican*, September 2, 1882, p. 2; September 16, 1882, p. 2; September 23, 1882, p. 2; September 30, 1882, p. 2; *Lincoln County Leader*, October 21, 1882, p. 2; October 28, 1882, p. 2; November 18, 1882, p. 2.
57. *Rio Grande Republican*, June 30, 1883, p. 2.
58. *Golden Era*, December 24, 1885, p. 1; *Rio Grande Republican*, January 23, 1886, p. 1.

59. Rasch, "Lynching of Wm. S. Pearl," 1956b; *Rio Grande Republican*, February 3, 1883, p. 4; February 10, 1883, p. 2; April 14, 1883, p. 2. For a considerably more detailed, and colorful, version see the *Rio Grande Republican*, May 10, 1884, p. 2.
60. Klasner 1972: 218–20; *Golden Era*, February 5, 1885, p. 1; October 1, 1885, p. 4; *Daily New Mexican*, July 16, 1885, p. 4; July 17, 1885, p. 4.
61. Garrett 1954: 153–54.

Chapter 14   *1885: Boom Times in Lincoln County*

1. *Rio Grande Republican*, October 6, 1883, p. 2.
2. *Golden Era*, April 16, 1885, p. 1.
3. *Golden Era*, July 24, 1884, p. 1; July 23, 1885, p. 1; *Rio Grande Republican*, January 23, 1886, p. 1.
4. *New Mexico Agricultural Statistics 1982*, p. 67.
5. NMSRCA, Territorial Archives of New Mexico, Roll 41. *Golden Era*, April 2, 1885, p. 1.
6. *Golden Era*, August 27, 1885, p. 1.
7. *White Oaks Golden Era*, March 6, 1884, p. 1; *Golden Era*, January 15, 1885, p. 1; January 22, 1885, p. 1.
8. *Golden Era*, September 18, 1884, p. 1; October 16, 1884, p. 1.
9. *Golden Era*, October 2, 1884, p. 1; November 20, 1884, p. 1; May 21, 1885, p. 1; July 16, 1885, p. 3.
10. *Golden Era*, March 5, 1885, p. 1; April 16, 1885, p. 1; June 11, 1885, p. 4; December 3, 1885, p. 1; December 10, 1885, p. 1.
11. *Golden Era*, February 4, 1886, p. 1.

12. Rasch 1957a: 61; Mullin 1968: 291.
13. *Golden Era*, July 23, 1885, p. 1.
14. *Golden Era*, October 29, 1885, p. 1.
15. *Golden Era*, November 12, 1885, p. 1; December 31, 1885, p. 1.
16. *Golden Era*, December 18, 1884, p. 1.
17. *Golden Era*, April 2, 1885, p. 1; April 16, 1885, p. 1; May 14, 1885, p. 1.
18. *Golden Era*, June 18, 1885, p. 1; October 22, 1885, p. 1; November 26, 1885, p. 1; December 31, 1885, p. 1.
19. *Golden Era*, February 19, 1885, p. 1; June 18, 1885, p. 1; October 15, 1885, p. 1.
20. *Golden Era*, September 3, 1885, p. 1; Caperton 1983: 156–62.
21. *Golden Era*, April 2, 1885, p. 1; Caperton 1983: 154.
22. *Golden Era*, February 19, 1885, p. 1.
23. *Golden Era*, June 11, 1885, p. 1.
24. *Golden Era*, July 2, 1885, p. 1.
25. *Golden Era*, July 31, 1884, p. 1; November 5, 1885, p. 1.
26. *Golden Era*, December 31, 1885, p. 1.
27. Ibid.

Chapter 15   *The Later Years, 1886–1913*

1. *Rio Grande Republican*, May 29, 1886, p. 1.
2. *Rio Grande Republican*, June 26, 1886, p. 2.
3. *Rio Grande Republican*, June 19, 1886, p. 3; October 30, 1886, p. 2; November 20, 1886, p. 1.
4. *Santa Fe Daily New Mexican*, March 17, 1886, p. 1.
5. *Rio Grande Republican*, May 15, 1886, p. 3.
6. *Rio Grande Republican*, May 8, 1886, pp. 1, 2; May 22, 1886, p. 2; June 12, 1886, p. 3; June 19, 1886, pp. 1, 3; July 3, 1886, p. 2.

7. *Rio Grande Republican*, May 8, 1886, p. 2; July 3, 1886, p. 2.
8. *Rio Grande Republican*, May 14, 1887, p. 1; *Pecos Valley Register* (Roswell, N.M.), September 5, 1889, p. 2; Reeve 1961: 212–14; Hinkle 1965: 16–17, 33.
9. *Rio Grande Republican*, January 29, 1887, p. 2; March 19, 1887, p. 3; April 16, 1887, p. 1; *Roswell Record*, June 27, 1894, p. 3; March 29, 1895, p. 1; January 29, 1897, p. 1; September 24, 1897, p. 3; Hinkle 1965: 33, 43–5.
10. Reeve 1961: 214; *Pecos Valley Register*,

December 20, 1888, p. 2.

11. New Mexico State Engineer Office 1967: 78; *Fourteenth Census of the United States* (1920), Vol. 7, p. 240.

12. Cassius A. Fisher, 1906: "Preliminary Report," pp. 26–27; Keleher 1962: 185–200; Metz 1974: 121–26; *Lincoln County Leader* (White Oaks, N.M.), May 31, 1890, p. 1; *Liberty Banner* (Lincoln, N.M.), March 19, 1891, p. 2; April 9, 1891, p. 3; July 9, 1891, p. 2.

13. F.H. Newell, 1894: "Report on Agriculture by Irrigation," pp. 196, 198; Fisher 1906: 27–8; Keleher 1962: 84, 150, 200; New Mexico State Engineer Office 1967: 79; *Pecos Valley Register*, December 6, 1888, p. 3; February 28, 1889, p. 3; March 7, 1889, p. 2; March 14, 1889, p. 3; April 18, 1889, p. 3; June 6, 1889, p. 3; July 25, 1889, p. 3.

14. *Pecos Valley Register*, December 20, 1888, p. 2.

15. Caperton 1983: 26.

16. *Pecos Valley Register*, October 24, 1889, p. 3; also July 4, 1889, p. 3; October 10, 1889, p. 2.

17. *Lincoln Independent* (Lincoln, N.M.), November 8, 1889, p. 3, quoting the Eddy, N.M. *Argus*.

18. *Lincoln Independent*, December 27, 1889, p. 3; *Liberty Banner* (Nogal, N.M.), January 22, 1891, p. 3; ibid. (Lincoln, N.M.), March 19, 1891, p. 2.

19. *Liberty Banner*, May 21, 1891, p. 2; see issue of May 7, 1891, p. 3 for similar remarks.

20. Caperton 1983: 26.

21. *Pecos Valley Register*, April 18, 1889, p. 3; May 9, 1889, p. 3; *Liberty Banner*, April 23, 1891, p. 2; May 7, 1891, p. 3.

22. *Rio Grande Republican*, February 12, 1887, p. 3; *Liberty Banner* (Nogal, N.M.), October 2, 1890, p. 3; Caperton 1983: 70–3, 160, 353, 356.

23. Broadside, *To the Voters and Taxpayers of Lincoln County* (1891), in Fulton Papers, Box 11 Folder 8; *Lincoln County Leader*, January 17, 1891, p. 1; January 31, 1891, p. 1; June 27, 1891, p. 1; *Liberty Banner*, June 25, 1891, p. 2; July 9, 1891, p. 2; Caperton 1983: 167.

24. *Roswell Record*, July 27, 1894, p. 3; March 29, 1895, p. 1; A.M. Gibson, 1965: *Life and Death of Col. Fountain*, pp. 219–23.

25. Gibson 1965: 223–37; Sonnichsen 1980: 112–30.

26. Rasch and Myers 1963; *Roswell Record*, August 16, 1895, p. 2; January 29, 1897, p. 1; September 24, 1897, p. 3; March 4,

1898, p. 3; May 27, 1898, p. 3. The Dolan family moved to the Feliz ranch in August 1895.

27. *Roswell Record*, September 24, 1897, p. 3; Reeve 1961: 212–14; Hinkle 1965: 43–46.

28. *Lincoln Republican* (Lincoln, N.M.), June 3, 1892, p. 1; August 26, 1892, p. 4.

29. NA, Microcopy T623 Roll 1001; Population Schedules, 12th Census (1900), Lincoln County, N.M., Precinct No. 1. New Mexico State Engineer Office, Hondo Hydrographic Survey (1908), Sheets 19 and 20.

30. *Capitan Progress*, August 23, 1901, p. 2; *1913 Year Book, Lincoln County* (unpaginated); Gorney 1969: 75.

31. Gorney 1969.

32. *Lincoln Independent*, December 13, 1889, p. 3; Shaler and Campbell 1907: 431–34; Wegemann 1914: 422–25, 447; Keleher 1962: 280–90; Myrick 1970: 76; Sonnichsen 1971: 48–49.

33. *Capitan Progress*, February 1, 1901, p. 1; March 8, 1901, p. 1; March 29, 1901, p. 4; Keleher 1962: 288.

34. *Capitan Progress*, October 18, 1901, p. 2.

35. *Capitan Progress*, May 2, 1902, p. 1.

36. *Capitan Progress*, Souvenir Number, March 20, 1903, p. 11. The population estimates were probably about 100 percent higher than the actual figures in this otherwise excellent special issue of the newspaper.

37. *El Capitan*, April 13, 1900, p. 1; *Capitan Progress*, February 1, 1901, p. 1; October 31, 1902, p. 4; January 30, 1903, p. 2; May 29, 1903, p. 4; June 26, 1903, p. 2.

38. *El Capitan*, August 6, 1900, p. 1; also August 13, 1900, p. 1; August 31, 1900, p. 4; September 14, 1900, p. 1.

39. *El Farol* (Capitan, N.M.), June 26, 1906, pp. 1, 2.

40. *Golden Era*, June 25, 1885, p. 1.

41. *El Capitan*, June 22, 1900, p. 1; *El Farol*, December 19, 1905, p. 1; April 24, 1906, p. 3; *Carrizozo Outlook*, February 10, 1911, October 11, 1912.

42. NA, Microcopy T623 Roll 1001; Population Schedules, 12th Census (1900), Lincoln County, N.M., Precinct No. 1.

43. *Capitan Progress*, November 22, 1901, p. 4; February 14, 1902, p. 1; December 5, 1902, p. 2.

44. *Capitan Progress*, November 7, 1902, p. 1; June 5, 1903, p. 1; June 26, 1903, pp. 1, 3; August 7, 1903, p. 1.

45. T.M. Pearce, 1965: *New Mexico Place Names*, p. 28; *El Farol*, February 6, 1906, p. 3; *Capitan News*, April 17, 1908, p. 8;

May 1, 1908, p. 8; *Carrizozo News,*
October 23, 1908, p. 6.

46. *Carrizozo Outlook,* August 20, 1909;
August 27, 1909.

47. *Carrizozo Outlook,* June 23, 1911, p. 1;
July 7, 1911, p. 1; *El Paso Herald,*

February 3, 1923, p. 1.

48. *Carrizozo Outlook,* January 24, 1913, p. 1;
January 31, 1913, p. 1.

49. *Roswell Register-Tribune,* August 22,
1911, p. 7.

Chapter 16   *The Community as a Historical Monument*

1. Emerson Hough, "Billy the Kid,"
1901; "Story of an Outlaw," 1907; Walter
Noble Burns, *Saga of Billy the Kid,*
1926.

2. Rasch, "They Fought for the House,"
1971; Ball, "What Became of Jessie
Evans?" 1979.

3. Rasch 1980. Susan Barber, "Notes of
correction on the Saga of Billy the Kid";
Fulton Papers, Box 1 Folder 4.

4. Wallace 1906; Rasch, "Men at Fort
Stanton," 1961; Nolan 1965: 464; Mrs. Tom
Charles, 1966: *More Tales of Tularosa,* p.
37; notes in Philip C. Rasch file No.
6—"Exit Axtell, Enter Wallace."

5. Amelia Bolton Church, "El Torreon,"
1935; Caperton 1983: 53–4.

6. Hendron 1939; Henn 1979: 138–39;
Caperton 1983: 173–74.

7. New Mexico State Planning Office 1974.

AN ESSAY ON SOURCES

L incoln was not a typical community and the materials for its history reflect this. For certain periods there is an abundance of records, to be found at a number of locations. Yet the only major author who has consistently cited his sources in writing about Lincoln is Philip J. Rasch. Maurice Fulton's history, edited by Robert Mullin, included neither notes nor bibliography; the only citations were occasional ones in the text. Keleher and Nolan used their end notes almost entirely for comments and biographical sketches. Nolan's bibliography was primarily of published books and articles, although his book relied mainly upon manuscript sources.

I surveyed the published literature before starting this history and found that it was impossible to judge the reliability or completeness of many writings because so few sources had been cited. Another limitation was the concentration upon the violence of the 1870s, especially the Lincoln County War, with a dearth of information before or after that. In order to produce a history that would cover the period from Lincoln's beginnings in the 1850s up to 1913, and do this evenhandedly, it was necessary to turn to primary sources.

In the end, these were relied upon almost exclusively. Fortunately the most important papers and copies of these are accessible in a handful of collections and consolidated files, all fairly well known and open to the public. The only two collections not personally examined were the Mullin Collection at the Haley History Center in Midland, Texas, and the Lincoln County court house records in Carrizozo, New Mexico. Dr. Robert Utley made available copies of a number of items from the Mullin Collection, while data from the county records may be found in the Fulton Papers and in Caperton's valuable Historic Structure Report (1983). Undoubtedly more sources will be found; indeed, as this was being written, several rare book and document dealers were offering for sale what appeared to be James J. Dolan papers. Military archives may have more to yield beyond the large and immensely valuable files that are already known.

Records of the U.S. Army were the single most valuable source for the history of Lincoln. Virtually all of the army reports originated at nearby Fort Stanton. The papers themselves are now at a variety of locations within the National Archives in Washington, D.C. The Letters Received by the Headquarters of the Military Department (later the District) of New Mexico from Fort Stanton may be seen on National Archives microfilms M1088 and M1120. Fort Stanton items are most easily found by first consulting the microfilmed Registers to the Letters Received. The army sometimes made consolidated files on controversial subjects. Two examples are a file on the Horrell War and another on the post trader controversies at Fort Stanton, now filmed on M666 Rolls 120 and 142. Many records relating to the Lincoln County War were placed in file No. 1405 AGO 1878, available on microfilm M666, Rolls 397 and 398.

That peerless military bureaucrat, Lieutenant Colonel N.A.M. Dudley, kept everything that crossed his desk as well as a copy of whatever he wrote. He entered hundreds of letters, reports, testimonies, et al. from the period after April 5, 1878, as exhibits in the Dudley Court of Inquiry, now filed in Record Group 153, Judge Advocate General's Office, Records Relating to the Dudley Inquiry (QQ1284). This court record is most easily seen on a two-roll microfilm made in 1968 for the University of Arizona Library. The army considered the Dudley file classified as recently as 1951, but Maurice Fulton and others had obtained excerpts from it probably by the early 1930s.

Complementing the military records were those of other government agencies. Frank Warner Angel, a special agent of the Departments of Justice and the Interior, compiled a huge report in the summer of 1878. Many prominent Lincoln County figures gave depositions and furnished copies of interesting letters and other documents. Angel seems to have accepted McSween's claims almost at face value. To buttress these, Mac appended a number of historically valuable "Exhibits" to his own testimony. Copies of the Angel report are in the Westphall Collection at the New Mexico State Records Center and with the New Mexico State Monuments Division; the original is in the National Archives in Washington, D.C.

U.S. Indian Inspector E.C. Watkins was at Lincoln and Fort Stanton virtually at the same time as Angel and likewise collected a large number of affidavits that related to affairs in Lincoln County, particularly with reference to the Mescalero Apache Reservation and supplies for the Indians. Watkins was less naive than Angel, and the depositions collected by the two investigators (some from the same individuals) complement one another very well. A little-used film of Internal Revenue assessments and license fees for New Mexico between 1862 and 1874 had some good personal financial data.

The voluminous Maurice Fulton Papers at the University of Arizona Special Collections Library were indispensable; these contained some original documents as well as photostatic and typescript copies of many other records, primarily from the Lincoln County War period. Frederick Nolan evidently did not have access to these while writing his biography of John Henry Tunstall; the original letters from Tunstall's father are in this file as well as photocopies of the son's correspondence. Fulton seems to have had a special talent for recognizing documents that would be the most valuable historically, and sometimes for acquiring them. The L.G. Murphy & Co. ledger and daybook at this same library are separate from the Fulton Papers. The Ealy Papers are there as well; these were not consulted.

Governor Lew. Wallace retained nearly all of the papers that related to his term as Governor of New Mexico. These included drafts of his own letters and reports, the correspondence that he received and a scrapbook of newspaper clippings. The Indiana Historical Society Library now houses the Lew. Wallace papers and has these available on microfilm. The surviving William Bonney letters are in this collection as well as some fascinating, if often cryptic, notes from the period when Wallace was prosecuting his "clean-up" in person at Lincoln.

The territorial newspapers were an invaluable source for all periods, particularly after the close of the Lincoln County War. Before the Horrell War, news items from Lincoln County appeared only occasionally in the Santa Fe and Mesilla Valley journals. After the violence started, letters from correspondents and newspaper editorials dominated the news coverage. Some valuable reports and documents also found their way into print. The Santa Fe *New Mexican* and *Mesilla News* were rabidly anti-McSween and pro-Murphy; the *News and Press* at Cimarron was pro-McSween; the *Mesilla Valley Independent* leaned towards McSween, and the other territorial papers were not so noticeably biased towards one party or the other. Correspondents wrote letters to promote the interests of their own side and much care is needed in deciding what to believe and what not to from the newspaper press.

The surviving Lincoln County records from the period after the county was formed in 1869 are in the county court house at Carrizozo. Before 1869 the same area was part of Socorro County. The early Socorro County records are now (except for Record Book "D") at the New Mexico State Records Center; these were examined, but apart from a few land transactions they contained little that pertained to Lincoln.

In territorial days Lincoln County was part of the Third Judicial District. The court records for territorial cases are also at the State Records Center. The Federal district court records are at the Denver Federal Records Center. Since the same judge and juries tried both territorial and Federal cases, it is necessary to know the jurisdiction in order to locate the case records. Records of the justices of the peace have, with rare exceptions, evidently not survived.

Lincoln State Monument has the Philip J. Rasch collection. This consisted of two long file cabinet drawers plus several boxes, primarily with typed transcripts of documents from most or all of the institutions and holdings listed above, including territorial newspapers. A single binder usually contained all of the background information for one of Rasch's articles plus a final draft of the article. I borrowed and examined this collection, thereby saving many hours of transcribing as well as finding sources that might otherwise have been missed.

In weaving together the documents from these myriad sources, the negligible duplication between the various collections was striking, even though many of the letters were themselves contemporary copies. For this reason it is difficult to say that one set of papers was more valuable than another; they all complemented each other and a document missing in one file might turn up in another. At the same time, the preservation of paperwork from the Lincoln County War period was little short of fantastic. The only significant missing document from that era may be the articles of co-partnership between John H. Tunstall and A.A. McSween, which were listed in an early inventory of property belonging to the Tunstall estate.

The published titles on Billy the Kid and the Lincoln County War are beyond counting. The most reliable author was Rasch, many of whose articles have been included in the bibliography. The other "big three" histories by Keleher, Mullin, and Nolan tended to be deficient in organization and completeness, in addition to the problems with documentation. Two of these works were also notably biased. With the exceptions of Pat Garrett's and Lily Klasner's books, the published reminiscences of participants have generally not been used, since these presented many problems in authenticating or disproving the writers' claims. Most of the principal characters of course never lived to write a book. The locations have been indicated for several rare or unique publications listed in the bibliography.

To wade through all of the source materials, select what to use, and present the results as a coherent history of the community of Lincoln has been a major challenge. The next researcher can draw upon the background already at hand and incorporate still more sources to make this story even more complete without, one hopes, being captured by the mythology of Billy the Kid.

My own files consist mainly of eight microfilm reels plus some two cubic feet of photocopies, microfilm print-outs, and typed transcripts of primary sources, with a few handwritten notes. Some sections of this history were written directly from microfilmed documents displayed on the viewer, without making notes or printing out copies. All of my files were submitted to the New Mexico State Monuments Division, for whom this manuscript was prepared, along with the final manuscript.

REFERENCES

Books, Articles, and Titled Manuscripts

Anderson, George G. (editor)
1907 *History of New Mexico; Its Resources and People.* Vol. I. Pacific States Publishing Co., Los Angeles.

Ball, Eve
1969 *Ma'am Jones of the Pecos.* The University of Arizona Press, Tucson.
1979 "What Became of Jesse Evans?" *True West* 26(3): 14–15, 48–49.
1981 "Don Florencio of Lincoln County." *True West* 28(10): 74–77.

Ball, Larry D.
1980 "Militia Posses: The Territorial Militia in Civil Law Enforcement in New Mexico Territory, 1877–1883." *New Mexico Historical Review* 55: 47–69.
1981 "The People as Law Enforcers: The 'Posse Comitatus' in New Mexico and Arizona Territories." *Quarterly of the National Outlaw Lawman Association* 6(2): 2–10, 22.

Beers, Paul
1970 "This Is Perfectly Gorgeous" (Civil War Income Tax). *Civil War Times Illustrated* 9(1): 21–27.

Bender, Averam B.
1974 "A Study of Mescalero Apache Indians, 1846–1880." In *Apache Indians XI*, edited by David A. Horr, pp. 61–310. Garland Publishing Co., New York.

Bender, Norman J. (editor)
1984 *Missionaries, Outlaws, and Indians: Taylor F. Ealy at Lincoln and Zuni, 1878–1881.* University of New Mexico Press, Albuquerque.

Bonney, Cecil
1971 *Looking Over My Shoulder: Seventy-Five Years in the Pecos Valley.* Hall-Poorbaugh Press, Inc., Roswell, N.M.

Bureau of Immigration of New Mexico
1909 *Lincoln County, New Mexico.* (Copy at University of Arizona Special Collections Library, Maurice Fulton Papers, Box 11 Folder 11.)

Burns, Walter Noble
1926 *The Saga of Billy the Kid.* Doubleday, Page & Company, Garden City, N.Y.

Caperton, Thomas J.
1983 *Historic Structure Report, Lincoln State Monument, Lincoln, New Mexico.* Office of Cultural Affairs, Santa Fe, N.M.
1986 "The McSween House Site, Lincoln, New Mexico." In *Prehistory and History in the Southwest*, edited by Nancy L. Fox, pp. 124–146. Papers of the Archaeological Society of New Mexico: 11. Santa Fe.

Carson, Wm. G.B. (editor)
1964 "William Carr Lane, Diary." *New Mexico Historical Review* 39: 181–234, 274–332.

Charles, Mrs. Tom
1966 *More Tales of the Tularosa.* Bennett Printing Company, Alamogordo, N.M.

Church, Amelia Bolton (Mrs.)
1935 "El Torreon." *New Mexico Magazine* 13(7): 53.
1982 "Early Days in Lincoln." *True West* 9(8): 20–23.

Clarke, Mary Whatley
1984 *John Simpson Chisum: Jinglebob King of the Pecos.* Eakin Press, Austin.

Cleaveland, Norman
1975 "The Great New Mexico Cover-Up: Frank Warner Angel's Reports." *Rio Grande History*, Number 5: 4–9. Las Cruces, N.M.

Coan, Charles F.
1922 "The County Boundaries of New Mexico." *The Southwestern Political Science Quarterly* 3(3): 252–286.

Commissioner of Indian Affairs
1861 *Report of the Commissioner of Indian Affairs, . . . for the Year 1861.* Government Printing Office, Washington, D.C.
1872 *Report of the Commissioner of Indian Affairs . . . for the Year 1871.* Government Printing Office, Washington, D.C.
1872 *Annual Report of the Commissioner of Indian Affairs . . . for the Year 1872.* Government Printing Office, Washington, D.C.
1874 *Annual Report of the Commissioner of Indian Affairs . . . for the Year 1873.* Government Printing Office, Washington, D.C.

Doolittle, J.R. (Chairman of Joint Special Committee)
1867 *Condition of the Indian Tribes.* 39th Cong. 2nd Sess. Senate Exec. Report 156. Washington, D.C.

Ellis, Bruce T.
1975 "Lincoln County Postscript: Notes on Robert A. Widenmann by his Daughter, Elsie Widenmann." *New Mexico Historical Review* 50: 213–230.

Fisher, Cassius A.
1906 *Preliminary Report on the Geology and Underground Waters of the Roswell Artesian Area, New Mexico.* U.S. Geological Survey Water-Supply and Irrigation Paper No. 158. Government Printing Office, Washington, D.C.

Frazer, Robert W.
1983 *Forts and Supplies: The Role of the Army in the Economy of the Southwest, 1846–1861.* University of New Mexico Press, Albuquerque.

Fulton, Maurice Garland
1957 "The Harrell War of 1873." *The English Westerners Brand Book* 3(3): 3–6.

Garrett, Pat F.
1954 *The Authentic Life of Billy, the Kid.* University of Oklahoma Press, Norman.

Gauss, G.
1890 "Reminiscences of Lincoln County, and White Oaks, by Old Sages and Stagers, No. XIV." *Lincoln County Leader*, March 1, 1890, p. 1. White Oaks, N.M.

Gibson, A.M.
1965 *The Life and Death of Colonel Albert Jennings Fountain.* University of Oklahoma Press, Norman.

Gorney, Carole
1969 *Roots in Lincoln: A History of Fort Stanton Hospital.* Submitted to the New Mexico State Planning Office (copies in Fort Stanton site survey file and with New Mexico State Monuments Division, Office of Cultural Affairs, Santa Fe).

Greenly, Dwight
1986 "The Military Career of Nathan Augustus Monroe Dudley, 1842–1889." Unpublished M.A. thesis, Graduate School at New Mexico State University, Las Cruces.

Haley, J. Evetts
1930 "Horse Thieves." *Southwest Review* 15(3): 317–332. Dallas.

Helbock, Richard W.
1981 *Post Offices of New Mexico.* Published by the author, Las Cruces, N.M.

Hendron, J.W.
1939 "The Old Lincoln Courthouse." *El Palacio* 46(1): 1–18. Santa Fe.

Henn, Nora
1978 "Lincoln County—An Historical Overview." *Rio Grande History*, Number 9: 2–5. Las Cruces, N.M.
1979 *An Historical Survey of Properties, Lincoln State Monument, Lincoln, New Mexico.* Manuscript on file (197 + unnumbered pp.), New Mexico State Monuments Division, Office of Cultural Affairs, Santa Fe.

Hinkle, James F.
1965 *Early Days of a Cowboy on the Pecos.* Stagecoach Press, Santa Fe.

Hinton, Harwood P., Jr.
1956 "John Simpson Chisum, 1877–84." *New Mexico Historical Review* 31: 177–205, 310–337.

Horn, Calvin
1963 *New Mexico's Troubled Years.* Horn & Wallace, Publishers, Albuquerque.

Hough, Emerson
1901 "Billy the Kid, the True Story of a Western 'Bad Man.' " *Everybody's Magazine* 5: 302–310.
1907 *The Story of the Outlaw.* The Outing Publishing Company, New York.

Hoyt, Henry F.
1980 Part Two from "A Frontier Doctor": "The Doctor Turns Cowboy." *Old West* 17(2): 49–66. Originally published 1929.

Jones, Fayette
1968 *Old Mines and Ghost Camps of New Mexico.* Reprinted. Frontier Book Co., Fort Davis, Texas. Originally published 1904, The New Mexican Printing Co., Santa Fe.

Jones, Oakah L.
1985 "Lew Wallace: Hoosier Governor of Territorial New Mexico, 1878–81." *New Mexico Historical Review* 60: 129–158.

Keleher, Michael
1974 "Lincoln, Its Past and Future." *Rio Grande History* 2(1–2): 12–15, 24.

Keleher, William A.
1957 *Violence in Lincoln County, 1869–1881.* University of New Mexico Press, Albuquerque.
1962 *The Fabulous Frontier.* University of New Mexico Press, Albuquerque.

Kelly, Daniel T.
1972 *The Buffalo Head: A Century of Mercantile Pioneering in the Southwest.* The Vergara Publishing Company, Santa Fe.

Klasner, Lily
1972 *My Girlhood Among Outlaws.* The University of Arizona Press, Tucson.

Lea, J.C.
1881 *New Mexico. Territorial Bureau of Immigration. Report as to Lincoln County.*

New Mexican Book & Job Printing Department, Santa Fe, N.M.

Leckie, William H.
1967 *The Buffalo Soldiers: A Narrative of the Negro Cavalry in the West.* University of Oklahoma Press, Norman.

(Lincoln County)
1913 *1913 Year Book, Lincoln County, New Mexico.* (Copy, less cover, at Museum of New Mexico History Library in uncataloged collection from Lincoln County Court House.)

McCright, Grady E., and James H. Powell
1981 "Disorder in Lincoln County: Frank Warner Angel's Reports." *Rio Grande History,* Number 12: 1–24. Las Cruces, N.M.
1983 *Jessie Evans: Lincoln County Badman.* Creative Publishing Company, College Station, Texas.

McKay, R.H.
1918 *Little Pills: An Army Story.* Pittsburg Headlight, Pittsburg, Kansas.

Mehren, Lawrence Lindsay
1969 "A History of the Mescalero Apache Reservation, 1869–1881." Unpublished M.A. thesis, Department of History, University of Arizona, Tucson.

Metz, Leon C.
1974 *Pat Garrett: The Story of a Western Lawman.* University of Oklahoma Press.
1978 *Books.* "The Lincoln War, a Bibliographic Essay." *Rio Grande History,* Number 9: 17–18. Las Cruces, N.M.

Miller, Darlis A.
1973 "William Logan Rynerson in New Mexico, 1862–1893." *New Mexico Historical Review* 48: 101–131.
1982 *The California Column in New Mexico.* University of New Mexico Press.
1986 "The Women of Lincoln County, 1860–1900." In *New Mexico Women: Intercultural Perspectives,* edited by Joan M. Jenson and Darlis A. Miller, pp. 169–200. University of New Mexico Press.

Mullin, Robert N.
1957 "Chronology—Lincoln County War Matters." *New Mexico Historical Review* 32: 69–74, 275–281, 363–367.
1968 *Maurice Garland Fulton's History of the Lincoln County War.* University of Arizona Press.
1973 "Here Lies John Kinney." *The Journal of Arizona History* 14(3): 223–242.

Myrick, David F.
1970 *New Mexico's Railroads—An Historical Survey.* Colorado Railroad Museum, Golden, Colorado.

Neel, Geo. M.
1932 *Tenth Biennial Report of the State Engineer of New Mexico, 1930–1932.* Santa Fe.

Newell, F.H.
1894 *Report on Agriculture by Irrigation in the Western Part of the United States at the Eleventh Census: 1890.* Government Printing Office, Washington, D.C.

New Mexico State Engineer Office (compiler)
1967 *Water Resources of New Mexico. Occurrence, Development and Use.* State Planning Office, Santa Fe.

New Mexico State Planning Office
1974 *Lincoln, New Mexico: A Plan for Preservation and Growth.* State Planning Office, Santa Fe.

New Mexico Territorial Engineer
1910 "Report on the Hondo Hydrographic Survey by the Territorial Engineer to the Court of the Sixth Judicial District of the Territory of New Mexico." In *Second Biennial Report of the Territorial Engineer to the Governor of New Mexico,* pp. 84–109. New Mexican Printing Company.

Nolan, Frederick W.
1965 *The Life & Death of John Henry Tunstall.* University of New Mexico Press, Albuquerque.

Parish, William J.
1961 *The Charles Ilfeld Company: A Study of the Rise and Decline of Mercantile Capitalism in New Mexico.* Harvard University Press, Cambridge.

Prince, L. Bradford (compiler)
1882 *The General Laws of New Mexico; Including All the Unrepealed General Laws from the Promulgation of the "Kearney Code" in 1846, to the End of the Legislative Session of 1880. With Supplement. Including the Session of 1882.* W.C. Little & Co., Law Publishers, Albany, N.Y.

Pearce, T.M. (editor)
1965 *New Mexico Place Names: A Geographical Dictionary.* University of New Mexico Press, Albuquerque.

Rasch, Philip J.
1955 "The Twenty-One Men He Put Bullets Through." *The New Mexico Folklore Record* 9: 8–14. Albuquerque, N.M.
1956a "Five Days of Battle." In *Brand Book of the Denver Posse of the Westerners for 1955,* Volume 11, edited by Alan Swallow, pp. 296–323. The Westerners, Inc., Denver.

Rasch, Philip J.
1956b "The Lynching of William S. Pearl."

West Texas Historical Association Yearbook 32: 70–74. Abilene.

1956c "The Horrell War." *New Mexico Historical Review* 31: 223–231.

1956d "The Pecos War." *Panhandle-Plains Historical Review* 29: 101–111.

1957a "The Rise of the House of Murphy." In *1956 Brand Book of the Denver Westerners*, Volume 12, edited by Charles S. Ryland, pp. 55–84. The Westerners, Inc., Denver.

1957b "The Gun and the Rope." *West Texas Historical Association Yearbook* 33: 138–142. Abilene.

1957c "Exit Axtell: Enter Wallace." *New Mexico Historical Review* 32: 231–245.

1959 "The Murder of Huston I. Chapman." *The Westerners Brand Book, Book Eight:* 69–82. Los Angeles Corral.

1960 "The Story of Jessie J. Evans." *Panhandle-Plains Historical Review* 33: 108–121. Canyon, Texas.

1961 "The Men at Fort Stanton." *Westerners' Brand Book* 3(3): 2–8. The Quarterly Publication of the English Westerners Society, London.

1962 "How the Lincoln County War Started." *True West* 9(4): 30–32, 48, 50.

1964a "War in Lincoln County." *The 100th Publication of the English Westerners' Society; The Brand Book* 6(4): 2–11. London.

1964b "The Loquacious Mr. Leverson." *The Westerners, New York Posse Brand Book* 11(4): 92–93. New York.

1964c "The Would-Be Judge—Ira E. Leonard." *The Denver Westerners Monthly Roundup* 20(7): 13–17.

1965 "The Trials of Lieutenant-Colonel Dudley." *The English Westerners' Brand Book* 7(2): 1–7. London.

1966 "The Governor Meets the Kid." *The English Westerners' Brand Book* 8(3): 5–12. London.

1968 "The Tularosa Ditch War." *New Mexico Historical Review* 43: 229–235.

1969a "The Hunting of Billy, the Kid." *The English Westerners' Brand Book* 11(2): 1–10, 11(4): 11–12. London.

1969b "Who Killed Who in Lincoln County, N.M." *Lincoln County News*, July 17, 1969, pp. 1, 2, 6. Carrizozo, N.M.

1970 "Prelude to War: The Murder of John Henry Tunstall." *The English Westerners' Brand Book* 12(2): 1–10. London.

1971 "They Fought for 'The House.' " In *Portraits in Gunsmoke*, edited by Jeff Burton, pp. 36–64. Special Publication Number Four, The English Westerners' Society, London.

1980 "These Were the Regulators." In *"Ho, for the Great West!"*, edited by Barry C. Johnson, pp. 50–69. Special Publication No. 6B, The English Westerners' Society, London.

Rasch, Philip J., and Lee Myers
1963 "The Tragedy of the Beckwiths." *The English Westerners' Brand Book* 5(4): 1–6. London.

Reeve, Frank D.
1961 *History of New Mexico, Volume II.* Lewis Historical Publishing Company, Inc., New York.

Rickards, Colin
1974 *The Gunfight at Blazer's Mill.* Southwestern Studies, Monograph No. 40. Texas Western Press, The University of Texas at El Paso.

Rickey, Don Jr.
1963 *Forty Miles a Day on Beans and Hay.* University of Oklahoma Press, Norman.

Sacks, Benjamin H. (editor)
1962 "New Evidence on the Bascom Affair." *Arizona and the West* 4: 261–278.

Sadlier, D. & J.
1869 *Sadlier's Catholic Directory, Almanac, and Ordo, for the Year of Our Lord 1869.* D. & J. Sadlier & Co., New York.

Samek, Hana
1982 "No 'Bed of Roses': The Careers of Four Mescalero Indian Agents, 1871–1878." *New Mexico Historical Review* 57: 138–157.

Sandoval, R. Jack (compiler)
1983 *History of St. Francis de Paula Church, 1862–1983, Tularosa, New Mexico.* Bennett Printing Company, Alamogordo, N.M.

Self, Juanita Sedillos
1981 "Sedillos and Brady Families of Lincoln County, N.M." *The Greater Llano Estacado Southwest Heritage* 11(2): 17–22. Hobbs, N.M.

Shaler, M.K., and M.R. Campbell
1907 *Investigations of the Coal Fields of New Mexico and California, by the U.S.G.S. in 1906.* Separate printing from U.S. Geological Survey Bulletin 316, pp. 376–438. Government Printing Office, Washington, D.C.

Shinkle, James D.
1966 *Reminiscences of Roswell Pioneers.* Hall-Poorbaugh Press, Inc., Roswell.

Simmons, Marc
1985 "History of Flying H Ranch Began Long Before Spread Got Its Name." *The El Paso Times*, July 21, 1985, pp. 7-B, 9-B.

Sonnichsen, C.L.
1958 *The Mescalero Apaches.* University of Oklahoma Press, Norman.

1980 *Tularosa: Last of the Frontier West.*
University of New Mexico Press,
Albuquerque.

Sonnichsen, C.L. (editor)
1971 *Morris B. Parker's White Oaks; Life in a
New Mexico Gold Camp, 1880–1890.*
University of Arizona Press, Tucson.

Stanley, F.
1964 *Fort Stanton.* Pampa Print Shop,
Pampa, Texas.

Theisen, Lee Scott
1976 "Frank Warner Angel's Notes on New
Mexico Territory, 1878." *Arizona and the
West* 18: 333–370.

Tittman, Edward D.
1929 "The Exploitation of Treason." *New
Mexico Historical Review* 4: 128–145.

**U.S. Bureau of Land Management, New
Mexico State Office**
Field Notes, Exterior Boundaries; Vol. R57.
Field Notes, Subdivision Lines; Vols. S976,
S1010.

**U.S. Department of Agriculture, New
Mexico Crop and Livestock Reporting
Service**
1983 *New Mexico Agricultural Statistics,
1982.* New Mexico Department of
Agriculture, Las Cruces, N.M.

**U.S. Department of Commerce, Bureau of
the Census**
1922 *Fourteenth Census of the United States,
Taken in the Year 1920. Vol. 7. Irrigation
and Drainage.* Government Printing Office,
Washington, D.C.

**U.S. Department of the Interior, General
Land Office**
1924 *Statutes and Regulations Governing
Entries and Proofs Under the Desert Land
Laws.* Circular No. 474. Government
Printing Office, Washington, D.C.

Utley, Robert M.
1961 "The Bascom Affair: A Reconstruction."
Arizona and the West 3: 59–68.
1967 *Frontiersmen in Blue: The United States
Army and the Indian, 1848–1865.* The
Macmillan Company: New York.
1986 *Four Fighters of Lincoln County.*
University of New Mexico Press,
Albuquerque.

Wallace, Andrew
1975 "Duty in the District of New Mexico: A
Military Memoir." *New Mexico Historical
Review* 50: 231–262.

Wallace, Lewis
1906 *Lew. Wallace; An Autobiography.* 2
vols. Harper & Brothers, Publishers, New
York.

Walz, Edgar A.
1931 *Retrospection.* 32 pp. Privately printed,
n.p.

Wegemann, Caroll H.
1914 Geology and Coal Resources of the
Sierra Blanca Coal Field, Lincoln and Otero
Counties, New Mexico. In *U.S.G.S.
Bulletin 541*, edited by Marius R.
Campbell, pp. 419–452. Government
Printing Office, Washington, D.C.

Westphall, Victor
1965 *The Public Domain in New Mexico,
1854–1891.* University of New Mexico
Press, Albuquerque.
1973 *Thomas Benton Catron and His Era.*
University of Arizona Press, Albuquerque.

Wilson, John P.
1983 "With His Boots Off: First Newspaper
Reports on the Death of Billy the Kid." *Rio
Grande History*, Number 14: 11–13, 23. Las
Cruces, N.M.

Congressional Documents

35th Cong., 2d Sess., *Senate Executive
Document No. 1*, "Report of the Secretary
of War, 1858–1859" (Serial 975)(1860).
37th Cong., 3d Sess., *Senate Rep. Com. No.
108*, "Report of the Joint Committee on the
Conduct of the War, Part III" (1863).
39th Cong., 2d Sess., *Senate Report No. 156*,
"Condition of the Indian Tribes" (Serial
1279)(1867).
46th Cong., 3d Sess., *Senate Report No. 829*,
"Report of the Committee on Military
Affairs on the manner of appointing Post
Traders, with a history of legislation and
regulations affecting same" (1881).
57th Cong., 2d Sess., *Senate Document No.
209*, "Federal Aid in Domestic
Disturbances, 1878–1903" (Serial 4430)(1903).

Maps

Map of the Territory of New Mexico,
Compiled by Bvt. 2nd Lt. Jno. G. Parke,
U.S.T.E., assisted by Mr. Richard H.
Kern, by Orders of Bvt. Col. Jno. Munroe,
U.S.A. Comdg. 9th Mil. Dept. Santa Fe
(1851).
New Mexico State Engineer Office, Hondo
Hydrographic Survey, Sheets 19 and 20
(1908).

Newspapers

The Borderer, Las Cruces, N.M., 1873.

Capitan News, 1908.
Capitan Progress, 1901–1903.
Carrizozo News, 1908.
Carrizozo Outlook, 1909, 1911–1913.
Daily Alta California, San Francisco, 1860.
Daily New Mexican, Santa Fe, 1872–1875, 1881, 1885–1886.
Eco Del Rio Grande, Las Cruces, N.M., 1878.
Daily Optic / Las Vegas Daily Optic, Las Vegas, N.M., 1882.
Daily Picayune, New Orleans, 1861.
El Capitan, Capitan, N.M., 1900.
El Farol, Capitan, N.M., 1905–1906.
El Paso Daily Herald, 1899.
El Paso Herald, 1923.
Golden Era, Lincoln, N.M., 1884–1886.
The Herald / The Grant County Herald, Silver City, N.M., 1876–1878.
Las Vegas Gazette, Las Vegas, N.M., 1878–1879.
Liberty Banner, Nogal and Lincoln, N.M., 1890–1891.
Lincoln County Leader, White Oaks, N.M., 1882, 1886, 1888, 1890–1892.
Lincoln Independent, Lincoln, N.M., 1889.
Lincoln Republican, Lincoln, N.M., 1892.
Mesilla News, 1874–1875, 1878–1879.
Mesilla Valley Independent, 1877–1879.
Mining Life, Silver City, N.M., 1873–1874.
Newman's Thirty-Four, Las Cruces, N.M., 1881.
News and Press, Cimarron, N.M., 1879.
Pecos Valley Register, Roswell, N.M., 1888–1889.
Rio Abajo Weekly Press, Albuquerque, N.M., 1863.
Rio Grande Republican, Las Cruces, N.M., 1881–1884, 1886–1887.
Rocky Mountain News, Denver, Colo., 1862.
Rocky Mountain Sentinel, Santa Fe, N.M., 1878–1879.
Roswell Daily Record, 1905.
Roswell Record, 1894–1895, 1897–1898.
Roswell Register-Tribune, 1911.
San Francisco Herald, 1860–1861.
Santa Fe Weekly Gazette / Santa Fe Gazette, 1853, 1855, 1861–1862.
Semi-Weekly Southern News, Los Angeles, 1861.
Texas Republican, Marshall, Texas, 1862.
Thirty-Four, Las Cruces, N.M., 1879–1880.
Tri-Weekly Missouri Republican, St. Louis, 1860.
Tri-Weekly Telegraph, Houston, Texas, 1861.
Weekly New Mexican, Santa Fe, 1875, 1877–1879, 1880.
White Oaks Golden Era, 1884.

Manuscript and Microfilmed Materials

1. **National Archives and Records Administration**
Civil Archives
Population Schedules, 8th Census (1860), Socorro County, N.M., Rio Bonito. Microcopy T7 Roll 158.

Letters Received by the Office of Indian Affairs, 1824–1881. Microcopy M234 Rolls 561, 562, 563.

Population Schedules, 9th Census (1870), Lincoln County, N.M. Microcopy M593 Roll 894.

Population Schedules, 10th Census (1880), Lincoln County, N.M. Microcopy T9 Roll 802.

Population Schedules, 12th Census (1900), Lincoln County, N.M., Precinct No. 1. Microcopy T623 Roll 1001.

Population Schedules, 13th Census (1910), Lincoln County, N.M., Town of Lincoln. Precinct No. 1. Microcopy T624 Roll 915.

Interior Department Territorial Papers, New Mexico, 1851–1914. Microcopy M364 Roll 8.

Records of the New Mexico Superintendency of Indian Affairs, 1849–1880. Microcopy T21 Roll 18.

Reports of Inspections of the Field Jurisdictions of the Office of Indian Affairs, 1873–1900. Microcopy M1070 Roll 29.

Internal Revenue Assessment Lists for Territory of New Mexico, 1862–1870, 1872–1874. Microcopy M782 Roll 1.

Record Group 60, General Records of the Department of Justice, Report on the Death of John H. Tunstall by Frank W. Angel, File No. 44-4-8-3.

Military Archives
Returns from U.S. Military Posts, 1800–1916, Fort Stanton, N.M. Microcopy M617 Roll 1216.

Compiled Service Records of Volunteer Union Soldiers Who Served in Organizations from the Territory of New Mexico. Microcopy M427 Roll 15.

Letters Received by the Office of the Adjutant General (Main Series), 1871–1880. Microcopy M666 Rolls 120, 142, 397, 398.

Letters Sent by the Ninth Military Department, Department of New Mexico, and District of New Mexico, 1849–1890.

Microcopy M1072.

Letters Received by Headquarters, District of New Mexico, September 1865–August 1890. Microcopy M1088.

Registers of Letters Received by Headquarters, District of New Mexico, September 1865–August 1890. Microcopy M1097 Rolls 1, 2, 3.

Registers of Letters Received and Letters Received by Headquarters, Department of New Mexico, 1854–1865. Microcopy M1120.

Record Group 92, Records of the Office of the Quartermaster General. Entry 1238 Vols. 16, 17; Entry 1239 Nos. 1, 2; Entry 1242 Nos. 1, 2.

Record Group 94, Records of the Adjutant General's Office, 1780s–1917.

Letters Received by the Appointment, Commission, and Personal Branch, 1871–1894. File 3172 ACP 1871.

Record Group 94, Records of the Adjutant General's Office, 1780s–1917.

Letters Received by the Appointment, Commission, and Personal Branch, 1871–1894. File 2461 ACP 1874.

Record Group 192, Records of the Office of the Commissary General of Subsistence. Entry 69, Vol. for the years 1863–1871; Entry 74 Vols. 2, 3, 4.

Record Group 153, Records of the Office of the Judge Advocate General, Records Relating to the Dudley Inquiry (QQ1284).

Record Group 393, U.S. Army Commands, Fort Stanton, N.M., Letters Received; also Letters Sent, Headquarters Fort Stanton, N.M.

2. **New Mexico State Records Center and Archives, Santa Fe**

Microfilm of Papers Relating to New Mexico Land Grants, Reel 56, U.S. Surveyor General, Letters Sent, Vol. I (1854–1866). Ibid., Reel 60, U.S. Surveyor General, Letters Received, 1854–1876.

Territorial Archives of New Mexico, Microfilm edition, Rolls 3, 21, 41, 87, 99.

Agricultural Schedule, 8th Census (1860), Socorro County, N.M., Rio Bonito.

Agricultural Schedule, 9th Census (1870),

Lincoln County, N.M., Precincts No. 1–4.

Agricultural Schedule, 10th Census (1880), Lincoln County, N.M., Town of Lincoln.

Socorro County Deed Records, Book A.

WPA Files

3. **University of New Mexico Library, Special Collections, Albuquerque**

First National Bank of Santa Fe Collection

Thomas B. Catron Collection

Michael Steck Papers

4. **Museum of New Mexico History Library, Santa Fe**

Manuscript Collection

Second National Bank of Santa Fe, Financial and Business Records

Journal of John A. Clark

WPA City Files

Manzano

5. **New Mexico State Monuments Division, Lincoln, N.M.**

Philip J. Rasch Collection

6. **Lincoln County Clerk's Office, Carrizozo, N.M.**

Record Book A

Book E — Misc.

7. **University of Arizona Special Collections Library, Tucson**

Maurice Fulton Papers

L.G. Murphy & Co. ledger, May 1871–December 1872

L.G. Murphy & Co. journal, May 1873–January 1874

8. **Indiana Historical Society Library, Indianapolis**

Lew. Wallace Papers

9. **Haley History Center, Midland, Texas**

J. Evetts Haley interviews with Susan E. Barber, Robert A. Casey, Frank Coe, George Coe.

Robert N. Mullin Collection, Tunstall Ranch Notes

Miscellaneous

War of the Rebellion: Official Records of the Union and Confederate Armies. Series I Vol. 1 (1880); Series I Vol. 4 (1882); Series I Vol. 15 (1886).

1885 *Compiled Laws of New Mexico, 1884.* New Mexican Printing Co., Santa Fe.

INDEX

Geronimo (Apache Chief), 137
Giddings, Gov. Marsh, 43, 44, 46, 50
Godfroy, Frederick, 49, 71, 73, 91, 92
Gomez, Francisco, 110 (photo), 111, 162; death of, 169
Gonzales, Florencio, 50, 53, 73
Gonzales, Juan, 46
Goodwin, Lt. M. I., 118, 122
Grant, President U.S., 34, 36
Gylum, L. J., 43, 50, 53

H

Hangings, in Lincoln County, 50–51, 151, 157 (photo)
Hardeman, Dick, 130
Hare, Captain, 14
Haskins, Joe, 46
Hatch, Col. Edward, 92, 113, 118–19
Hatch, Gen. Edward, 111
Hayes, President Rutherford B., 82, 85, 91, 107; proclamation of, 109
Higgins, Frank, 20
Hill, Tom, 69–70, 79–81, 82, 85. *See also* Evans, Jessie, gang of
Hindman, George, 87; death of, 89, 90
Holmes, Oliver Wendell, 164
Horrell, Ben, 43
Horrell, Samuel, 47
Horrell Brothers, 43, 44, 45–46, 47, 57
Horrell War, xi, 41, 43–48; Washington's response to, 44, 46; 50, 53, 73, 103
Hough, Emerson, 169
House, The. *See* Murphy, L.G., & Co.
Hudgen, Will, 105
Huff, Daniel, 97
Hunter, R. D., 56, 57, 67; involvement of, in Lincoln County War, 69, 76; in league with Jessie Evans, 116
Hurley, John, 142, 146

J

Janes, John, hanging of, 151
Johnson, D. C., 151
Johnson, S. A., 145
Jones Boys (John, Jim, Tom, and Billy), 108–09

K

Kautz, Lt. Col. August, 30
Kimbrell, George: election of, to sheriff, 109; 114, 117, 118, 122–23, 130, 132
Kinney, John, 93–95, 103, 104, 134, 137; death of, 169
Kiowa Indians, 15
Klasner, Lily Casey, 22 (photo), 23: *My Girlhood Among Outlaws*, 23; 27, 29, 31, 34, 43, 44, 51, 53, 57, 137

L

Lamy, Archbishop, 138
La Placita. *See* Lincoln (town)
LaRue, J. A., 29; Tunstall store rented by, 129, 131, 140, 152
Laws, Dr. J. W., 160
Lea, J. C., 146–47
Lee, Oliver, 155
Leonard, Ira, 118, 123, 124–25; retained by Sue McSween, 129; 130, 132; defense of Billy the Kid by, 132; 134–36

Lesinsky, Henry, & Co., 29
Leverson, Montague, 82, 85, 89, 91, 102
Lincoln (county), boundaries of, 5 (map); 10 (map); 11 (map); census for: in 1860, 6, 8; in 1870, 31, 33, 43; in 1880, 130–32, 145; in 1885, 143; in 1900, 156, 162; creation of, 24; delinquent taxes in, 50; 192; farming in, *see* Agriculture; Corn; gold, discovery of, 9, 19, 130, 156–58; land titles in, 53; liquor, selling and trading of, 4–6, 7, 12, 16, 29, 31, 41; livestock in, *see* Livestock; mining in, 41, 76, 107, 130, 137, 142, 153, 156–58; principle locations in, 83 (map); war of, *see* Lincoln County War
Lincoln (town), Anglo-Americans at, 6–7, 23, 44, 130–32, 143; County courthouse, *see* Courthouse (Lincoln County); county jail, 69, 146–47, 161 (photo); county seat at, *see* County Seat (Lincoln); Hispanics at, 6–7, 23–24, 44, 130–32, 143; historical monument, xi, 169–72; Klasner's description of, 23; L. G. Murphy & Co. at, 30; Murphy & Co. relocate to, 37, 39, 40 (photo); settlement of, 4–6, 7–8, 15; resettlement of, 17, 19–23
Lincoln County Bank, 67–69; letterhead of, 68
Lincoln County War, xi-xii, 27, 40, 41, 43, 48, 56; mercantile opposition and the, 67–76; prominent locations during, 98 (map); roots of, 58–59, 62, 63, 66, 73–76; 79–125. *See also* Blazer's Mill, Battle of; Five-Days Battle
Lincoln Hotel. *See* Wortley Hotel
Livestock, raising of, 7, 19–20, 21 (report); for beef contracts, 27, 29, 34–35, 38, 41, 56–60; 71, 131, 136–37, 142, 143; Linclon Co. brands for, 144 (photo), 145; purchase price of, 27–41, 56–59, 65–66; 152–53, 155–56, 158; stockmen's associations for, 137, 155. *See also* individual ranchers.
Long, Jack (John), 87, 93, 114, 124
Lynde, Major, 12–14

M

Manuelito, Chief (Mescalero Apache), 16
Martin, W.W., 36 (photo)
Martinez, Atanacio, 147
Martinez, Atencio, 82
Martinez, Juan, 43
Mathews, J. B. "Billy": involvement of: in Lincoln County War, 79, 80 (photo), 81; 87, 89; indictment of, in Tunstall murder, 90; 114, 118, 124, 129, 134; death of, 169
Maxwell, L. B., 29
McCarty, Henry A., Jr., 162
McGowan, Timothy, 6–8
McKibbon, Capt. Chambers, 39, 43, 48
McKinley, President William, 156
McNab, Frank, 87, 90; death of, 90, 91, 124
McNew, Billy, 155
McSween, Alexander A., 40, 49, 51, 53, 54 (photo), 65–66, 67, 69–70, 73–76; arrives in London, 53–56; house of, 95, 98 (map), 171 (map); meets J. H. Tunstall, 60; Emil Fritz insurance policy and, 58, 63, 67, 74, 90; law offices of, in Lincoln, 67–69; involvement of, in Lincoln County Bank, 69; Fritz estate vs., 74–75; involvement of, in Lincoln County War, 79, 82, 84–85, 87, 89, 90, 91–102; death of, 95, 101–102; 105, 109; estate of, 111, 129
McSween, Sue E. (later Sue McSween Barber): arrives in Lincoln, 53–54, 55 (photo), 56; 60, 67, 84,

Photo Credits

The publisher gratefully acknowledges the following institutions for permission to reproduce photographs from their collections: University of Arizona Library, Special Collections, Tucson, pages 40, 48, 49, 64, 68 (top), 72 (top right), 80 (bottom right), 88 (left), 96 (top), 110, 148, 154 (bottom), 161 (bottom), 163, 167 (bottom). University of Oklahoma Western Historical Collections, page 68 (bottom). State University of New Mexico, Western History Collections, pages 28, 167 (top). The Aultman Studio, Trinidad, Colorado (State Historical Society of Colorado), page 13. The Lincoln County Heritage Trust, Lincoln, New Mexico, pages 100, 135. University of Arizona Press, Tucson, for permission to reproduce from the book *My Girlhood Among Outlaws*, by Lily Klasner; edited by Eve Ball, © 1972. Photographs from the Museum of New Mexico Photo Archives, Santa Fe, may be referenced by the following negative numbers: 11656, 11677 (pg. 28); 16371 (pg. 32 top, by Ben Wittick); 90634 (pg. 32 bottom, by Edwin A. Bass); 11668 (pg. 38); 105048, 105385, 91336 (counterclockwise, pg. 54); 30769 (pg. 61); 104923 (pg. 70); 105130, 50364 (bottom, from left pg. 72); 93148 (top, pg. 80); 105400, 104857 (bottom, left and center, pg. 80); 92936 (right, pg. 88); 11657 (bottom, pg. 76); 15295 (pg. 120); 49576 (pg. 121); 4876 (pg. 133); 105473 (pg. 154); 78418, 93117 (pg. 159); 104917, 89722 (pg. 165). Photos of weapons by Art Taylor, Courtesy Museum of New Mexico History Unit. Maps on pages 5, 10, 11, and 98 by Jeffrey Horton.

About the Author

For the past twenty-five years John Wilson has worked in New Mexico, initially as an historical archeologist with the Museum of New Mexico. He holds a doctorate in anthropology from Harvard and currently runs a business specializing in innovative historical and anthropological research. Many of his writings on Spanish Colonial, Indian, and military history of the Southwest appear in professional journals and in his own research series. He has been a director in the Council on America's Military Past and currently serves on the board of the Historical Society of New Mexico.